# THE LAST DAY
# OF CREATION

# THE LAST DAY OF CREATION

WOLFGANG JESCHKE

*Translated by Gertrud Mander*
Afterword by Brian Aldiss

St. Martin's Press
New York

Library of Congress Cataloging in Publication Data

Jeschke, Wolfgang.
    The last day of creation.
    Translation of: Der letzte Tag der Schöpfung.
I. Title.
PT2670.E75L413    1984        833'.914        83-27235
ISBN 0-312-47061-4

First Published in Great Britain by Century Publishing Co. Ltd.

First U.S. Edition

10 9 8 7 6 5 4 3 2 1

And the evening and the morning
were the fifth Day.
And God said, Let the earth bring
forth the living creature after his
kind, cattle, and creeping things and
beasts of the earth after their kind:
and it was so.
And God made the beasts of the earth
after his kind and cattle after their
kind, and every thing that creepeth
upon the earth after his kind: and
God saw that it was good.
And God said, Let us make man in our
image, after our likeness...

1 Genesis 1, 23-36

# CONTENTS

*Prologue*

### PART ONE
## TRACES 11

1   Drilling Holes     13
2   Artefact 3: The Flute of Saint Vitus     15
3   Artefact 2: The Chariot of Gibraltar     23
4   Artefact 1: Tiefenbacher's Gun     34

### PART TWO
## PROJECT CHRONOTRONE 47

### PART THREE
## DROPPED 61

1   Volunteers     63
2   Enterprise Western Basin     79
3   Dropped     89
4   The Place of the Skull     110
5   The Fortress     124
6   The Dark Barge     144
7   A Lost Lot     160
8   Journey to Atlantis and Other Places     187
9   Regards to Leakey     200
10   The Encounter with the Angel     209
    *Afterword*     220

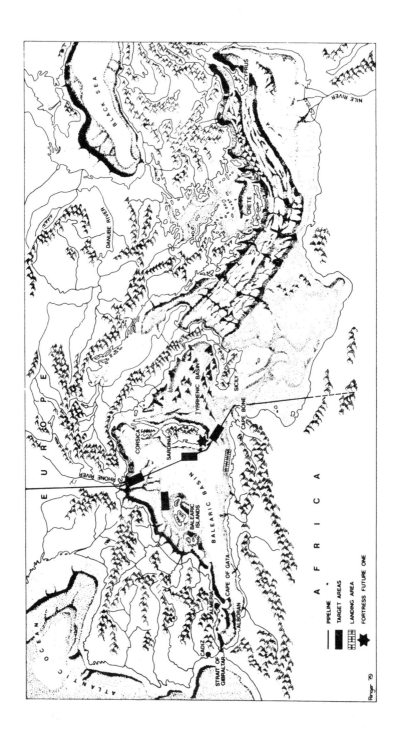

Roger '79

# PROLOGUE

In 1959, Steve Stanley was sixteen. He spent his childhood in Rome and Paris, where his father worked as the representative of an American pharmaceuticals group. Back in the States he studied aircraft engineering at Springfield College and his ambition was to become a pilot. After his exams he joined the Air Force.

In 1959, the American intelligence service discovered in the Western Mediterranean traces of a project that was to transform reality as we know it.

In 1968, Steve Stanley was twenty-five and had become one of the best pilots in the US Air Force.

In 1968, the United States Navy and NASA jointly embarked on a top-secret project, surrounded by the most elaborate security measures. It was to be unique in the history of mankind.

In 1977, Steve Stanley was thirty-six and was working as a test pilot for Rockwells. He lost his job when President Carter decided to cancel the B-1 project, and applied for a job with NASA, where experienced pilots were needed for projected shuttle flights.

In 1977, the top-secret NASA/Navy project was going ahead at full speed, though for some time now a number of scientists working for it had been issuing warnings of possible serious consequences. By that time, everybody who knew about the project was aware of the fact that it had not developed entirely as planned.

Yet the military project leaders disregarded the warnings and ordered work to continue. By then even outsiders had got wind of strange happenings in the Atlantic west of Bermuda. The CIA were, however, not at all unhappy about the wild speculations concerning the so-called Bermuda Triangle, and positively encouraged the rumours already circulating. The result was that soon no serious scientist remained interested in the strange phenomena.

A little later, the name of Steve Stanley appeared on a computer print-out among the names of candidates shortlisted for the secret project. The list contained specialists from various fields of science including engineering and logistics, as well as former members of the fighting forces with specific qualifications.

At that time Steve Stanley did not yet know what would be required of him, nor did any of the other people whose names were on the list drawn up by project-leader Admiral William W. Francis. They did not know that their lives were to be utterly changed – or that they were about to embark on experiences beyond their wildest dreams. Steve Stanley and his colleagues had been chosen to enter paradise. Yet they were not to witness Genesis. They were to witness Apocalypse.

One day Steve Stanley disappeared without trace, and with him most of the other people whose names had been printed out by the computer.

Without trace?

They did leave *some* traces.

Yet it was very difficult to recognise these traces and even more difficult to decipher their meaning – particularly for those who were not their contemporaries.

# PART ONE

# TRACES

# CHAPTER ONE

# DRILLING HOLES

When, on 13th August 1970, the *Glomar Challenger* left the port of Lisbon on an expedition to conduct sea-bed drillings in the Balearic depression, many people had high hopes of it; not only scientists, in search of answers to some strange happenings which had been observed in the fifties and sixties, but also biologists and oceanographers hoping for clues to an important event that had taken place about five and a half million years ago, at the transition from the Miocene to the Pleocene age. At around this time a biological revolution had taken place in the Mediterranean resulting in a drastic change of climate in Europe as a whole.

The *Glomar Challenger* expedition was funded by the National Science Foundation and was carried out under the supervision of the Scripps Institute of Oceanography. On the evening of 23rd August, with the research vessel electronically anchored a hundred miles south of Barcelona, the first drilling was made down to a depth of two thousand metres. Further drillings followed between Barcelona and Mallorca, south of Minorca, at the eastern slope of Sardinia and south of Malaga.

The results confirmed the hypothesis made by William E. B. Benson of the National Science Foundation, and by Orville L. Bandy of the University of Southern California. They also confirmed some rather extravagant guesses by high Pentagon officials who were working on a project that took shape around the late sixties, when the Apollo programme was at its height. During the press conferences in Paris and in New York where the expedition results were released, some information was deliberately withheld. This concerned material found during the drillings, and was later to prove crucial in deciding the fate of the project. It decided President Nixon in mid-February 1971 (when Apollo 14 had just finished its successful flight) to reduce the NASA space flight budget drastically and to provide funds instead for the NASA/Navy project – now operating under the cover name of Sealab.

The results of the sea-bed drillings confirmed some inexplicable data which had been collected by the US intelligence service over a long period. The first clue dated back to 1959 and had been provided by the French War Ministry; it was considered highly mysterious and no explanation for it could be found. It was filed as 'Artefact 1'. Admiral Francis, then an expert working in the Navy department of armament technology, was directed to continue researching into it. He made little progress in his investigations until 1968. This time the clue came from Switzerland, and was filed as 'Artefact 2'. In 1969 another piece of information filed as 'Artefact 3' was collected by the intelligence service in the Vatican. Piece by piece, the mosaic was put together. A picture emerged and slowly a scientific basis for the enterprise took shape as Francis and his assistants had always known it would. For more than a decade, all publications in the field of theoretical physics from everywhere in the world were gathered by Francis and his team and evaluated.

CHAPTER TWO

# ARTEFACT 3: THE FLUTE OF ST VITUS

'Anachronisms' are difficult to recognise. One either has to categorise them according to their function and appearance, or one has to place them through documentation or tradition. To the primitive mind, such objects are either curiosities or they are endowed with magical and sacred power, depending on the credulity or scientific knowledge of those who find them.

In fact, there was evidence for hundreds of years that at some time in prehistory there had been an event in the Western Mediterranean that could be called a 'time fracture'. Strange objects had been found in the coastal areas of Southern Spain and Southern Italy, in Malta, Sardinia, Corsica and the Balearic Isles, and particularly in Sicily. Because they appeared almost indestructible and were of mysterious origin, these objects were universally worshipped as sacred relics; some of them still are to this day. They consist as a rule of fragments of light material, dirty white or yellowy brown in colour and easily mistaken for old ivory or bits of skull and bone polished over the centuries by sea and sand and thereby rendered unrecognisable. All the more reason, then, for attributing sacred powers to these bony fragments and for regarding them as relics miraculously saved from the bodies of saints who had once walked the earth.

In San Lorenzo, near Reggio in Calabria, a twenty-centimetre-long piece of this material was worshipped for more than five hundred years as the Prophet Jeremiah's index finger. In Algeciras near Gibraltar, a square-shaped fragment about twelve centimetres across was kept as a relic and revered as the skull-top of John the Baptist, whose severed head was supposed to have been washed up miraculously on a Spanish beach. And in thirty-seven Sicilian churches there were fingers and toes, upper and lower jaws, ribs and shins of at least twenty-seven saints, prophets and similarly worthy persons.

The strangest find, however, was kept in a silver shrine at *Sta*

Felicita in Palermo: the sexual organ of St Vitus, now revered as the patron saint of brewers and miners, cripples and boiler-makers, actors, pharmacists and wine-growers, and prayed to in cases of bed-wetting, fire, snakebite and rabies, St Vitus' dance and epilepsy, distress and threatened loss of chastity. Vitus came from Mazara del Balla on the south-western coast of Sicily and, as is well known, suffered at the hands of Emperor Diocletian's soldiers around 304 AD. He was the son of a wealthy pagan by the name of Hylas and to his father's distress, became a member of the Christian sect at the tender age of seven. In order to escape his father's wrath, he fled with his nurse Crescentia and his tutor Modestus to Lucania. Here, sadly, he was recognised and arrested and brought to Rome, where he was sentenced to die the particularly cruel death of being thrown into a pot of boiling oil. Fortunately the poor little boy was saved by angels and brought back to his distant home country, where he is said to have died soon after.

In 583 AD, his mortal remains were broken up, and his body was taken to Lower Italy, while his severed genitals remained in Sicily. The energetic Abbot Fulrad of St Denis had his dismembered body brought to his monastery in 756, but not all his successors seem to have shared his devotion to the saintly Vitus, for Abbot Hilduin made a gift of the corpse to the Monastery of Corvey in 836. There the martyr's body was further dismembered. In 922, Duke Wenceslav the Holy received an arm when he built a church in Prague in honour of Vitus, on the very spot on the Hradschin where now stands the Cathedral of St Vitus. In 1355, Emperor Charles the Fourth, a great admirer of St Vitus, who had since been promoted to patron saint of the Empire, tried to gather together the dispersed moral remains of the unfortunate saint, but only succeeded in acquiring a few bones in Pavia, of whose authenticity the fathers of divinity have never been completely convinced. Today there are more than one hundred and fifty places in Central and Southern Europe which claim to possess some part of the saint's body.

That most delicate relic, to which Vitus owes his patronage of chastity, reappeared in Palermo in the 10th century. It is mentioned in a document in 938 in connection with the construction of the church of *Sta* Felicita, where it found safe refuge. The legends are silent about the uncertain fate it had suffered in the course of the intervening 355 years – a mysterious omission, since legends are unusually numerous in the case of this youthful martyr.

A local tradition gives the following story of its origin, which may be fairly close to the truth. A fisherman named Rosso was surprised by a storm one night and driven far out to sea. For two days and two nights he was in great danger, until at last, on the morning of the third day, the storm abated, and he sighted his native coast again. When he hauled in his net he found twelve fish – an auspicious number, since it is obviously a symbolical allusion to the twelve disciples – and a strange curved, hose-like, ribbed object, one and a half feet in length and half an inch in diameter, made of an unknown material which seemed to be elastic and brittle at the same time and pale grey in colour.

Grateful for his miraculous rescue, the fisherman handed over his find to the prior of *Sta* Felicita, who locked away the curious object, specifically from the eyes of the ladies, as he feared it might give rise to unchaste thoughts. This happened in the middle of the 9th century.

As if by miracle, the object survived intact when a fire destroyed the old church of *Sta* Felicita. In 932 the new building which still stands, was begun.

In 1277, Ambrosius, a young and ambitious prior of *Sta* Felicita, obtained permission from the archbishop of Palermo to have the relic authenticated by the Holy Father. Pope Nicholas III was unable to decide, although he did send two parties of experts to Palermo to examine the object on the spot. After that the petition remained on the files until Bonifatius VIII sent a third party of experts in 1296. But even then the Holy Father waited until 1303, shortly before his death, before he finally made up his mind and gave his apostolic blessing.

Ever since then, the strange piece of hose, which was confirmed by the highest authority in the Catholic Church to be a symbol of Christian chastity and a proof of astounding Sicilian manhood, has been kept in a skilfully chased and silk-lined silver shrine and only opened once every hundred years on the anniversary of *Sta* Felicita, Only once a century are the public given a chance of laying eyes on the miraculously preserved saintly genitals.

In 1439, Professor Angelo Buenocavallo, teacher of medicine in Palermo, wrote a learned tract on the relic, which in popular parlance was called 'The unmentionables of St Vitus', or more vulgarly, '*il gazzo di Santa Felicita*'. He denied that the said object could possibly be a human sexual organ, let alone that of St Vitus, no matter how miraculously it might have been changed by the boiling oil. Anatomically, he claimed, there was no similarity at all – to say nothing of its length. Pigs' tails, when fried in boiling oil, tend to swell and acquire a blistery hardness which makes them appear bigger and harder; yet, argued Buenocavallo, the said object was not made of baked flesh, but appeared to be made of ivory. All the evidence, he maintained, pointed to the fact that this was one of those musical instruments made from ivory which Muslim musicians use to produce those dreadful noises which were so popular at the court of King Frederick II of Sicily.

Buenocavallo was denied permission to print his tract by his faculty, and was denounced by envious colleagues in the church and accused of heresy for having compared the genitals of St Vitus with baked pigs' tails. The tract was confiscated and burnt in public. The courageous little professor managed to escape the charge of heresy and was forbidden to teach for two years. He went to Padua where he practised anatomy for three further productive decades. His fame travelled far from his chosen place of exile.

Meanwhile the musical instrument of St Vitus continued to lie in its silver shrine and survived the centuries almost forgotten.

When in 1938 the shrine was opened for the thousandth anniversary of *Sta* Felicita and the holy relic was exposed once more to the public gaze, a certain Luigi Risotto, a grammar school teacher in Tarento, who had been wounded in the First World War in the very same part as the famous Abelard of Paris, was one of those who took a particularly close look at it. In 1939, the *Tarento Journal for Teacher Training* published an article in which Luigi Risotto emphatically denied the relic's authenticity. He waxed indignant at a church which had the impudence, in the 20th century, to pretend that a piece of hosepipe of this length and consistency could possibly be the sexual organ of a saint and allow it to be worshipped as such. This, he wrote, is a continuation of the Dark Ages and an affront to simple, credulous people. It was particularly serious, also, at this crucial stage in the history of the great and cultured Italian nation, shortly to become politically one of the most important nations in the world.

The object, in Risotto's view, was nothing but a ribbed piece of hosepipe made of hard and brittle rubber resin, probably the connecting piece of a waterpipe of Muslim origin. In his enthusiasm, however, Risotto overlooked the fact that this piece of rubber was documented as far back as the 10th century and was sanctioned in 1303 as a relic, while among the Moors tobacco was not heard of until the middle of the 16th century. As for the waterpipe, this was not invented until 1612 by Ziad Kawadri of Damascus, an ingenious coffee house proprietor who produced the 'nargileh', after intense thought, for the greater comfort of his customers. From Damascus, this instrument of Oriental pleasure started its huffing and puffing triumphant march all over the Muslim world, from Budapest to Casablanca, from Dar-es-Salam to Hyderabad.

In 1961, Pope John XXIII called a commission of scholars to weed out the jungle of holy relics. Its task was to investigate in particular cases where unworthy, indecent, tasteless or ridiculous objects were venerated. In the course of more than five years the commission collected 3,786 such cases, 1,284 of which were speedily forgotten and 1,544 of which were recommended to be quietly shelved for the time being and therefore remain officially unmentioned. The final 958 relics were tacitly tolerated, yet only mentionable in exceptional circumstances.

An unexpected result of the investigation was the discovery that more than a thousand of these relics were of a material that was dirty white or yellowy brown in colour, and – as the official description had it – 'looked like very old, cracked ivory'.

The papal commission asked for samples of this material and sent these to the physics laboratory in the Vatican, where they were examined by the latest methods, including radio carbon testing. The latter technique brought an astonishing discovery. Every one of the radio carbon tests was negative. This could only mean one thing: assuming the matter in question was organic, *i.e.* bone or ivory, rubber or amber, then all these samples had to be more than thirty thousand years old, since radio carbon dating cannot be done beyond this date. Probably the samples were over a hundred thousand years old. It was therefore no longer possible to revere them as the index finger of

Jeremiah, or the skull-top of John the Baptist, nor the right foot of St Geneviève nor the chest bone of St Paul.

Predictably, the flute of St Vitus was among the embarrassing relics instantly to be relegated to oblivion. Though in colour and consistency it was different from the majority, it proved on examination to be of a similar prebiblical or rather unbiblical age. The genitals of St Vitus, which had survived boiling in oil and the wear and tear of centuries, therefore had to be given up for lost. The object the fisherman had retrieved from the depths of the sea in his net after the storm was no saintly relic; it was something far more interesting, even to the scholars in the papal physics lab. The insignificant cloud that now appeared on the horizon threatened to grow into a storm which would shake the foundations of history. If the guesses of the scientists proved right, this discovery could assume immense significance.

And they were to be proved right.

On 2nd March 1969, a deputation arrived in Palermo sent by Pope Paul VI. Pope John had died in 1963 without ever becoming aware of the importance of what he had initiated. The deputation carried a personal letter from the Holy Father to the archbishop of Palermo, in which his eminence was requested 'for reasons which he had the most urgent cause to keep secret' to have the relic of St Vitus brought immediately from *Sta* Felicita to Rome. 'It was with the greatest distress that he had to acknowledge signs to the effect that the Anti-Christ was about to eliminate with a stroke of his pen thousands of years of the history of human salvation, thereby robbing the world of its longed for and deserved salvation and taking possession of it retrospectively.'

His Eminence the archbishop was at first indignant about the apparent lack of trust the Holy Father showed in him by not telling him what connected the curious relic with the imminent take-over of power by the anti-Christ; and yet he was deeply worried about the urgency of the request. He therefore ordered the immediate opening of the shrine of *Sta* Felicita and the hand-over of the object to the deputation – well wrapped up, of course.

After more than a thousand years of rest, the flute of St Vitus – *alias* the hose connection of a nargileh, *alias* the pagan musical instrument – started on a long journey. Suddenly identified as

an 'anachronism' after a thousand years, it now excited
enormous interest among physicists, moral theologians and
politicians.

On 5th March, the relic reached Rome and was immediately
taken to the Holy Father, who, after inspecting it with growing
discomfort, realised that his most horrible fears were confirmed.
Uttering a moan which sounded almost like a growl, he retired
to pray.

Meanwhile in the physics laboratory, more samples of relics
had been examined and the investigators had come to the
conclusion that the material of which they were composed was
neither organic nor inorganic, but synthetic. The same was
found to be true of the slightly different material of which the
relic of Palermo was composed. Moreover, '*il gazzo di Santa
Felicita*' bore an astonishing resemblance to the ribbed hosing
on the oxygen masks usually worn by jet-pilots.

The question of how it was that a material like this – which
showed traces of extremely old age – could have appeared
centuries before the invention of synthetics remained at first
unanswered. The Vatican scientists were baffled. There was no
scientific theory and no imaginable technical explanation
which could solve the mystery. Yet the consequences the
discovery threw up were highly alarming.

Pope Paul VI met in conference with his scientists and
advisers almost without interruption, only leaving when called
on unavoidable duties, or to retire to his private chapel for
prayer. After long hesitation he finally announced his decision:
all the samples of the materials at hand should be locked up in
the Vatican archives *in eternitatem*, and the strictest secrecy was
to be observed concerning their existence.

Thus the flute of St Vitus disappeared for ever, lost among
the biggest collection of strange objects, curious gadgets,
documents and artefacts which had ever been gathered
together in the course of fifteen hundred years.

In his wise decision, however, Pope Paul VI overlooked the
fact that the CIA is interested in everything and that its spies
are everywhere – even under the Holy Chair. With the help of
the CIA's man at the Vatican, Washington was soon informed
of the strange finds and the distress they had caused the Pope. A
short time later packets of photographs and samples of the
strange material arrived at the Pentagon.

Admiral Francis stuck his chin out belligerently while he examined the photos spread out on his desk with a magnifying glass. The unexpected shipment from the Vatican perfectly matched the drawings, and the two artefacts found in 1959 and 1968 in Algiers and Gibraltar. The *Glomar Challenger* would supply the last pieces of the mosaic by its drillings in the Balearic depression. Preparations for the deep-sea drilling project by the National Science Foundation were to start soon and the funds for the research project had now become available.

Francis felt satisfaction at the upward turn the project had taken with the consignment from Rome. It would take him right to the top, too. Now nothing stood in his way.

Taking aim carefully with his plastic ruler, he swatted a fly that had settled irreverently on the sharply focused photograph of Vitus' oil-fried organ. A small smear disfigured the martyr's unmentionables, but Francis did not mind.

He scratched the ridge of his nose with the side of the ruler and smiled, curling his upper lip and narrow moustache and pushing the tip of his tongue between his incisors and his lower lip.

He was very, very confident.

CHAPTER THREE

# ARTEFACT 2: THE CHARIOT OF GIBRALTAR

While the Austrians and the French were busy fighting each other in the War of the Spanish Succession, the British, with their strong instinct for essentials, took possession of the most important strategic points in the Western Mediterranean. In the morning of 4th August 1704, German mercenaries attacked Gibraltar, took it at the first attempt, and hoisted the Union Jack.

Djebel al-Tarik, the rock of Tarik – so-called after a famous Arab general who crossed over there with his troops in 711 and set out to conquer the Iberian Peninsula – is a block of Jurassic limestone which once, together with Djebel Musa, west of Ceuta on the African coast, formed a narrow ridge of land separating the Atlantic and the Mediterranean. Since more water vapourises in the Mediterranean basin than is supplied by rivers emptying into it, there is a constant flow of water into it from the Atlantic. This massive water input produced, in the course of millions of years, a breach more than three hundred metres deep and twenty-four kilometres wide: the Straits of Gibraltar. The waters ate into the southern flank of the rock of Gibraltar, forming the terraced ridges of Windmill Hill and Europa Flats which fall away towards Punta de Europa and are thus ideally suited for fortification. After the Treaty of Utrecht in 1714 confirmed their proprietary rights, the British began to construct a naval base.

There have been continual demands from Spain for the return of Gibraltar; there were even some attempts at re-conquest, which failed miserably. Since the British were often welcome allies for the Spanish against France – for instance, during the Napoleonic Wars – the British position remained unchallenged and they thus retained control of the movements of all ships between the Mediterranean and the Atlantic.

When the great Napoleon left the stage of history, there were renewed demands to liberate the rock, but these remained unfulfilled. Soon Spain's political radicals were fully occupied with the Liberal Revolution, with the French intervention and, after that, with a bloody civil war between Carlists and followers of the Prince Regent and the Infanta. Even so, there was always a spontaneous outburst of patriotic passion in Spain whenever the *reconquista* was mentioned, and the British presence in Gibraltar remained cautious and discreet. The slightest friction between Britain and the Gibraltarians was invariably seized on by European powers who were envious of the strategic position held by the British, and the Spanish cause hailed as a legitimate fight for freedom against colonial oppression. In 1843 the commander of the base, Sir Walter Griffith, therefore decided to strengthen the fortifications overlooking the sandy spit of land to the north-east of the Moorish Castle. The first trenches were dug in the autumn of that year.

The intention was to proceed with the work as inconspicuously as possible, in order to mislead the nationalists and to prevent embarrassing questions being asked at the court of Madrid. The work was directed by Colonel Frank Gilmore, an officer with much experience in fortification engineering. Gilmore was also an enthusiastic amateur archaeologist and had participated in excavations in Nubia, where his fellow officers nicknamed him 'Gilmore Pasha'.

Gilmore's men began by clearing the thin beech forest and digging trenches – ostensibly to expand the catchment area of the water reservoir situated to the south-west, and to make some canals. So as to be able to lay the foundations for the fortifications on solid rock, Gilmore made his men dig up the tree stumps and remove the top soil, which consisted of marl and clay slate. At a depth of about eight feet they met a stratum of hard clay. Gilmore sank a vertical shaft in order to find out its full extent. After digging three feet down, the pick-axes struck rust, apparently mixed into the clay.

The colonel stopped the work immediately in order to investigate the find. The clay in fact contained heavily weathered iron, yet there were traces of other substances, too, blunt fragments of a grainy material which might have been glass.

Gilmore decided to have an area of twenty feet square dug out vertically and inch by inch, because he guessed rightly that he had hit some kind of artefact. At a depth of about two feet, the digging produced further traces of rust, and a day later the site of the excavation exposed the outline of a rectangle measuring about six feet by twelve.

Gilmore now made a scale drawing of the outline and continued the inch-by-inch excavations. After every five inches the outline was measured carefully and another scale drawing made in order to help towards an eventual vertical reconstruction of the object, which was now of course completely disintegrated. When, at a depth of two and a half feet, the rectangular outline started to show traces of rust first on one side and then, at three and a half feet, over the whole area, Gilmore began to make out the remnants of a box-like shape, possibly a cart, perhaps an antique chariot which had sunk into the mud. The mud had apparently entered the vehicle and completely filled the inner space, like the supporting core of a mould. The vehicle had thus been preserved in an upright position.

Armed with a trowel and a brush, Gilmore Pasha searched around the sides of the 'box' for remnants of wheels, at first without success. He was about to give up, assuming that the iron vehicle must have had wooden wheels which had vanished without trace, when he discovered lateral protuberances in front and at the back of the 'box', which were metallic in character and might well have been wheels or rollers. Thus, the vehicle must have had four wheels – a rather unusual feature for an antique chariot.

When Gilmore started the vertical reconstruction of the 'chariot' with the help of the horizontal sketches, the result was a curious object resembling a low-slung light carriage rather than an armoured chariot as depicted in ancient representations.

On the side which Gilmore instinctively called the 'front', there seemed to have been a largish metal block which had reached about halfway up the side walls of the bodywork. He hesitated to state whether this was a passive platform for the charioteer or archer to stand on, or perhaps a weapon, a kind of battering ram. Either way, the vehicle seemed to be of a rather squat design, unnecessarily massive in its body and particularly in the platform, and yet carelessly and weakly armoured at the flanks. It might have had wooden or leather shields there, which had disappeared completely, the colonel concluded. Yet he was disappointed with the result, since he was unable to place and date his find satisfactorily.

Gilmore naturally informed the base commander, Sir Walter Griffith, of the affair and the latter, secretly rather amused, yet as always rather formal in his manner, allowed him to interrupt the works at the site of the find for some time in order to let him ride his 'Egyptian hobby horse,' as he called it. Sir Walter was of the opinion that the mysterious 'rusty spot' was probably a vehicle which the Moors had left to drown in the mud when they stormed the Djebel al-Tarik, from which they controlled their supply lines.

The colonel did not contradict the commander, yet he was enough of an archaeologist to know that Griffith was hopelessly wrong; the 'rusty spot', judged by the stratum and depth at which it was situated, was an artefact of pre-Christian, perhaps Càrthaginian age – and probably it was much older even than that.

Gilmore's guess was confirmed when, on further investigation of the excavation site, he discovered some badly decayed bone fragments, among them a skull which showed a hole the size of a thumbnail. The driver of the vehicle had apparently died a violent death.

What intrigued the colonel was the fact that the state of the bone fragments indicated that they were more than three or four thousand years old. In Egypt, Gilmore had seen skeleton finds which had been almost completely preserved for five thousand years under circumstances much less favourable than here. The clay in which the vehicle was found ought to have preserved a corpse for a time span ten or even twenty times longer.

Colonel Gilmore was baffled, and asked Sir Walter for his permission to sent a message to the Royal Society in London, inviting an expert to come and inspect his find.

'Out of the question, Colonel,' Sir Walter declared peremptorily. 'Completely out of the question. I cannot take responsibility for a horde of scientists getting in the way of my military duties. The fortification works to the north of Moorish Castle have already been delayed far too long while you've pursued your archaeological interests. I insist that they are now speedily completed.'

'With your permission, Sir . . .'

'Of course. But you have to understand, Colonel, that I cannot risk a discussion in the press about archaeological finds made during fortification works on the territory of Gibraltar.'

'During canalisation works for the reservoir, Sir.'

Sir Walter dismissed this impatiently. 'Even archaeologists or whatever you call these people would be able to distinguish between fortification works and canalisation works, Colonel Gilmore.'

'Sir, it is possible that we are dealing with one of the most important prehistoric finds in Europe – and on territory belonging to His Majesty!'

'On *military* territory belonging to His Majesty, with the safety of which I happen to have been entrusted.'

'I am aware of that, Sir. But please try and understand my position. I am not a professional archaeologist; I do not have the tools and the means to conduct a thorough investigation, particularly for purposes of more exact dating. This could mean an irreparable loss to knowledge. I would not care to bear the responsibility for this on my own shoulders . . .'

'You can leave the responsibility to me, Colonel. Moreover, I fear you exaggerate the importance of your find. You talk as if you had found the skeleton of an elephant in Hannibal's army. Most probably a Spanish peasant lost his way on his way home after a night on the tiles and drowned in the swamp with his cart. We shouldn't make so much fuss about a rusty spot. I assume you take my point, Colonel?'

'Yes, Sir.'

It was useless to protest. Sir Walter stuck to his decision. Yet he did allow Gilmore Pasha to write to a photographer in London who had been assistant to Fox Talbot in Reading for a while, and to invite him to Gibraltar to make a few photographs of the site.

Three weeks later, Archibald Wesley arrived and exposed about forty plates in order to preserve the rusty spot for posterity and for posthumous scientific evaluation. Both he and Colonel Gilmore were ordered not to publish anything about the matter 'for the time being'. What exactly this meant remained undefined. Then the fortification works resumed and the remainder of the clay stratum was excavated.

When Colonel Gilmore retired in 1846, it is doubtful if anybody actively tried to prevent him from reporting his find.

Yet, strangely, he did not act. Perhaps the conflict between his scientific interests and his military loyalty had finally been settled in favour of the latter. More probably he had reached the conclusion that as an amateur he would not be able to convince the experts with his sketches and his technically rather unsatisfactory photographic documentation. Perhaps also he feared heavy criticism for his failure to impress on Sir Walter Griffith the importance of the find and the necessity of a thorough scientific investigation by specialists.

It is curious, also, that he never heard of a further find in Gibraltar two years after his retirement. For in the building of further fortifications, the skull of a prehistoric man was found, which for decades was held to be that of a primate. Sir Walter Griffith was now no longer Commander of Gibraltar and this time the find did become known in the archaeological world. But it was not until a hundred years later, after Leakey had made his discoveries, that the experts became interested in it.

When the aged Gilmore Pasha died in his country house near Chatham on 25th December 1874, his notes concerning the mysterious chariot of Gibraltar fell into oblivion.

His grandson, Edward George Gilmore, a successful young architect and enthusiastic automobilist, decided to give up the country house near Chatham in 1898 and set about modernising it with a view to selling it to a rich textile manufacturer from Manchester. But before he moved into his new house in the West End of London, Edward Gilmore went through the piles of documents and letters in the spacious attic of the house, deciding which of them he should burn. It was then that he came upon a bundle of thirty-two yellowed photographs inscribed on the back in his grandfather's handwriting. Now all that was legible was the decorative stamp of 'Archibald Wesley, Calotype Studio, Chiswick' in the lower right-hand corner. Alongside the photographs was a small carefully wrapped-up paper parcel containing greyish-brown crumbly dust – bone dust, Edward thought, before throwing the stuff away carelessly – and a packet of sketches in his grandfather's hand, among them a drawing of an automobile.

Edward Gilmore held his breath. The paper was dated 12th March 1844. Could the old colonel have been a secret inventor? Had he been on the point of designing a car in 1844? As far as he knew, the old gentleman had been less interested in technology than in excavations and in publications of Champolion, who deciphered the hieroglyphic script, and Schliemann, who had made such sensational finds in Greece and Asia Minor.

Gilmore looked at the first sketch with the eyes of an expert. The others were outline drawings which showed the vehicle in various sections and elevations. It was certainly not a carriage but a car, though of a rather curious shape, with front-wheel drive apparently indicated by the motor block in front. Edward went through all his grandfather's other papers to find further information on his activities as an inventor, but without success. Probably this was meant to be a machine for moving earth, or a military vehicle designed for some special mission such as constructing fortifications.

After a while, however, Edward Gilmore lost interest. But he did consider his discovery important enough to mention in his diary; he also kept the sketches and photographs and took them with him to London when he moved into his new house a few weeks later.

There the papers of Gilmore Pasha rested, until one rainy Saturday afternoon in September 1968, when Patrick Geston, who had married Edward Gilmore's granddaughter Catherine, picked up the diaries of his wife's grandfather in a mood of nostalgia and started to read. Soon his eye fell on the entry concerning the car-like vehicle sketched in 1844 by Edward's ancestor. Underneath it he read in the clear handwriting of the successful *art nouveau* architect: 'There are a few more sketches of elevations, cross-sections, design drawings, and about thirty-two photographs, which unfortunately have been badly fixed. Only the occasional smudges can be recognised on them.'

Patrick Geston, teacher of German and English and occasional translator, a science fiction enthusiast with a keen interest in all forms of literature dealing with the frontiers of science, stopped in his tracks. After finishing his beer, he went up to the attic and opened all the chests and boxes he could find. At last he discovered what he was looking for:

A firm brown envelope, on which Edward Gilmore had written in ink: 'Grandfather Gilmore Pasha's automobile'. Inside were the documents mentioned in the diary. The sketch of the 'automobile' lay on top.

Geston started up as if hit by an electric charge.

The object was unmistakable, even though the shape was not

quite right; it was a Jeep or a Land Rover. The fenders and wheels were missing and the bonnet was lower, as if it had sunk. Where in the world could Colonel Gilmore have come across a *Jeep* in 1844? The combustion engine had not even been invented then!

Geston took a deep breath and held the papers with the greatest care, fearing they might turn to dust between his fingers. Mad ideas immediately flashed into his mind – ideas about time-leaps and time-travel, as in Dean McLaughlin's *Hawk among the Sparrows*, which had been published two months ago in *Analogue*, or the time-travel story by a German author whose name he couldn't remember which he had read in another Science Fiction magazine.

He went down to his study and spread out the photos on his desk. At first sight they were a bitter disappointment – they were completely faded and covered with brown stains – but on closer inspection, some of them showed regular structures, though he could not make out what they represented.

Later he put the twenty-eight sheets in chronological order following the dates written on the back. It was at once evident that they were cross-sections of the 'jeep', arranged in the order of height, starting at the top and finishing at the bottom. Finally he discovered similarities between the stain structure on some of the photos and the sketches which represented the lowermost cross-sections. He was dealing with the documentation of an excavation!

Geston burst into the sitting room and asked his startled young wife, 'What was Colonel Gilmore's profession? Old Gilmore, I mean – your great-great-grandfather?'

Mrs Geston looked up from the book she was reading. 'What do you mean, profession? He was an officer. I think he was an engineer – something to do with fortifications. Why the sudden interest?'

'And why was he called Pasha?' Patrick continued, ignoring her question.

'How should I know? Oh, yes, wait a minute. Wasn't he posted to Egypt for a while? I believe he was in Egypt.'

*Egypt!* The word affected Patrick like a magic charm. He hurried into the kitchen, fetched himself another beer from the refrigerator and opened the can with trembling fingers.

'And when was that?' he asked when he returned.

'I've no idea, but it ought to be easy enough to find out.'
And indeed it was.

At the time in question Colonel Frank Gilmore was not in Egypt. As Patrick Geston soon discovered, he had returned to London from Alexandria in 1840 and had been posted to Gibraltar a year later, where he had directed the new fortification works until he retired.

*Gibraltar?*

Geston was disappointed. But he did not give up. He wrote to the Royal Society and to the National Geographic Society to ask whether there had been archaeological excavations in or near Gibraltar in the mid-eighteen forties. Both institutions informed him that they did not know of any archaeological excavations either at the time in question, or at any later date, although in 1848, during excavations for some military trenches, fragments of a primate skull had been found, now considered to belong to a hominid.

Geston's enthusiasm had by now diminished. By 1848, Gilmore Pasha would have left Gibraltar and been living in retirement at Chatham. Geston was stuck. However, he knew a German writer who had published a successful book on mysterious prehistoric finds – Geston had translated it into English and had corresponded with the writer in the course of this. He now offered the material to him, indicating that he might be on to a big thing, but did not have the ways and means of following it up himself. The writer, an amateur archaeologist like Gilmore Pasha, showed a keen interest and after examining them thoroughly, offered to publish the sketches and photographs in his next book. This might also produce further information.

As Geston was reluctant to entrust the valuable material to the post, he suggested a safer method of putting it into the writer's hands. In the German Club in London he had met some German Embassy officials, one of whom travelled two or three times a week with the diplomatic bag from London to Bonn. The latter offered to take the envelope containing the material with him on his next trip to Germany.

Another employee of the German Embassy had the routine task of filming the material he packed into the courier's baggage, and sending copies to the American intelligence service.

Three days later, the Pentagon was informed about the strange find in Gibraltar, which matched exactly the other strange find that had been made in Algeria and handed over by the French War Ministry in 1959.

Since the copies of the photographs were of extremely poor quality Captain Francis decided to set about obtaining the original material and restoring the calotypes by the computer technique of contrast-heightening. He saw, too, that it was absolutely essential to prevent publication of the material. Perhaps it would be possible to stop the writer from publishing for a while. The project had by now reached a stage at which it would have been highly dangerous if the other side had received the merest hint of the activities the US Navy was engaged in.

On 16th October 1968, the envelope with the photographs and sketches reached Bonn, but the writer was unable to collect the package in person as he was on a lecture tour, so he asked his publisher to send somebody to fetch it for him.

On Monday 21st October, the publisher sent an editor to Bonn who was handed the package. On Friday of the following week it was passed on to its addressee, who opened the envelope, only looking briefly at the contents as he was in a hurry and already late. He put the envelope into his suitcase and took a taxi to the station.

Four hours later, in the train between Karlsruhe and Basel, the writer left his first-class compartment for about ten minutes. When he returned from the toilet, his suitcase had disappeared from the luggage-rack. He informed the guard who alerted the railway police. A baggage check at the frontier station of Lörrach brought no result, nor did another at Basel Hauptbahnhof.

When the writer arrived home that evening, he found his suitcase had got there ahead of him. An unknown man, using his name, had asked a taxidriver to deliver the case to his home and tell his wife that he had been held up and would'return an hour later.

Nothing was missing from the suitcase except for the envelope with the photos and the sketches.

The police never found a trace of them and soon gave up their investigations. Three weeks later the writer was arrested under a trumped-up charge and held for one and a half years.

Captain Francis looked out at the snow driven by violent gusts of wind past the window, without really noticing it. It seemed that his eyes were focusing on a very remote point in space. 'Why Gibraltar?' he murmured. 'The weakest point . . .'

Behind him on the desk, the sketches and calotypes of 1844 were spread out. Next to them there was a shapeless, heavily corroded piece of metal which almost looked like charcoal but had a matt sheen in some places, where samples of the material had been chipped off.

So there will be casualties, Captain Francis thought. Well, you can't have anything for nothing. And something big is going to happen. We are about to start the biggest coup in the history of the world – quite literally.

The Captain smiled, optimistic as always.

# CHAPTER FOUR

# ARTEFACT 1: TIEFENBACHER'S GUN

Axel Tiefenbacher, born in 1934 in Hanau near Frankfurt, had been a gun fanatic ever since childhood. He stole and bought guns wherever he could find them. And finally a gun was his undoing.

In 1949, he served a two-year sentence for shooting and severely injuring a US Army sergeant during a pub fight between civilians and soldiers of the occupying army in the Frankfurt district of Bockenheim. When Axel's parents' flat was searched, the police – who had been tipped off by a neighbour – found a collection of arms in the unused laundry room of the bombed-out tenement such as they had never seen before. As well as forty-two revolvers from all over the world, there were guns from former German Army supplies and from American supplies, a machine pistol of Russian origins, ammunition of every conceivable calibre, the barrel of an anti-tank grenade-launcher, plus propelling charge and several hand-grenades of American origin.

Asked where his collection came from, Tiefenbacher remained stubbornly silent. When he was let out of prison in 1951, his life went steadily downhill. He was constantly watched by the police, and his suspect or crooked activities were rarely overlooked.

In 1952 he was in jail for another eight months, this time for resisting the law – using a gun, he had threatened a municipal police officer who had been about to arrest him. The police conducted a thorough search and found in his possession two British Army automatic guns and fourteen pistols from American Army supplies, parts of an MG-34 Wehrmacht machine gun and a French anti-tank grenade which had been stolen two months earlier in Rastatt.

In spring 1953, Tiefenbacher was caught attempting to steal a car in Central Frankfurt and, before escaping, shot down a passer-by and a policeman on duty. This time he realised that the judge would not exercise mercy; five years in jail was the least he could expect.

The same night, before a police search could be fully mounted he fled south, swam across the Rhine north of Kehl and arrived in Strasbourg. When he ran out of money, as he did quite soon, he put his name down for the Foreign Legion.

After a short period of training near Perpignan and Oran, he was shipped to Vietnam. After barely three months at the front, a shell fragment severed two fingers of his left hand, thereby saving him from Dien Bien Phu. He spent two glorious months of debauchery and convalescence in Marseilles until his hand was in working order again, and then three less enjoyable months being treated for VD. Returning to Vietnam, Tiefenbacher distinguished himself as a sharpshooter, was promoted to corporal, and was awarded a medal for his courage.

Those troops remaining after the defeat were shipped to Algeria, where after suffering one defeat after another, the *Grande Nation* finally allowed the frustrated legionnaires to take it out on the civilian population. Here, too, Tiefenbacher distinguished himself by conducting a few delicate pacification missions in the Atlas Mountains, and was promoted to Senior Corporal in 1956.

Tiefenbacher's unit had been posted to Quarglia, where its task was to secure the oil fields of Hassi Messaoud and to accompany transports from the eastern trail through the Grand Erg Oriental to the drilling sites of Bourarhet at the Libyan frontier.

On 18th January 1957, Tiefenbacher was on his way back to Quarglia with two armoured cars and eighteen men, after accompanying a convoy of lorries as far as Hi Bel Guebbour and handing them over to another security unit there. It was almost dusk when they were ambushed south of Cassi Touil. The first car hit a mine. The explosion was so heavy that the vehicle's front axle was torn off and the driver was killed instantly. When the soldiers jumped off the loading platform, they found themselves being shot at from a dune. During the shooting, Tiefenbacher lost another one of his men and three others were wounded. The co-driver, whose legs had both been torn off underneath the knees by the explosion, died soon after.

The rebels took flight on camels and Tiefenbacher saw there

was no point in following them into the pathless terrain in the
dark. It was impossible to return to Quarglia with the rest of his
men, the three wounded soldiers and the weapons, since only
one vehicle was still intact. Tiefenbacher assumed that the
rebels knew this, and that they would not miss an opportunity
to overwhelm the decimated unit. Since there was no hope of
relief for eight or ten hours, he searched for some higher terrain
and ordered his men to dig in on top of a dune. Meanwhile he
sent a coded radio message informing the commander at
Quarglia of the ambush and asking for help.

The detonation of the big and probably hand-made mine had
torn a big crater into the sandy soil. Tiefenbacher towed the
badly damaged vehicle over to the side and investigated the
hole. Here he discovered a heavy, badly corroded metal object
which had been half-exposed by the explosion. It was about
forty centimetres long and seemed to be a gun barrel whose wall
had been eroded on one side. It was evident that the object had
nothing to do with the mine and had only accidentally been
exposed to the light of day. Yet Tiefenbacher recognised at first
glance that it was a fragment of a heavy anti-tank weapon. He
guessed it was a lost relic from the German Africa campaign,
but he was baffled by the heavy corrosion the metal had
suffered. In his experience, steel objects covered by sand in this
extremely dry climate stayed shiny for decades without showing
any trace of rust. This object looked as if it had been lying in salt
water for centuries.

According to an order then in force, all weapons and parts of
weapons found had to be sent to the government in Algiers to be
examined. This was because the Arabs repaired and used even
the most ancient guns in their fight against their hated colonial
masters – and also because the government wanted to know
where the desert rebels got their arms from.

Tiefenbacher interpreted this order in his own way: he
requisitioned the evidently ancient object for his private
collection, wrapped it in a blanket and put it under the driver's
seat. Then he climbed up the dune, where his men had now dug
in and were about to position their machine guns. Towards the
west the last light of the day was vanishing; the stars were
brilliant above their heads. The night proved extremely cold,
the wounded men, in particular, were suffering badly. Every
now and then there were groans or murmured curses, and even

those who were not on guard duty could not sleep. Every now and then somebody crouched behind the dune and lit a cigarette.

Tiefenbacher was positioned behind one of the machine guns, his fingers numb with cold. He had judged the situation correctly. Shortly before daybreak he heard the characteristic *chak-chak-chak* of trotting camels a short distance away. Ordering the machine guns to be turned in the direction of the noise, he listened. A few seconds later his experienced ear heard the crunching of quick feet in the sand.

In a soft voice he gave the order to shoot off a flare. The moment it popped with a dull flop and illuminated the dunes with its chalky light, Tiefenbacher opened fire. In the uncertain light he thought he could see human shapes falling and eight or ten camels about a hundred metres away. Suddenly they reared up in fright and pulled at their reins, dark patches like bullet wounds appearing on their milk-white skins. Then the light went out.

While the other machine gun continued to fire, Tiefenbacher turned his weapon in the opposite direction to counter an eventual attack from there. It never came.

The enemy had not shot a single shot. Had they all been killed instantly? Tiefenbacher listened in the darkness, but could hear nothing except for the chattering teeth of his men, who were miserably cold under the starlit sky, and the groans of the wounded as they changed position. Far away, almost out of earshot, a busy thin whisper could be heard; it was the night wind swishing over the dune, patiently moving one grain of sand after the other in the limitless hourglass of time.

It seemed an eternity until morning came. Then, finally, there was a bright shaft of light on the eastern horizon. Gradually the contours of the land appeared, but still Tiefenbacher could only make out the edges of dunes. The camels and the nocturnal shapes had disappeared, as if they had been apparitions. Taking a machine pistol, he climbed from the trench and cautiously approached the area they had fired on in the night. He could see the craters their bullets had made, yet no dead bodies, no trace of blood; only the footprints of men and camels.

'*Merde!*' Tiefenbacher said. With four of his men, he climbed into the one vehicle and followed the track for about six kilometres, before it petered out in the rocky terrain. Then he moved south in a circle and after about three kilometres came to two black nomad tents. In a thornbush enclosure a dozen sheep and goats were grazing among the sparse blades of dry grass that poked up between the stones.

Tiefenbacher stopped, ordered his men out of the truck and surrounded the tents.

'Everybody out – *quick!*' he shouted, raising his machine pistol and shooting in the air to give his order more emphasis.

There was a loud noise and two old women and two young ones appeared with four children.

'Typical,' he said. 'Not a man in sight. They're sure to be the families of the people who attacked us. Well, they'll have a surprise when they get home.'

Tiefenbach ordered the women and children herded together and cautiously approached the tents to search them for hidden arms. The first tent was empty apart from some kitchen utensils and earthenware pots on the floor, which Tiefenbacher pushed aside with his foot. When he entered the second tent he noticed a movement in the darkness. Instinctively, he fired in the direction of it. When his eyes had got used to the gloom a few seconds later, he saw an old man sitting on the floor at the back of the tent, apparently unable to walk. He had scored a direct hit.

The old man lifted his brown skinny arm and stretched out his hand as if to beg for something, while with the other hand he clutched the dirty white burnous close at the chest. Tiefenbacher saw that it was already soaked with blood. The old man gazed up with fear in his watery blue eyes, his thin cracked lips forming some inaudible words. Suddenly a stream of bright bubbling blood erupted from his mouth, ran down his chin, dyeing his wispy beard and dripping onto his chest, while he babbled on, still holding out his hand.

'Get him out of here. *Quick!*' Tiefenbacher shouted in disgust, somewhat nervous now.

Two of his men dragged the dying man into the open.

'I said, everybody out!' he shouted at the women, who immediately burst into loud wailing sounds when they saw the old man. Now the children started to join in the lamentation, crying loudly.

'Quiet, for God's sake,' Tiefenbacher shouted.

He had two sheep loaded into the vehicle and shot the other animals; then they poured petrol over the tents and set them alight.

The piercing wails of the women could still be heard as they drove back to rejoin the rest of the party.

'And these people claim to be human beings!' Tiefenbacher said to his men. 'They live in the dirt like gipsies and whine like coyotes.'

When they returned to their temporary dugout on the edge of the trail, they found the relief had arrived – ten men in three vehicles, one of which was an ambulance. In their absence, the wounded had already been taken care of, and the bodies of the driver and his co-driver had been laid into simple, flat pinewood coffins by the roadside.

'Nothing,' Tiefenbacher reported laconically.

'Nice mess,' the major commented.

'Certainly is,' replied Tiefenbacher.

Before he settled behind the steering wheel, he made sure that the antediluvian weapon which he had found in the sand was still under his seat.

It was. Nobody had taken any notice of it. They would soon enough.

In March, Tiefenbacher's unit was moved to Oran to help enforce law and order in the town. Tiefenbacher enjoyed the city life after the months he had spent in pest-infested desert quarters. One evening after a good meal and a bottle of champagne, he had gone upstairs with a plum Arab tart and had a good screw; after another drink to help him cool off he was feeling pleasantly tired in mind and body, content with his miserable existence and the miserable state of the world. It was at this moment, just as he was leaving the brothel, that he was hit by a rooftop sniper. The first bullet hit him in the shoulder, and a second in the abdomen – and that felled him. As he dropped, he pulled out his pistol and tried to roll over on his belly to get a better aim on his target, but it was no good. Lying on his back, he shot two Arab boys who had taken cover in a nearby entrance when the shots rang out and were trying to cross over to the other side of the street. Then a third shot from the darkness shattered half his jaw.

Tiefenbacher lay gasping in a fast-growing pool of blood, and by the time the ambulance came he was dead. Yet even in death he still held his weapon firmly, as if he still had the enemy in his sights.

When the dead man's locker was opened in the barracks, the collection of captured weapons found inside would have been sufficient to have brought the senior corporal before a court martial. Among them was the rusty fragment of the weapon he had found on the trail south of Cassi Touil. Tiefenbacher had cleaned it with a wire brush as best he could, and after removing all loose bits of rust, had oiled it and wrapped it into a piece of woollen blanket. Now it had a dull black colour like a piece of charcoal.

Tiefenbacher's arsenal was shown to a weapon specialist at the prefecture, who identified the pistol and automatic weapons immediately. Finally he examined the rusty fragment, which at first he had almost overlooked. It seemed to be part of a weapon, a mortar or something like that. After consulting a number of handbooks he established that it was not German Second World War. Now he was baffled; all his efforts at identification remained in vain. Finally, after a few weeks, he sent the object to the department of weapon technology in the War Ministry in Paris.

The experts there were just as baffled – particularly when they discovered that the metal was a compound which contained vanadium and wolfram and an unusually high amount of titanium, an expensive and little-known material which was used in compounds for its anti-corrosive qualities.

After long deliberation, the ministry decided to approach a US arms specialist from NATO who had taken up residence at the Palais Chaillot at the time. He became interested when he saw the results of the material analysis, because he knew that experiments with similar compounds were being made in rocket technology. He insisted that Tiefenbacher's gun was flown across the Atlantic. In September 1959 it ended up at the Navy Department for Weapon Technology in Oakland, California, where ever since the war in the Pacific the most modern materials were being developed and tested for military uses.

There, the insignificant piece of metal immediately created confusion, since it resembled part of a Navy weapon which was still being tested, and of which only four prototypes existed: a portable thrower which could be charged with tactical atomic grenades.

Commander Francis's hour had come. He had served in the Pacific Fleet in the Second World War and during the Korean War was considered one of the most outstanding experts on Russian and Chinese weapons. He was rumoured to be able to tell simply by looking at an object in flight which type of weapon had discharged it. He had a cool and brilliant mind, with a mixture of shrewdness, persistence, push and unsentimentality that is commonly called assertiveness – and is rewarded as such. He always remained optimistic with regard to his career, which he pursued with cunning and singlemindedness. Between 1954 and 1958 he had been involved with experiments undertaken by the Navy in connection with the hydrogen bomb explosion on the Eniwetok and Bikini Atoll, during which a number of materials on wrecked ships were exposed to heavy radiation.

Commander Francis was sent to Oakland by the Navy and entrusted with the mysterious and frightening unidentified object.

'Any doubts?' Commander Francis asked, scraping the ridge of his nose with the brass setting of his magnifying glass, forehead contracted to a gloomy frown which appeared to make his grizzled crewcut hair stand on end. He explored with the tips of his fingers the badly corroded surface, as if trying to reconstruct the original shape of the weapon.

'No doubt at all, Sir,' the engineer replied, and pushed his glasses from the plump rosy-cheeked face over his sweaty forehead.

Francis's eyes rested uncomfortably on the long white bristles which peeped over his partner's collar, looked at the stained lab coat which covered his voluminous paunch and seemed to burst at the buttons, until his gaze came to rest on the red, immensely broad hands. A white ape, Francis thought; a majestic, grizzly, furry, well-fed animal. In his mind's eye he recalled an image he had seen in his youth: two peasant lads rolling a freshly-slaughtered pig into a wooden trough full of boiling hot water before they shaved off the bristles from its skin with their knives . . .

'It's quite mad,' the engineer snorted and broke into a chuckle that made his enormous belly tremble.

'And what makes you say that, Mr Manley?' Francis asked.

'We've been testing the prototypes for the throwers for four months now. There've been a number of problems which have made us think it might be better to use some other material. For weeks on end we've been trying to work out which compound might meet all the demands, and at last we found a really ideal solution. And just at that moment . . .' Manley dropped his broad grey-haired paw on the table. 'Just at that moment, this . . . this *thing* lands on our desk. And it consists of the very same compound we've come up with!'

'O.K. Let's sum it up like this: most probably we're dealing here with . . .'

'Most probably? *Certainly*, Sir!'

'. . . a weapon developed by the US Navy which is in the process of being tested here at this very moment. Yet it must have been exposed to the influence of wind and weather for at least ten thousand years, according to your estimate. And as far as the composition of materials is concerned, not a single sample of this particular compound has yet been produced. Is this correct, Mr Manley?'

'Absolutely correct. But isn't it crazy?'

'You know, there's a saying of Sherlock Holmes: "When you have discounted the impossible, whatever remains, even if it cannot be proved, must be the truth." In my opinion, that's a rash maxim. I wouldn't care to discount *anything* as impossible.'

Manley dropped his bull-like head and stared at the Navy officer for a moment. 'May I ask you a question, Sir?' he said.

'Go ahead.'

'Do you read science fiction, Sir?'

'Are you asking this in a tone of reproach, Mr Manley?'

'Not at all, Sir. On the contrary . . .'

'Sometimes it's my duty to investigate things which are not susceptible to rational explanation.'

The engineer nodded and suddenly gave a radiant smile. Commander Francis's face remained completely unmoved.

'I think that's all for the moment, Mr Manley. Unless there are any more questions?'

'No-no, Sir,' the engineer said, picked up his papers and hurried out.

The Americans were still recovering from the shock caused by the launching of Sputnik I in 1957, when on 12th April 1961, at 07.07 hours Central European Time, Major Yuri Gagarin in

Vostok I orbited once round the earth in 108 minutes and landed safely near the village of Smelovka in the district of Sarstov. There was an outcry in the Western press, and in order to boost the nation's morale after this defeat in the space race, John F. Kennedy announced six weeks later, on 25th May 1961: 'Our nation should set itself the aim of sending a man to the moon and back before the end of the decade.'

The United States accordingly set their sights on the moon.

In mid-November 1962 a conference took place in Detroit, attended by NASA specialists, technologists from the aeronautical and space flight industries and specialists from Army, Air Force, and Navy. The subject under discussion was the behaviour of materials under severe stress conditions. Commander Francis had been sent there, too, and reported on information gathered by the Navy during the hydrogen tests in the Pacific. His subject was *The Behaviour of Surfaces under Extreme Radiation Charges.*

The mood of the conference was more than merely subdued. Eighteen months after Kennedy's epoch-making announcement, the US did not have a single success to its credit; on the contrary, it had been one setback after another. In November 1961, Ranger II had failed to achieve its flight path towards the moon. Towards the end of January, Ranger III missed the moon by 36,000 kilometres; Ranger IV had finally hit the moon in April and exploded on its surface as planned, but the cameras had failed. Now Ranger V had again fallen short of its target, if only by 720 kilometres. The NASA officials seemed depressed; the military officials did not hide their discontent, and there were some heated exchanges. The representatives of industry insisted that the programme had been over-hasty in its implementation, but pretended to be optimistic in the hope of attracting lucrative orders.

In the evenings, among the specialised working groups, the discussion turned to more general topics. There was a lot of talk about the 'conquest of space'.

'Tell me,' Francis casually asked Dr Thomas Winter of NASA, 'do you think it will be possible one day to conquer time, too?'

Dr Winter looked at him for a moment as if sizing him up over his rimless glasses; then he glanced at Francis's name-tag and replied, with a tiny trace of superiority in his voice: 'You must know, Commander, that the history of science is very cruel to those of us who are too ready to use the word "impossible". I personally believe that time travel is theoretically and practically improbable.'

'Improbable, but not impossible?'

'I might even go further than that,' Dr Winter replied. 'I believe it is unthinkable.'

Francis nodded.

'You see . . .' Winter continued, 'if you open up this possibility, you get into an infinity of paradoxes. Every logical step will then end in insoluble contradictions. A journey into time would do away with logic. To assume this possibility is already to fly in the face of logic.'

'So in your opinion, time travel is improbable, unthinkable, and against logic. Yet you still do not maintain that it is impossible?' Dr Winter looked at him thoughtfully, then nodded silently. 'Forgive my asking, Doctor,' Francis continued, 'but are you saying this out of exaggerated respect for the verdict of posterity?'

Dr Winter found himself warming to this Navy man, whom he had considered rather foolish at first. 'You see, Commander,' he answered patronisingly, 'probabilities and unthinkabilities do not really matter in the formation of scientific theories. They are an expression of empirical experience and of habits of thinking. And as for logic – logic reflects our human ability to perceive, not the laws of the universe.'

'I understand,' Francis said.

'It is the impossibilities, the forbidden realms of science, so to speak, which allow the mind its most fascinating speculations.'

Francis nodded thoughtfully. As soon as he returned to Washington he would have to get some of his people to dig out some more of these fascinating speculations. He continued to nod mechanically, letting his thoughts run away with him, and was hardly listening at all, when a sentence of Dr Winter's suddenly brought him back to the present.

'All decisive breakthroughs in the sciences,' the NASA official was saying, 'began life as fascinating speculations . . .'

### PART TWO

# PROJECT CHRONOTRONE

A thunderstorm raged over Huntsville, Alabama. Flashes of lightning lit the sky, followed by claps of thunder, making the rain-blanketed window-panes tremble. Outside, it was as dark as if night had fallen, although the luminous digits on the electric clock over the door said only 14.47.

In the conference room of the inner sanctum, the strip-lighting was on, as it always was, even when the sun was blazing outside. The soft breeze and whisper of the air-conditioning neutralised the noonday heat and the refreshing shower, and produced a stale, yet carefully humidified chill, which was taking its toll on those present.

Admiral William W. Francis jerked his chin forward energetically, as if to put a symbolic full stop to the debate. 'Gentlemen, I cannot understand –' A flash of lightning lit up the faces of the people present and a clap of thunder followed immediately. The admiral lowered his head and waited for a few seconds until the windows had stopped shaking; then he continued. 'I cannot understand your objections. Sooner or later, other scientists will discover that gravity and the dimension of time are interdependent. Now, we might be able to prevent others from working on this problem too intensively, but why shouldn't *we* use the advantage *we* already have? Gentlemen, the survival of our nation – the survival of Western civilisation – is at stake. We happen to be on the right track, and we ought to make the most of our good fortune. We possess the means to ensure the welfare of the Western world and we ought to act immediately, before other people beat us to it. This is the only argument that counts, gentlemen.'

Professor Samuel Fleissiger, a tall, slightly awkward-looking man in his late thirties wearing a slightly soiled polo neck sweater and a shabby brown corduroy jacket, raised his eyes from the papers in front of him and looked at the admiral. The expression in his light-grey eyes was that of a schoolmaster confronting a slightly dim-witted pupil.

'And that's why I object, Admiral,' he said, with an unmistakable trace of sarcasm. '*Because* we're concerned with the continued existence of Western civilisation and the welfare of the Western world, we must plan this project with the utmost care  Besides, it's completely unnecessary to rush into things – any so-called advantage we might gain is quite illusory. We would be like the hare in the race with the hedgehog. No matter how fast we run, the hedgehog will always be there before us.'

'Then *we* ought to be the hedgehog,' said the admiral, failing to grasp the allusion. He leant back in his chair and looked to the two technical directors from NASA for support.

Dr Herbert H. Hollister merely smiled and turned his head in the direction of Fleissiger, while Dr Walter W. Berger stared at his papers in glum silence. He was only interested in the technical aspects of the project; the facts and theoretical speculation of the academics he considered a total waste of time.

'If only it were *that* easy,' Fleissiger answered, putting together the tips of his long, narrow fingers. 'What do you think, Kafu?'

Professor Nobuyuki Kafu, a small, squat Japanese with bristly hair, was about the same age as Samuel Fleissiger. In spite of his immaculate white shirt and elegant navy-blue pin-striped suit, which softened his bull-necked, short-legged appearance, he could almost have been a middleweight boxing champion. Together with Fleissiger, he had been working on a project concerning gravitational fields and gravitational waves. While calculating models of extreme gravitational conditions found in black holes and pulsars, the two of them had discovered certain curious chronometric phenomena. In the course of their investigations they had been led to the astonishing conclusion that in gravitational fields of extreme force it is possible for particles of matter to disappear in the direction of the past.

With the help of their findings, Kafu and Fleissiger had laid the theoretical foundations of a *chronotrone*, a hypothetical device by which such gravitational fields could be produced artificially with the help of vast amounts of energy. These investigations were by now more than eight years old.

In spite of the almost unpleasant chilliness of the room,

Professor Kafu was perspiring freely. He turned his blinking slit-eyes first on his friend and long-standing colleague, then, one by one, on the other gentlemen present; then he announced in a high and slightly nasal voice: 'I believe we should first discuss the problems of what is technically possible and leave out the theoretical implications. Otherwise the gentlemen from NASA will get impatient.'

Berger flashed him a grateful look.

'I do not share this opinion at all,' Fleissiger remarked. 'All persons present ought to be quite clear about the consequences of the chronotrone project before the technical production is forced through and further millions are spent.'

'You can let *me* worry about money,' Admiral Francis interrupted him angrily.

'Oh, I know, you military people are never concerned about money when weapons are needed. But I'd remind you that it's also *my* tax money that's being spent, Admiral,' Fleissiger said pointedly.

'Does this question really belong on our agenda, Professor?' the admiral asked impatiently. Dr Hollister gave a subdued snort. Fleissiger looked at him furiously and then returned to his papers, without bothering to answer the admiral.

'The fact is,' Francis continued, 'that we've cut down other projects for years in order to have enough money for the chronotrone, and now we're about to start a big project under NASA cover. We've kept a low profile on manned space flights for ten years now, and put the Mars project back into the drawer – even though the Soviets could steal the show from us every time they launch a new space project. Are you seriously telling me you want us to put the project on ice and lose *more* time?'

'Maybe the Soviets are having the same problems as us. They could be working on something similar too,' Berger dared to interject.

The admiral was visibly taken aback, then he shook his head decisively. 'There's not the slightest reason to assume that anybody else is working in this particular field.'

'Are you saying that you're monitoring *all* research on this subject?'

The admiral leant back in his seat, a smile of forbearance on his face. His narrow white moustache formed an exact horizontal line. 'You ought to know, Professor, that for more than fifteen years I've kept close tabs on anyone and everyone working on these problems. I know precisely who has access to material which could lead him to the solution you and Professor Kafu have found.'

'Even in the Eastern bloc!'

'Even in the Eastern bloc. At least, to a large extent.'

'But surely even you can't stop more and more people becoming interested in these problems?'

'And why not, Professor?' The admiral smiled triumphantly, ignoring the expression of alarm which crossed Fleissiger's face. 'After all, we always need fresh blood. Either the person concerned is our man, and by God, we do everything in our power to help him, or . . .' Francis snapped his fingers, 'he isn't. It's as simple as that.'

'Hm,' Kafu spoke up. 'What puzzles me is the behaviour of the Soviets. They've abandoned their space station project; they're no longer planning to go to Mars; they suddenly say they want to resume the SALT talks. I can't help wondering what in heaven's name they're doing with all their money.'

'They need it to buy our wheat,' Hollister remarked.

'Right,' Francis nodded. 'They've had one bad harvest after another. But that doesn't alter the fact that we ought to press on with our project. I can't understand your hesitations, gentlemen.'

Fleissiger threw the Japanese a helpless glance and shook his head wearily. 'This is not a race, Admiral – the winner doesn't take all. In fact, there are clear advantages in letting others take the lead.'

'What? And let our actions be dictated by the opposition?'

'Admiral, the game we're involved in is rather like a game of chess where both partners are equally strong: you always have to react to your opponent's moves. The difference here is that unlike chess, the first move could prove fatal . . .'

The admiral grunted impatiently. A clap of thunder rang out. Fleissiger lit a cigarette with his spindly fingers and turned once more to face Francis.

'Look here, it's like this: supposing you sent a US commando unit to Alaska in the sixteenth century with orders to cross over to Khamchatka and secure a large part of Eastern Siberia which is rich in natural resources, before the Czar's officers turn up and take possession of it.'

'Then the history of the world would have taken a different course. And our strategic position *vis à vis* the Soviets would be vastly improved,' the admiral exclaimed triumphantly. 'That's precisely my point, professor.'

'But that's total fantasy,' Berger said impatiently. 'In the sixteenth century the only people on the Eastern seaboard were a handful of English, French and Dutch colonists who were dying of starvation and were barely able to fight off the red-skins. And anyway, how could they act on behalf of the United States? The United States didn't even exist until two hundred years later! You're speculating wildly.'

'Wait a moment, Mr Berger. Anybody can claim territories provided he's able to defend them,' Fleissiger answered. 'And if a *future* United States could somehow return to the sixteenth century . . .'

'Now I like you much better, Professor,' Francis said in a conciliatory tone.

The Japanese studied the admiral with curiosity from under the heavy folds of his eyelids, then he sank back into his chair with a contemptuous snort. 'The trouble is, the enemy can wait for another five hundred years and then send an infantry battalion to the same spot on the exact date when your un-suspecting men are about to land – and give them a very bloody reception indeed. It would be like a troop of crusaders pitted against Hitler's Wehrmacht – they'd be five centuries ahead of your men in their weapons technology. Your commando unit, Admiral Francis, would be decimated. Now do you understand what Fleissiger meant?'

Francis's triumphant smile froze on his face. Hollister lowered his eyes sadly. Berger looked more sullen than ever.

'And so far we haven't even considered the Aloysius effect,' Fleissiger remarked.

'The *what?*' asked the admiral.

'The Aloysius effect,' Fleissiger repeated, looking at Francis reproachfully over the rim of his glasses. 'So-called after Raphael Aloysius Lafferty, the inventor of the phenomenal Ktistec machine.'

'A science fiction writer of the sixties and seventies,' Kafu added by way of explanation, noticing the irritated look the admiral gave the two NASA scientists. 'Among other things,

Lafferty wrote about time travel and other consequences of time fractures.'

'Look, what's all this about?' Berger barked. 'Are you having us on, gentlemen?'

'Not at all, Dr Berger,' Fleissiger replied. 'Lafferty maintains – and his argumentation is absolutely logical – that it is impossible to use the past at will. People in the present who send somebody or something into the past in order to cause a change will never be able to find out whether this change happened, because the alternative version will become historical reality the moment the change occurs. In other words, everybody will think that things were *always* that way and no different. For example, if you send somebody back into the year 1775 to shoot George Washington before he was nominated Commander in Chief of the Armed Forces by the continental congress, then all the history books will tell you is that George Washington was a superb general who might have defeated the British, and that he was shot in 1775. That's the way it'll be. And you, gentlemen, wouldn't know any different, because that's the way you'll have learnt it at school.'

'Are we talking about the abstruse ideas of a science fiction writer or about the chronotrone project?' the admiral bellowed angrily.

'About the chronotrone project, Sir,' Fleissiger answered calmly. 'You see, Admiral, you want to use the chronotrone to put your country at a strategic advantage. The trouble is that nobody will thank you for it. No contemporary, yourself included, will ever notice any change to our advantage. And even if you were successful and improved the situation for the United States and its allies in strategic, economic, political and other respects, people will simply say: Oh, how good things are for us. They'll also wonder what in the devil's name this man Francis wants. Here he is, putting millions of dollars into an expensive project *that has no effect!* Why is he spending all that money? they'll ask. Answer: in order to make things even better for us. But isn't it unfair that *we* should be so well off and the *others* so badly off? Wouldn't it be better to use the money to help the poor mushics who are suffering under the Czar's autocratic regime? Or the millions of Chinese who are still living in serfdom and are dying of starvation in their hundred thousands every year while the rulers in Petersburg and Peking are enjoying themselves? You see, I'm assuming here that you'll have succeeded in eliminating Lenin and Mao – something I guess will be considered of the most vital importance to the Western world, if I know how our leaders' minds work.'

'You're mistaken,' Hollister blurted out. 'Our aims are quite different.'

'Aha? So there are specific objectives,' Fleissiger said, astonished.

The admiral kept his lips pressed together and threw the engineer a gloomy look, then he turned to the professor. 'Things can't go on like this. We'll be blacking the oil sheikhs' boots sooner or later – either that, or the Communists will take over altogether. Look at us: one recession after the other. And now we've got anti-nukes and eco-nuts protesting every time an oil-rig is towed out to sea. All this, while the Arabs are buying golden toilets for their desert palaces. It has to be stopped – once and for all.'

Hollister nodded agreement. Fleissiger looked irritably around the table. He had never known the cool Francis to show such emotion. 'So that's the way the wind blows,' he said, hesitantly.

'But surely,' Kafu threw in, 'the costs of the enterprise will be inconceivably high?'

'So what?' Francis replied with indignation. 'The country is capable of making sacrifices if its security and welfare are at stake.'

'And the gains will be remarkable,' Hollister said – but nobody listened.

'What you propose, then, Admiral,' said Kafu, 'is to enter every conflict in history and alter the outcome in our favour. It is an equation – I almost said *game* – with an infinity of variables. No country could possibly see such a project through. Think of the economic cost. Quite possibly our civilisation, perhaps even the whole world as we know it, will perish in the attempt.'

'We have faced threats from other quarters before now,' Francis replied. 'We shall do so again, Professor – even if we have to place military bases all along the time-line as far back as the pre-Cambrian age.'

'A base for every hundred, every thousand, every ten thousand years?' Fleissiger asked sarcastically. 'You'll need quite a few men . . .'

'I want to see who'll win the game,' the admiral barked.

Kafu shook his head. 'But don't you see? It won't be of any use to us. It'll be useless if the others are only *one* day earlier than you.'

'Then we shall be there one day earlier *still*,' Francis shouted angrily, and hit the pile of papers in front of him with the palm of his hand. 'Even if we have to send a fleet of aircraft-carriers and atomic submarines into the Algoncium age and have them cruise on the original ocean!'

Fleissiger looked at him with concern. 'My God,' he murmured. 'You really are serious.'

'Thank you, Professor. I take that as a compliment.'

'Perhaps we ought to turn to the technical details then,' Hollister suggested, giving the admiral an uncomfortable look. 'We haven't even considered those yet.'

'We have positive proof that the project will be a success,' Francis retorted. The NASA man looked startled. 'We have . . .' – the admiral counted the objects that had been found on the fingers of one hand – 'the rocket-thrower from Algeria, the Jeep from Gibraltar and the fragments of plastic material collected by the Pope.'

'And the drilling samples made by the *Glomar Challenger*,' Hollister hastened to add.

'And the drilling samples from the *Glomar Challenger*,' the admiral nodded.

Fleissiger seemed doubtful. 'But how do you conclude from these that the enterprise will be a success?'

Berger saw that his moment had come and was about to launch into his speech when Professor Kafu got up, filled a plastic mug at the water fountain and drank from it noisily.

When he had sat down again, Fleissiger said: 'It's your turn now, Berger.'

'Well,' Berger began, 'it would be best if I summed up the position first. So far we've made thirty-eight experiments with the small cage, all of which were successful. We've sent atomic clocks welded into plastic spheres back between five hundred and five thousand years. They were all placed in the surroundings of the institute and recovered from low depths. With the bigger cage in Arizona we achieved distances of between one thousand and one million years. Out of fourteen time devices, twelve have so far been recovered. However, in the case of the third and largest cage, which is also sited in Arizona and started operation six months ago, we've found a high incidence of scatter.'

'What's its range?' Kafu snorted, impatiently twisting his plastic mug. Hollister glared at the plastic shape, hoping to discourage the Japanese from manipulating it, but to no avail.

'The highest so far,' Berger said. 'Sixty million years. Two devices, though identical in structure, form, and matter, and identical in the force of gravitational field at the start, were found almost exactly seven million years apart.'

'116,666 per cent,' Kafu murmured. 'What exactly do you mean by identical field force, Doctor?'

'Down to a millionth of total energy.'

'How much is that?'

Berger hesitated a moment and looked questioningly at the admiral, who didn't react. 'About nine hundred thousand megawatt hours.'

The Japanese nodded with a smile. Fleissiger whistled through his teeth. 'Quite a steep electricity bill you'll be having.'

'It took us weeks to recover the two probes,' Berger continued. 'We had to consider all the orogenetic factors and calculate a simulated continental drift. This does not stay constant at all times and is slowed down by the blockage caused by the mountain ranges in the test area. One of the probes was dug out one hundred and fifty-eight miles away, the other had a deviation of a hundred and eighty-two miles. Both were found at a depth of about eighty metres.'

'Remarkable', Kafu declared.

'Yes, remarkable,' confirmed Admiral Francis, and pushed out his chin defiantly in Fleissiger's direction.

'Tell me, Dr Berger,' Fleissiger said slowly. 'Have you ever tried to dig out one of your atomic clock spheres *before* you put it into the cage and dropped it?'

Berger's face twisted into a grimace, as if he had bitten into a mustard seed unawares. 'Well, I don't know . . .' he said uncomfortably, turning for help to Hollister, who looked at Fleissiger uncomprehendingly.

The professor raised his index finger and looked at Berger over the rim of his glasses disapprovingly. 'Aloysius.'

'This is indeed an interesting aspect of the matter, Doctor,' Francis intervened. 'We should really have tried this occasionally. Perhaps . . .'

'. . . The egg appears before the chicken has laid it,' Fleissiger completed with a grin.

Berger glanced at the admiral briefly and shrugged his shoulders sullenly. He flipped through his papers until he had found the thread again, and resumed: 'Our most important problem now is to drastically lower the scatter in the range between five and six million years. We'll need to get it below the hundred-year mark we've so far managed to reach – if possible to ten or even five years.'

'And I'm quite confident we will,' the admiral added, bowing and tapping his papers with his pencil for emphasis, as if this could give more weight to his words.

'Why between five and six million years?' Fleissiger asked, astonished. 'Do you mean to say that the project is already geared to specific target dates?'

'Yes, indeed it is, gentlemen. With your help we've been able to progress to the point where success is very nearly within our grasp. Cage four is already under construction, and its Kafu field will be strong enough to transport men and materials as far into the past as the period named.'

'Did you say *men?*' Fleissiger asked, aghast. 'But you know very well that these people couldn't possibly be brought back into the present! We're still at the testing stage of a theory whose consequences are still incalculable – and yet you intend to risk human lives? I hope I've misheard you!'

'Now, now, Professor, you're being far too pessimistic,' Francis said, trying to sound conciliatory. 'I don't usually turn people's attention to contradictions in their own arguments, but you said yourself that there was no need to rush anything. Although we don't yet have the means to get something back from the past into the present, we *shall* be in a position to do so in ten, twenty, or fifty years at the latest. And then we shall get back the men from *everywhere*, wherever in the past they may be.'

'Do you realise the implications of your statement, Admiral?'

'Of course I do, Professor. The human mind stops at nothing – you yourself have proved this triumphantly. Ten years ago, everybody would have considered time travel an idle fantasy. and even today if I allowed you to publish your findings, you'd meet with ridicule and mockery. But soon you'll be able to prove your theory.'

'Mr Francis,' Fleissiger' said with great seriousness. The admiral frowned indignantly; he was not used to being addressed as plain Mister Francis and hated it passionately. 'You could be compared to the optimist in the smart restaurant, who, although completely broke, orders oysters by the dozen in the firm belief that one of them will contain a pearl with which to pay for his meal. Do you realise the risks involved in this project? And the cost – in human and financial terms – of proceeding with it?'

In the course of his speech, Fleissiger had raised his voice more and more and had ended up by virtually shouting his questions into the admiral's face. When he had finished there was an uncomfortable pause.

Finally Francis cleared his throat. 'I realise you'll probably never forgive me, *Mister* Fleissiger, for advising you not to publish the results of your research.'

'Pshaw,' Fleissiger grunted.

'You and Professor Kafu would certainly have received the Nobel Prize for your discoveries.'

'We were very generously compensated, if that's what you mean,' Fleissiger said, with a sarcastic little bow. 'I could retire right now and write my memoirs – except that I wouldn't be allowed to publish them.'

'I hope you understand that we cannot allow any leaks or breaches of security.'

'Of course I understand, Admiral.'

'Am I right in thinking that the experiments using the fourth cage will not be made on United States territory, but on the ocean? said Professor Kafu, in an attempt to bring the conversation back to a more objective level.

'Why do you assume that?' Francis asked suspiciously.

'Well,' the Japanese said with an impenetrable smile. 'Wherever I look I see the Navy. It seems a reasonable conclusion.'

Francis looked at him for a few moments with a frown, then his face brightened up. 'You're right, Professor. There'll be more than one cage of type four; they'll be deployed at various points, all in international waters.'

'And how will you solve the energy problem?'

'In the course of the experiments, two nuclear ships will be launched disguised as supply ships. Eight more are in the docks, and they'll be available in the middle or towards the end of next year. Every one of them will carry a cage of type four.'

'And what about the field of action?' asked Kafu.

'You'll be informed of this in good time, gentlemen,' the admiral said smoothly. 'We couldn't manage without your cooperation'.

'And what about the poor sods on board those ships?' Fleissiger asked softly.

'They are without exception volunteers,' the admiral replied. 'You can leave the question of men and materials to me, Professor. I can understand your misgivings, but I don't share them. We shall spare no effort or expense to get our boys back from wherever and whenever in the past they may be after the work is done. And you shall help me in this, gentlemen. The Navy is about to construct a large structure which will be erected at a depth of forty metres underwater near our base in the north-eastern Bermudas. There it is far enough removed from the mainland to avoid the risk of gravitational anomalies triggering off earthquakes. The structure will be used exclusively to reverse the effect of the Fleissiger generator and so produce a negative Kafu field. With the help of which we shall be able to transport matter from the past into the present.'

'And do you know what a Kafu field is?' Fleissiger asked, aghast.

'That's not within my area of competence,' Francis answered with indignation, looking to Hollister and Berger for help.

Fleissiger groaned. 'A Kafu field is an artificially-produced gravitational anomaly which, when the critical field force is reached, propels matter situated in its centre from our universe and through time. The surplus of gravitational energy which results from the anomaly balances itself out in the space-time continuum in the direction of the past, like a longitudinal wave. The greater the surplus in proportion to the matter supplied, the further into the past the matter is transported; the matter will re-enter the universe where the carrier wave peters out – in other words, when its energy surplus is used up. The decisive aspect of this balancing process is the fact that it runs counter – and *only* counter – to the time-flow direction. Are you with me, Admiral?'

'Then you'll simply have to turn the goddam effect around,' the admiral shouted angrily.

'But,' Kafu said slowly, 'that would be like putting a pot full of water onto a hotplate and trying to turn the water into ice.'

Fleissiger pushed back his chair and jumped up. He hurried over to the water fountain, filled up a plastic mug with trembling hands and drained it greedily, as if dying of thirst. For a moment he felt he was going to be sick.

Suddenly outside the sun broke through and the raindrops on the window-pane were fractured into hundreds of glittering particles by the light.

PART THREE

# DROPPED

# CHAPTER ONE

# VOLUNTEERS

For some reason Steve Stanley had an uncomfortable feeling when he got a phone call from General Snydenham late one afternoon.

'I have to talk to you, Major. Come over immediately.'

'Yes, Sir'.

Steve put on his uniform jacket, combed his hair, and set out for the general's bungalow. The sun was already low on the western horizon, but it was still very hot. Somewhere in the suspended camouflaged hangars, the engines of a fighter plane were being tested noisily, and the hot, dry desert air was heavy with the acrid stench of burnt kerosene. On the other side of the runway five helicopters were lined up, their narrow rotor-blades drooping sadly, trembling in the wind like giant steel feathers.

Steve knocked at the door of the bungalow and entered.

'Hi, Major,' Snydenham said, baring his dentures and gesturing peremptorily to the shabby green leather armchair in front of his desk. The general was a very tall, skinny man in his mid-fifties with full snow-white hair, remarkably long for a military officer of his rank, a small, well-groomed and equally snow-white moustache which looked as if it had been glued to his narrow, deeply tanned face, and an unusually broad mouth. His fleshy, almost protruding lips suggested that he was a gourmet; but the deep grooves running from the sides of his strong, hook-like nose to the corners of his mouth indicated also that ulcers detracted from his enjoyment of rich food.

'Won't you sit down, Major Stanley?' he said with a smile, pushing the thick full hair from his forehead.

'Thank you, Sir,' Steve said, and abandoned himself to the enormous armchair.

'It seems NASA are looking for astronauts again,' the general said, waving a document in the air.

Get to the point, Steve thought, and attempted a quick look

at the letter heading, but without success. The noise of the engines outside had been softened to a whine by the sound-proofed windows of the bungalow, yet the gentle noise remained disturbing. Out beyond the runway, a flock of sheep were grazing peacefully. There was no shepherd in sight.

'If you decide not to take it, we'll meet again next week – if you do, I'll see you in five years' time,' Snydenham declared. 'That's about as much as they let on in their letter.'

Steve was thoughtful. Did this mean that at last they were preparing for a manned flight to Mars? The rumours of an impending Soviet expedition had never been completely quashed – in fact, they had been deliberately nurtured by NASA – yet the government had never been able to make up their mind. For once, though, it had seemed that those on the side of caution had been in the right: the Russians had launched one space probe after another from Baikonur, yet none of them ever got beyond the orbit of the earth. So what had happened in the meantime? Had the doubters been proved wrong? Would the project go ahead?

Outside, two training planes came gliding in to land, one close to the other, passing the window like shadows and suddenly starting up again with whining engines. The helicopters on the other side of the runway seemed to melt for a moment in the ripple of the exhaust fumes.

'That's as much as I can tell from the letter of request, Major Stanley,' Snydenham said. 'There's also a flight ticket to Miami.'

'Thank you, Sir', Steve nodded, not quite sure what he was being thankful for.

'NASA are looking for volunteers, apparently for a big project. You're the ninth pilot they've asked for from my units.'

'Oh,' Steve said, with some disappointment.

'I hope we shall meet again next week, Major.'

'If you want me to reject the offer, Sir, I shall do so,' Steve said.

The general looked at him for a few seconds, somehow managing to smile and frown disapproval at the same time.

'No, no, Major. You must do what they want you to do, unless you have good reasons not to. Naturally I'm reluctant to give you up because I consider you one of my very best men; but you're also a qualified astronaut and your training has cost a lot of money. If you're needed, it's your duty to make yourself available.'

Snydenham got up. Stanley jumped from the armchair and saluted, but the general did not respond, merely stretching out his tanned right hand in a friendly gesture over his desk. Stanley seized it and shook it warmly.

'Good luck, Steve.'

'I'll do my best, Sir.'

Returning to his room, Steve threw the ticket and the travelling documents on to his tiny formica-topped desk and stared at them. He put his uniform jacket on the bed and sat down in the cool draught of air from the ventilator.

He had never expected to be reactivated again as an astronaut. After all, he was forty years old; though physically in peak condition, he had long realised that his best years lay behind him. He had nothing to feel bitter about; God knows, he had had all the luck – even though it had not necessarily made him happy. After being trained as a pilot in his youth, he had been sent to Guam when President Johnson's fears of a North Vietnamese invasion had become so strong that the B-52 seemed the only answer. He had been on the point of being recalled, when Tricky Dicky had appeared on the scene.

After ten wasted years, the boys finally came home – or at least those who were still alive. And Steven B. Stanley was fortunate enough to be among them. For a time he flew the B-1 prototypes from Rockwells, but then, in spring of 1977 after the failure of the SALT II talks, the United States under President Carter embarked on a new arms race, putting all their hopes into the unmanned Cruise Missile and scrapping the expensive B-1. Out of a job, Steve volunteered to join NASA, where experienced pilots were needed as fourth-generation astronauts. To call them 'astronauts' was something of a euphemism; they were being trained as shuttle-pilots, and as such, they would hardly ever get further than a hundred kilometres beyond the earth's atmosphere, although NASA kept them interested with rumours of an impending expedition to Mars – a plausible enough story, since the Soviets were suspected of preparing a manned mission to the Red Planet too.

In 1977, the American intelligence service dropped hints that the Soviet Government was placing extensive orders with heavy industry and electronics industries; these, it was reported, were not directly connected either with armaments production or with the vast production of 'Backfires'. After that, rumours about a Soviet expedition to Mars spread like wildfire each time they launched a space rocket. Since the two US Viking landers launched in 1976 had not brought back definite information about the existence of life on Mars and had only added to the problems already faced by eco-biologists, chemists and geologists, a number of prominent scientists were now calling for a manned expedition to the neighbour planet. NASA entered into the debate in a spirit of cooperation and called for volunteers. Every now and then some NASA directors, under pressure from industry, would revive the old slogans of 'US prestige', 'national honour' and such like, and the plans drawn up by the late Wernher von Braun would be taken from the drawer and dusted. But the objectives would only be pursued half-heartedly. The orders given out to industry were tentative: project studies, alternative solutions, preliminary costings. Congress kept a tight hold of the purse-strings. Nobody really believed in the race to the Red Planet, and nobody ever really knew for certain whether the Russians were seriously pushing ahead with *their* preparations. And Congress was tight with its money for another reason; for although only a few people knew, money was being constantly diverted into other channels – channels which were proving to be insatiable.

In 1981 regular shuttle flights were started and Spacelab began its work. When, soon after that, the date for the launch of a Mars expedition drew near and the Soviets *still* did not seem to be planning a manned mission, the United States temporarily put their own project on ice. The Soviets' inactivity in this field was a mystery to them. Meanwhile, the military officials responsible for the chronotrone project considered the situation serious and urged a speeding-up of their project. The construction of cage carrier ships was accelerated, and the scientific staff expanded.

Steve B. Stanley was unaware of these developments, of course. All he knew was that the government had lost interest in space flight and were withdrawing more and more scientific and technical personnel. In 1983, after going into orbit half a dozen times and returning safely to earth, he left NASA, finding the work there not to his taste. Twenty hours of tests and instrument checks, and then barely an hour's flight – that was the first part of the mission. Then came two hours of the same procedure, in constant radio contact with space station and ground control; then, before you knew it, it was time to head back to earth, push the button to dispose of containers on re-entry into the atmosphere, and prepare for the landing.

By his third mission, Steve had come to feel like a taxi-driver. All through the flight he was ordered about by nervous metallurgists, biologists, geographers, meteorologists and astronomers, all of them over-anxious for their own safety and that of their instruments and only too ready to blame him whenever something went wrong. On his sixth return flight, when he emptied a full toilet bucket into space and saw it burn up like fireworks, he finally made his decision. He would go back to the Air Force as a pilot instructor.

Two years ago he had come to New Mexico.

The flight ticket was made out for Friday, which gave him two days to put his affairs in order. His few belongings fitted easily into two metal suitcases and an army holdall. The following afternoon he called up Lucy, his girlfriend for the past six months. She was an intelligent girl in her late thirties with auburn hair and inviting green eyes a little too far apart, and she worked as a secretary in a lawyer's office in Albuquerque.

After collecting his marching orders, Steve was taken by jeep from the Air Force base into town and took a taxi to the lawyer's office.

Like most short men Steve liked his women tall, and Lucy fitted the bill. She jokingly called him 'Frankie boy' because of his remote resemblance to Frank Sinatra in such oldies as *From Here to Eternity* and *The Man with the Golden Arm* and maintained that he must have some Italian blood. Steve could not imagine how an Italian could have forced his way into the pious Baptist family of the Stanleys, but he had to admit there was something in it. After all, his parents had often been to Europe early in their married life. He could barely remember his mother, and most of what he knew about her he had learned from his father. She had died in an accident before he reached the age of two. Only her voice had stuck in his memory, a clear, high-pitched, melodious voice which for some reason he associated with colourful autumn leaves and the smell of overripe fruit on calm sunny afternoons.

Steve had planned to ask Lucy out for a meal and take her to a bar afterwards, but she insisted on cooking something for him. So they went shopping in Lucy's VW and afterwards Lucy prepared a delicious and hellishly hot dish from her Mexican repertoire. Soon the conversation turned to Steve's trip to Miami. When they had reached their second bottle of Los Reyes, Lucy looked at him with her clever green eyes and said: 'Benedict', (his hated middle name: she always called him Benedict when she wanted to say something serious) 'you must be the one to decide. It's your job – the choice is yours. I should hate you to feel you've missed out on something big because of me. It would be bad for both of us.'

'Listen, Lucy, I just don't want to make a decision without talking it through with you . . .'

She put her hand on his arm, looking at him with a smile in which he detected a tiny trace of sadness. 'You've long since made your decision, Steve. Even if you haven't admitted it to yourself yet.'

'But Lucy, I . . .'

'Maybe a pair of stubborn old mules like us shouldn't be put in harness together.' When he looked at her helplessly, she continued: 'But call me from the Cape. Tell me what's happening – just so that I know.'

In the morning, lying exhausted beside her, Steve asked himself seriously whether he wouldn't much rather be in harness with Lucy than work for NASA in any capacity. Then they both snatched some sleep before daybreak.

When Steve woke up, Lucy had already left for the office. She had deliberately made it easy for him; that was her way. He took his time over breakfast, even allowing himself one of Lucy's cigarettes. He put on a record of Italian lute music which he found on top of the pile and tried to settle down and listen to it; but soon he got up again and began idly studying the postcards Lucy had stuck on the wall with drawing-pins. His thoughts were going round in circles; he felt a strange restlessness which he could not explain to himself. It was almost like that time when they posted him to Guam. His father had died shortly before, of lung cancer.

Overcome by nausea, Steve stubbed out the second cigarette he had lit and went through into the kitchen to wash the dishes from yesterday evening. Then he got dressed, took his two suitcases and army holdall and set out for the airport.

He arrived there far too early. The plane from Miami was two hours late because of a storm low over the Gulf. The return flight was via Memphis, not Houston.

He called Lucy and said goodbye. She was very busy and couldn't talk for long – which he guessed was a good thing.

Towards four in the afternoon the plane finally took off, and when it touched down in Miami dusk was falling. After the dusty dry air of New Mexico, the sultry atmosphere of Florida felt like a slap in the face with a wet towel.

'Major Stanley?' asked a gentleman in civilian clothes as he approached the exit.

'That's me, yes,' he said.

'Would you follow me, please?'

'My luggage is still . . .'

'Leave that to us. Could I have your ticket, Major?'

'But . . .'

'My name's Walton, Commander Alan S. Walton, Navy, at present seconded to NASA. We've been waiting for you for two hours.'

'The plane was delayed.'

'We know, Major.' Steve took an instant dislike to the Navy man. But almost as if he had read his thoughts and intended to improve on the unfavourable impression he had made, the commander suddenly turned round and smiled at him. It was a stereotyped smile without warmth.

The guy's as charming as a deep freeze, thought Steve. He was puzzled too, as to what a Navy man was doing, mixed up in NASA affairs. The Navy had often lent a hand recovering landing capsules and recently, shuttle boosters from the sea – and they had always asked a high price for their help, too – but a Navy man acting as escort to a NASA astronaut? It was new to him. If the Navy were recruiting for their Sealab experiments, they had come to the wrong man. He swore he would take the next plane back to Albuquerque.

He was taken to a room in the old part of the airport which was usually reserved for transit passengers from second- or third-class airlines. There were about fifty men there. An elderly grey-haired waiter in a burgundy jacket, light gabardine trousers and crêpe shoes was clearing away empty coke bottles and beer cans and emptying over-flowing ashtrays into a large trashcan.

While Steve was looking around for familiar faces, he heard a voice he knew.

'I should have known old Steve would be here, too!'

The voice belonged to Jerome Bannister, with whom he had taken his NASA training, a tall, broad-shouldered man in his early forties with pronounced cheek-bones, sparkling black eyes and a complexion like a cowboy from a Marlboro commercial. He gave Steve a friendly punch on the shoulder. They had not met for more than two years. Bannister had left NASA at about the same time as Steve and had become an instructor in a private flying school in Tucson, hoping to save enough money to open a school of his own.

Bannister was accompanied by a young, rather plump-looking man with sparse fair hair, a cheerful grin on his red-cheeked face and a dashing reddish moustache, evidently his pride and joy, judging by the way he constantly tugged at it. He seemed to be sticking to Jerome like a burr to a woollen sweater.

'Harald Olson,' Bannister introduced him. 'The best aero-nautics engineer I've ever met. Give him a toolchest and a little time and he'll make a bus fly.'

The fair-haired young man nodded enthusiastically and giggled cheerfully. Steve was taken aback by this reaction and gazed at Olson in surprise before finally giving him a friendly nod. He certainly seemed rather strange if not a little mad. This was not at all like Jerome, who usually chose his friends very carefully and was notoriously sparing in his praise. Perhaps they had both been drinking.

It was only now that he realised how thirsty he was; but it was too late. Everyone must have been waiting for him, because three minutes later they were led to two airport buses which took them to an old 737 charter plane belonging to Eastern Airways which was parked a little out of the way.

They rolled onto the runway immediately and soon they were flying high above the coloured lights of Miami. Then the plane turned north.

'Do you know what they're planning for us?' Steve asked

Jerome, who was sitting next to him.

Bannister pursed his lips and shook his head slowly. 'Hard as I've tried, I can't find rhyme or reason in it.'

'To Mars?' The moment Steve asked this question he became aware how stupid it was. If it had been *that*, they would have known by now.

Jerome looked at him askance. 'Are you serious?'

'No, not really,' Steve admitted.

'Look at these people,' Jerome said softly. 'I know some of them. A few pilots with or without fighting experience; a few trained astronauts; lots of first-class technicians – but most of 'em haven't a clue about rocketry, let alone space flight. The Navy seems to come into it in a big way, though; there are lots of Navy pilots, good men. So far the Navy have only done recovery jobs for NASA, but this time it looks as if they're really in charge. But can you think of a reason why they should be interested in Mars?'

'Maybe they want to cruise about in torpedo boats on the Mars canals.'

Jerome did not respond. He merely shook his head and stared into space absentmindedly.

When they arrived at Cape Canaveral they were welcomed by a horde of officials and led into a plain room lit by yellow neon lights, where they were issued with luncheon and drink vouchers and assigned to their quarters. Finally they had their pictures taken by a polaroid camera and received a plastic card with coloured portrait, name and military rank. Each man also received a plastic folder and pen. On the cover of the folder, under the NASA emblem, were the words *Symposium: New Goals of Navigation* embossed in gold.

Wondering what he could possibly have to contribute to the new goals of navigation, Steve wandered off to his quarters, one of many small bungalow-style huts shaded by eucalyptus trees and separated by closely cropped hedges, well-kept lawns and flower beds. There were distant flashes of lightning over the sea. The air was hot and humid. Not a leaf was moving. Close by there was the croaking of a chorus of frogs.

Steve was dead tired. He took a hot shower, went to bed naked and fell asleep within a few seconds.

.

On Saturday morning the participants in the 'symposium' met in the large conferènce room of the space flight centre. Normally this was where working committees sat when a major project had reached its technical completion phase, so as to check on coordination issues before starting montage.

Steve was surprised to see how many participants had been asked to the conference: there must have been between a hundred and sixty and a hundred and eighty altogether, including about two dozen women.

A tall, slim white-haired official by the name of Francis came in, looking very impressive in his admiral's uniform and flanked by a number of Navy bigwigs, their assistants and a few civilians, too – presumably NASA personnel. Several security officers were also in attendance, behaving with deliberate casualness and studied indifference. They all sat down at a table at the far end of the room, occasionally glancing at the audience with curiosity and studying the papers spread out in front of them.

'This looks like a gala performance,' Jerome mumbled. He had sat down next to Steve and Olson was on his other side.

'I'll be interested to see where it's all leading to . . .' Steve said softly. 'With a turn-out like that . . .'

'I don't like the look of it,' Jerome answered, with a shake of his head. The expression of dislike on his face deepened when Francis leapt energetically onto the speaker's rostrum and grabbed the desk with both hands. With the US flag on one side and the NASA standard on the other, he welcomed the audience with a winning smile and after adjusting the microphone, proceeded to speak for thirty minutes without once mentioning anything more specific than the 'country's honour' and the fact that 'the best brains of the nation' had been gathered together for some purpose intimately connected with the 'future of the nation'. The only factual revelation was that the mission to which they had been called would probably take five years and that during this time they would not be able to have contact with their 'home country'.

'Excuse me, Sir,' somebody in the audience asked. 'Does this mean that during the time specified there won't even be radio contact with earth?'

'No comment,' the admiral answered. 'I repeat: during the course of the mission, which will take about five years, there will not be any contact with the home country.'

'Sir, is this interruption of contact due to technical . . .' the questioner continued relentlessly.

'No comment,' Admiral Francis replied, evidently a little irritated. 'You will understand, ladies and gentlemen, that at this stage of the project I am not in a position to give you any more specific information. The project is top secret. Only when you have taken a positive decision – and you will be given till tomorrow to do so – will you obtain further information concerning your mission from me.'

There was a general murmur of indignation at this, and somebody shouted something about 'a pig in a poke'.

'Ladies and gentlemen . . .' The admiral raised his voice. 'Ladies and gentlemen . . . I admit that I'm asking you to take an unusual decision. Yet the risks are no greater than those involved in any technological enterprise in space. Everything in our power will be done to ensure your safety – I give you my word of that.' He waited for the noises in the room to subside, then continued: 'The persons gathered here in this room have been chosen from the most diverse technological and scientific disciplines, and from technological units of the Air Force, the Navy, Army, and the Marines. But there's one thing you all have in common: you're all either unmarried or divorced and without family. You're therefore largely free of responsibilities. But I want to add one more thing.' He lowered his white-haired head and raised an index finger for emphasis. 'We've invited many more people that we actually need. For the moment, at least. Therefore, any one of you who isn't absolutely sure that he wants to take the decision, or feels that he can't go along with the mission whole-heartedly, ought to return his card. Nobody will bear him a grudge; nobody will blame him; nobody will ask him for his reasons. The decision is entirely in your hands, ladies and gentlemen.' Francis pushed his chin out in a challenging way and looked around the audience. 'Yet if you *do* decide to accept this challenge, ladies and gentlemen; if you *do* come back at ten o'clock tomorrow morning, you will have an opportunity of belonging to an élite, of accomplishing something hitherto totally inconceivable. You will guarantee the safety and the well-being of our nation by your work. You will set the course for a better, more glorious future for our country, the Western world, the Christian tradition, perhaps

the whole of civilisation. Ladies and gentlemen, I thank you.'
Jerome turned to Steve with a look of consternation, as if he
had lost a filling in a tooth.
'Jesus!' said Olson. 'What crusading zeal. Even St Bernard
couldn't have put it better.'
Jerome looked at Steve questioningly.
'He was some kind of Christian demagogue who lived in the
twelfth century and mobilised armies of knights against the
Saracens,' Steve explained.
'I can almost hear the sabres rattling,' Jerome said grimly.

'Does anyone know what this bullshit about setting the course
for the future is all about?' Steve asked. He and a few others had
gathered in Bannister's hut that evening.
'Search me,' Geoffrey 'Moses' Calahan answered, leaning
with his back to the door and twirling his whisky glass so as to
melt the ice cubes. He was one of those tall black men who seem
to have been bred specially for basketball teams.
As well as Moses, Jerome, Steve, and Harald, there was Paul
Loorey. He had arrived well-prepared, with a suitcase full of
whisky, knowing the Cape from his time as an astronaut. 'It's
not only the swamps that are dried up round here, boys,' he had
said as he opened his case. 'You have to drive a hundred miles
to find a decent drink.' Paul had been a shuttle pilot, like Steve
and Jerome, but had lasted a year longer than them before
returning to the Air Force.
Steve looked up and into the amber-coloured eyes of
Calahan, whom he had met for the first time only a few minutes
ago. Moses lowered his close-cropped head and took a sip from
his glass.
'And what'll happen once this mysterious course has been
set?' Steve asked.
'Don't ask me, man,' Moses said. 'I'm no clairvoyant. You
any ideas, Paul?'
Paul Loorey was a sullen-looking man in his mid-thirties,
slightly shorter than Steve, but strongly built and squat;
judging by his appearance, he could have been a clerk or school
teacher. In answer to Moses' question he shrugged his
shoulders, toying indecisively with his glass, and lay back on the
bed.
'I've kept my ear to the ground for rumours,' Jerome said

hesitantly. 'The hottest tip is that the Navy are cooking something up in the Bermudas – top secret, of course. Some complicated affair concerning gravitational waves, artificial gravitational anomalies.'

'Artificial gravitational anomalies?' Moses asked, baffled. 'What the hell are *they*?'

Jerome shrugged his shoulders. 'Nobody knows anything specific. It's impossible to find out.'

'Then there must be something in it,' Moses said. There were nods all round.

'Gravity disturbances, gravity suspension, gravity anomalies, gravity wave interferences . . .' Steve meditated aloud. He was now beginning to feel the comforting warmth of the whisky in his bloodstream. He had been sunning himself all afternoon behind his bungalow until the sky had clouded over. He had felt chilly before, and the drink was welcome. 'And NASA is mixed up with it, too,' he said, whistling through his teeth.

'What's it all mean?' Harald Olson asked.

'Gravitation means matter,' Loorey said, 'and matter means gravitation. What effect would a gravitational anomaly have on matter?'

'How anomalous is this anomaly?' Moses interrupted.

'Considerable,' Jerome replied, 'judging by the amount of energy used. It's said to be in the region of giga watts . . .'

'Of what?' Harald asked.

'In an extreme case, a gravitational anomaly,' Lorey continued, 'could have the effect of making matter disappear altogether.'

While Jerome spoke, Harald Olson had been working feverishly on his pocket calculator and making notes in his NASA folder. He now lifted his head, amazed.

'Disappear *where*?' he asked.

'Good question,' Loorey said.

Suddenly they all fell silent and the room was still, except for the hum of the air conditioner.

'Aha. Well, now, we could be getting closer,' Jerome said, sharing out what remained of the bottle into the glasses. 'So who's joining up?'

'Me,' Harald Olson answered like a shot. 'It's something new for a change.'

'As I'm already one of the country's élite,' Moses declared, in a mocking reference to Francis's speech, 'I guess I'll have no choice but to accede to my country's demands.'

'We can't leave it all to the Navy, now can we?' Loorey said, contemptuously. 'And anyway, I'm curious to see what it's all about.'

'What about you, Steve?' Jerome asked.

Steve shrugged his shoulders. 'You?' he asked, throwing the question back.

Jerome put a hand on his shoulder. 'I don't think I can let you all handle this project on your own. After all, if we're to believe the admiral, the traditions of Western civilisation are at stake.'

'Fuck him,' Moses said.

'So we intend to give our lives,' Loorey said sullenly, 'in the service of our country?'

Jerome snorted with contempt.

'That's right, man,' said Moses with a grin. 'In order to prepare the way for a better, more glorious future.'

'I'll drink to that,' said Steve. And they all raised their glasses.

'The Navy defending Western civilisation,' Loorey suddenly spluttered. 'That must be the funniest thing I've heard in years!'

Steve lay in the darkness, on the verge of sleep, his alcohol-numbed brain plagued by questions. Where could matter affected by gravitation disappear *to*? What happens when gravitational anomaly occurs? But his thoughts were lost in an impenetrable maze. Every time he thought he discovered a way out and ran towards it he came up against a brick wall. His head and legs felt as heavy as lead.

Soon he fell into a fitful sleep and dreamed about a story he had read many years ago. It was about a time-traveller who returned to Shakespeare's England and found himself in a nightmare world. Steve himself was the time-traveller. In front of an inn, in a muddy road among the rubbish, he found a half-rotting severed hand and on its grey wrinkled palm, an eye which opened and stared at him attentively.

In the large panelled hall on the first floor of the inn, which was lit by one narrow window and from which strange narrow doors led off into the adjoining rooms, sat a tall, slim, white-haired man at an enormous desk. He was dressed from head to foot in dark leather, and covering his face was a cracked mask like the masks once worn by lepers. His eyes were twinkling throught the narrow slits and his mouth was covered with a large-toothed zip which gave his lifeless face the appearance of a grinning skull. In front of him on the desk stood a precious vase of Venetian glass, beautifully cut and holding a bouquet of lilies, each flower containing an eye which studied Steve with curiosity. The man pointed authoritatively to the gloomy room behind him, and Steve turned round to see that a door had opened in the semi-darkness. From the narrow room no deeper than a coffin, a woman stepped forward. When she turned her face in his direction he recognised her.

It was Lucy.

He ran up to her. The ancient floorboards under his feet creaked in protest and for a moment he was afraid he might break through the ceiling into the room below.

'Lucy!' he called, opening his arms to greet her. At the same moment one of the lily plants popped up between her breasts and stared at him.

Steve recoiled in horror, but the masked man had come up from behind, put his arms round him, tightening his grip on his rib-cage until he was barely able to breathe.

'*Lucy,*' he groaned, while the masked man kept him in his merciless grip and the ghostly flower on its fleshy stem craned towards him. Steve noticed that Lucy's half-bared breast was covered with tiny drops of sweat, yet however hard he tried, he was unable to make out her face in the growing gloom. In the background a crackling noise which he had heard for quite some time without being able to discover where it came from was getting louder and louder.

It took a moment before Steve regained consciousness and managed to switch on the light. The air in the small room was hot and sticky. He had turned off the air conditioner before he went to bed because he regularly woke up with a sore throat from the cold draught.

The penetrating crackling noise he had heard in his dream continued. It was raining. Steve opened the door. A dense tropical rain was falling, like a cascade of millions of tiny silvery fish, drumming on the large leaves of the bushes growing in front of the bungalow. Near the wall of the house, a group of large, dark toads had gathered for shelter. They looked like black stones, the size of fists, only their staring eyes glittering attentively. Far out over the sea there were dark-red flashes of lightning amid the tangle of clouds.

In a flash Steve grasped the significance of the decision he had taken and a feeling of anxiety gripped him around his chest for a moment, as if the masked man were still standing behind him, holding him tight. He breathed in the fresh, wet night air until the pressure abated.

Before he fell asleep again he remembered that all the lilies in his dream had looked at him with Lucy's eyes.

CHAPTER TWO

## ENTERPRISE WESTERN BASIN

By the time they went over to the conference centre next morning, the sun had almost dried the rain from the night before, and only a few drops still sparkled in the grass, on flowers and bushes. The air was bright and refreshing and heavy with the scent of flowers.

In the conference room, yesterday's pattern was repeated: the same procession, the same entourage, the same seating arrangement. Admiral Francis climbed on to the platform in front of the enormous projector screen, positioned himself between the star-spangled banner and the NASA flag and triumphantly flourished a small pile of conference cards.

'I expected nothing less of you, ladies and gentlemen,' he announced with a big smile. 'Thank you. Only eighteen have decided not to participate in the project. I assume they have good reasons for their decision, and I promise to respect their decision and not to enquire any further. The persons in question are as follows . . .' He now began to read out the names of sixteen men and two women from the conference cards, pausing meaningfully after each one, as if to indicate that they were now forever dishonoured. Steve found this performance deeply distasteful.

'I have to remind you, ladies and gentlemen,' the admiral continued "that from now on you are under an obligation to observe the strictest secrecy; you will be subject to all the security measures customary in such cases. The information you are about to receive is not to be divulged to outsiders and I assure you, ladies and gentlemen, that we shall take every measure – I repeat, *every* measure – to prevent information from being leaked to outsiders.'

Thrusting out his chin, he cast his eyes around the audience as if hoping to unmask an enemy agent and order him out for summary execution. The tension in the room rose.

'Ladies and gentlemen, you will be the advance guard of a

splendid enterprise which will guarantee the survival of our Western world and the well-being of all nations allied to us. Your task will be . . .·ah . . . to set the course for the future – the better future we all wish to see. Commander Walton will now speak to you and give you the technical details. Thank you, ladies and gentlemen.'

Steve did not immediately recognise the dashing young officer in full uniform who now got up on the platform and bent over the microphone. It was not until he heard his voice that he realised that it was the unpleasant official who had met him at the arrival lounge in Miami.

'In the last few years,' Walton began, 'science has managed a decisive breakthrough on the basis of research into the foundations of physics and mathematics carried out from the mid-sixties onwards. We can now talk of a *pioneering* discovery.' He hesitated for a moment; there was an expectant hush in the room. 'It is no exaggeration to say,' he continued, 'that the discovery of fire, Einstein's theory of relativity and the first moon flight will all pale into insignificance beside this new discovery.'

There was a murmur of scepticism from the audience, and one audible jeer. The mood in the room had by now reached the point when tension begins to turn into laughter and levity.

A map was rolled down over the projector screen: a huge contour map of the Mediterranean region about eight metres wide and three and a half metres high. There was silence again, and Walton continued. 'This map shows the physical structure of the area underneath the Mediterranean.'

'Hey,' somebody called out, 'don't tell me the Navy are going to pump the water from the Mediterranean?'

There was general laughter.

'That won't be necessary,' Walton said, quite unperturbed. 'There have been times when the Mediterranean basin *was* dry. The Mediterranean is an evaporation basin: in other words, it loses more water than it receives from its tributaries. When the Straits of Gibraltar are closed – and this has happened a number of times in the history of our planet – the Mediter-ranean basin turns into a desert dotted with salt lakes and swamps about two or three thousand metres under sea level, particularly around here . . .' He pointed to a ditch south of Crete, where the Nile flows through a deep canyon between

Wadi Halfa and Alexandria. 'And here.' Walton pointed again
– this time to the wide fan of the Rhône delta, off Barcelona,
where the river once poured into a deep gorge from a height of
over two thousand metres. From here the river flowed into a
sickle-shaped sea which started about two hundred miles south
of Nice, its eastern shores running parallel to the western coast
of Corsica and Sardinia, curving around the Balearic Isles
towards the west and gradually tapering to a point just south of
Cartagena.

'Now, you're probably thinking: all this is very interesting,
but what does it have to do with *us*? What interest do *we* have in
a salt desert that was obliterated millions of years ago?'

There was a murmur of agreement.

'Well, precisely 5.3 million years ago the land connection
between the Iberian peninsula and Africa broke, probably due
to an earthquake. The waters of the Atlantic gushed in and
filled up the basin.'

'So what?' somebody shouted.

Walton looked at the questioner with infinite patience.
'Because we can get you to this area before it was at the bottom
of the sea,' Walton said, carefully stressing his words. 'We have
a device which enables us to do this: the chronotrone.'

For a moment Steve thought his heart had stopped beating.
He turned to Jerome who was sitting next to him, as if he had to
make sure that he wasn't dreaming. Jerome stared back at him
with frightened, wide-open eyes. There was a breathless silence
in which the drop of a drawing-pin would have been heard;
then a sound like a gasp, almost a groan of astonished dis-
belief.

'The western dip,' Walton continued, gesturing to the area
between Sicily and Gibraltar, 'will be your operational base.
We shall send you five and a half million years into the past and
you will correct a few faults which God in his infinite wisdom
seems somehow to have overlooked.'

Walton was grinning. Little rat, Steve thought: a greedy little
rat – greedy for power at any price.

'As the saying goes,' the commander continued, a trace of
cynicism in his voice now, 'God helps those who help themselves.' He raised his eyes from his papers and gave a
triumphant grin. 'And this is exactly what we intend to do. We
will help ourselves, ladies and gentlemen. And you will be the

crack troops of the operation. Your task will be to supervise the logistics and technical organisation – and to look after security, of course.'

'Security from what?' somebody asked.

'Well, naturally you will have to protect the building construction units from wild animals and from our ancestor, apeman. You and the technical units will be the first human beings in that era. We shall be sending geologists, geophysicists, pipeline specialists and drillers too. Your task will be as follows.'

The commander took up a pointer and turned to the map. A red line ran straight across the western Mediterranean basin forking just south-west of Tripoli; from there, one line ran east-south-east, while the other ran south-south-west.

'Ladies and gentlemen, we intend to pump the oil away before the sheikhs can lay their hands on it.'

The boldness of this notion deprived the audience of speech for a moment. Then there was a chatter of voices.

'Unbelievable!' Jerome murmured.

'It's complete nonsense!' Steve said.

'It's a simple matter of justice,' Walton continued, with a complacent smile. 'We simply correct a fault in creation. Or you could say we'll be giving it a geophysical facelift.' He turned back to the map. 'Enterprise Western Basin will be concerned with the oil deposits in North Africa – in other words, present-day Libya and Algeria. The main finds are here . . .' – he followed with the pointer the eastern branch of the line '. . . between the Great Syrte and the Al-Haruj al-Aswad near Beda, Waha and the Jalo Oasis in southern Benghazi. The other sources are here . . .' the pointer circled the area where the southern branch petered out '. . . east of the Tinrhet Plateau at Erg Bourarhet, near the present Algerian-Libyan border. The pipelines from these two drilling areas will meet here, near Bi'r al Ghanam, and run north-north-west, reaching the coast near Zuwarah, then across the flat shelf between Malta and the Tunisian coast up to here, north-east of Cape Bône. From there it will bend west-north-west, south of the island of San Antioco, round the steep slope of the mountain range which is now Sardinia, and curve north-west off the little island of Mal di Ventre, crossing the basin in the north and ending up at the mouth of the Rhône area, which, at the time in question, was more than two hundred kilometres further south, roughly off Barcelona. The pipeline will then be carried north through the canyon of the Rhône, following the river to the mouth of the Saone, then continuing in the valley of the Saone right through the Burgundian gate, following the course of the Marne through northern France and Belgium, and right through the Netherlands. It will probably reach the coast near Maastricht. We are not sure of the exact shape of the coastline in those days, but as the climate was considerably warmer and there was less ice in glaciers and on the pole caps, it is reasonable to suppose that the level of the sea must have been correspondingly higher; on the other hand, the tectonic plateaux which frame the Mediterranean, the Eurasian, the Adriatic, the Aegean, the Turkish, the Arabian and the African coasts must have been higher too, at that time. They were later compressed downwards by the enormous weight of the waters which form the Mediterranean, and this led to vast tectonic upheavals in the adjoining areas.

'In the coastal area near Liège, Maastricht, Aachen, Bonn and Coblenz, our pipeline will meet a second pipeline which runs across Europe from the Persian Gulf and Saudi Arabia via Anatolia and along the Black Sea Coast, following the course of the Danube. The two lines will be joined and led towards the mainland shelf of the North Sea, where a number of chronotrones disguised as oil-rigs will pump up the oil from the past into the present.'

'And the oil sheikhs will sit back and let this happen?' somebody asked.

'There is not the slightest indication that anybody other than ourselves knows anything about the project,' Walton said, 'either the scientific research behind it, or its practical realisation.'

The commander was not completely truthful there. In fact, there were suspicions that the Soviets had been occupied with a project of a similar nature. Ever since the mid-seventies the Soviet aircraft carrier *Kiev* had been cruising the eastern Mediterranean, and four more units had joined her. Their exact function was a mystery to the experts at the Pentagon.

'Nevertheless,' Walton continued, 'we shall not take any chances. We will be prepared for all eventualities. The security measures I mentioned will also include defensive measures against potential enemies. Military equipment will be provided. Your duties will also include the providing of fresh meat for the technical units, so those of you who are fond of hunting will have a field day. You will find a genuine wilderness at your disposal, completely untouched.'

Moses put up a hand to ask a question. He was sitting two rows behind Steve and Jerome with Loorey and Olson. Steve turned round and saw that Loorey had apparently struck up some kind of relationship with one of the NASA girls sitting next to him. She looked carefree and young, twenty-five at the most, snub-nosed, her flaxen hair tied in a bun, sun-tanned and with freckles dotted over her face and neck. She was wearing a low-cut white summer dress. Loorey was looking her up and down with obvious pleasure and seemed much less sullen than normal; evidently he was far more interested in her than in what the commander was saying. Steve smiled and when their eyes met, Loorey gave him a grin back and raised a conspiratorial eyebrow. Meanwhile Moses had stood up to put his question.

'What about the equipment for bringing us *back* from this wilderness, Sir?'

'Let's take one thing at a time,' Walton answered defensively. 'We'll have to talk about that problem later.'

'So it is a problem, then, Sir?' Moses insisted.

'No, not at all,' Walton assured him. 'There are a few . . . ah . . . experiments which haven't been quite concluded yet. But we are . . . ah . . .' he lowered his head to his papers, 'very confident we'll soon have any difficulties ironed out.'

'What do you mean, Sir?' Harald Olson interrupted. 'You're saying you haven't sent anybody out and brought them *back* again yet?'

'Listen, Lieutenant,' Walton said, irritated, 'if you'd allow me to continue I'm sure I can clarify this point to your satisfaction.'

'I sincerely hope so, Sir'.

'The Sixth Fleet has two nuclear reactor vessels which are disguised as supply ships. They are carrying the technical apparatus with which you and your equipment will be sent into the past: the so-called chronotrones or "cages".'

'Very apt,' somebody called out.

'These cage carriers have been operating off the south coast of Sardinia for some time.' The commander pointed to a rectangular, red-coloured area stretching from about fifteen miles south of Cape Sperr to about forty miles south-east. 'Here they are, close to the west coast.' A second red rectangle appeared on the map north-west of San Pietro, and a third and fourth south-east of Toulon and north-west of Mallorca and Minorca. 'For about three years now, regular consignments of materials have been dropped into the past over these target areas: pipes, machines, petrol, geological apparatus, food, medical supplies, tents, inflatable shelters, armaments, ammunition and everyday necessities.' Walton glanced over in Olson's direction and continued: 'As for the return journey, there's not the slightest reason for worry. A research institute has been erected in the Eastern Bermudas which is equipped with the most sophisticated chronotronic machinery. From there we've already sent a number of scientists and technicians into the past. They are working to clear an area measuring a few square kilometres which will serve as the retrieving zone, and constructing the necessary installations. We shall certainly get you back from there as soon as you have finished your work.'

'But so far you haven't brought anybody back,' Olson insisted. 'And yet if what you say is true, this so-called retrieving zone ought to have been ready for the past five million years.'

'In essence, getting people back to the present involves the same procedure as transporting them into the past,' Francis replied smoothly. 'The process is simply reversed. The best brains in the country are working hard to perfect the in-stallations and make your safe retrieval one hundred per cent guaranteed. I am completely confident that in five years you will all be back home again, ladies and gentlemen. I give you my word for it.'

'Of course, we haven't quite solved *all* the problems of retrieval', Walton confessed, carefully avoiding going into further details. 'But those needn't concern us now. Even if only *one* of our installations functions, it'll be quite sufficient. In theory, once your time is up, we *could* bring you back five years later to the very day, or even further back in the past; but that would be impossible for security reasons, and as I'm sure you will understand, it also could be psychologically harmful. Subjective and real time ought to be of about the same duration. If we didn't insist on that, we'd be faced with social and legal problems I can't even begin to describe here.'

'I must say, I'm touched by your concern,' Moses said.

'I am pleased to hear it, Major Calahan,' the commander answered with a smile.

'Clever chap, this Walton,' Jerome said softly. 'I wouldn't be surprised if he already knows everybody in the room by name.'

'He's a rat,' Steve grunted. 'He'll chew his way through anything until he gets what he wants.'

'Any questions?' Walton called out.

'You said we were going to be retrieved from the Bermudas,' somebody said in an unmistakable Southern accent. 'How do we cross the Atlantic? Obviously there won't be any airlines.'

'But there will be ships,' Walton answered, unperturbed. 'We intend to build a harbour in the neighbourhood of what is now Cadiz and open a once-yearly ferry service between Europe and the Bermudas. We're about to build a cage which will be able to expedite objects of the size of ocean-going units and to organise a supply line of fuel and crews.' Walton paused. 'I want to mention one more point. We shall return to it in more detail in our briefings with individual units, but we ought to raise it right at the start. The chronotrones which are going to transport you into the past have a scatter which we are able to reduce significantly but not eliminate entirely. In our target area it amounts to about six to eight years. Thus, two transports which are being dropped at the same second and sent over an identical time-distance may arrive up to eight years apart. This raises some logistical problems; they're not insurmountable, but they *do* mean that we're forced to select mixed groups. In other words, each group will include one armed man with some military experience. We'll be sending groups of twos and fours, depending on the equipment they're carrying; they'll be fully motorised and completely self-sufficient and if necessary able to operate for years on their own. Remember: any group could be the first on the spot – and they *could* have to wait for months before the next group joins them, though it's unlikely.'

'It looks as if this is going to be a fascinating game of blind man's buff,' Steve murmured. Jerome nodded.

'You'll be landing here,' Walton said, pointing to a narrow green-coloured rectangle situated about thirty miles north of Cap de Fer running forty miles parallel to the Algerian coast. 'We chose this area between the North African plateau and the

Balearic basin because it fulfils three important conditions: first, the territory is relatively flat, sloping gently from south to north towards Lake Balearic; second, it's between a thousand and fifteen hundred metres below sea-level, which means it can be reached by glider from the present sea-level. Third, it's currently situated in international waters.

'When you arrive at your target time you'll find bases already there – provided you're not one of the first units. The nearest one ought to be about here.' He pointed to the steep slope south of the Gulf of Palma on the south-western tip of Sardinia. 'With luck they'll already be waiting for you in the landing area, but if you're in need of help and find your radio messages unanswered, don't panic. Remember you may be the first on the spot. Get down to work and prepare for the arrival of the next unit. You can console yourself with the proud thought that you're the first to take possession of a virgin earth on which no human being has ever set foot before you.'

'Very uplifting,' somebody shouted.

'Drivel,' Steve grunted.

Jerome giggled. 'Don't get so worked up,' he said. 'The guy's very good at his job.'

'Thank you, ladies and gentlemen,' Walton concluded.

Admiral Francis got up and stepped up to the microphone.

'Do you know what this is?' he asked, triumphantly holding up a handful of dirty yellow objects looking like oversized gambling chips. 'This is plastic,' he announced, wide-eyed, like Santa Claus bearing gifts. 'And it is plastic material 5.3 million years old – the same material we'll be using for the pipeline. In 1970 the *Glomar Challenger* retrieved these fragments a hundred miles south of Barcelona. They were two thousand metres down, at the bottom of the sea, at exactly the spot where we now drop the stuff. You see, ladies and gentlemen, this is the best proof of the success of our project.'

'Sir,' interrupted Moses, 'I'm afraid I don't find that very encouraging. If the *Glomar Challenger* had drilled into a pipeline at a spot where no material is being dropped I would be more convinced.'

The admiral's triumphant smile seemed to freeze at the corner of his mouth. Nimbly Walton came to his rescue.

'Naturally we drop much more material than we shall ever need, Major, so that we always have enough material to hand.

It's obvious that some material is still lying around the target area because not all of it has been used. I can't see anything strange in that.'

Francis's triumphant smile had melted again. 'We have other proof that the project has been successful – and we've had it in our possession for quite some time,' he announced. 'Therefore we have good reason to go to work confidently. Together we shall tackle a project which promises to change our future. May God be with all . . .'

Steve lost interest in the admiral's rhetoric and the voice trailed away. When he left the windowless room a few minutes later he was startled to step into bright sunshine. For some reason he had had the feeling that it ought to be pitch-dark outside. He was quite numbed and had a headache; he decided to miss lunch and get a few hours' rest.

Lying under the cool sheet, his limbs feeling like weights, he watched the chromium-plated protection grille on the pale blue ventilator, which turned with the patience of a robot at an angle of ninety degrees from one direction to the other. A short while later he fell asleep.

He was woken by a knock at the door. Jerome was standing outside, Harald and Moses by his side.

'We're celebrating our new status as temponauts,' Harald Olson said with a twinkle in his eye. His sparse blond hair was still wet from the shower, and his moustache was neatly brushed. He looked like an inquisitive young seal and had even managed to acquire a tan after a few minutes in the Florida sun.

Steve had a cold shower, dressed and joined them. He was ravenously hungry and thirsty, but all they could find to drink was frozen canned beer, which tasted foul. Later they managed to persuade Paul Loorey to part with the remainder of his whisky. He excused himself from the gathering in favour of spending the evening with the NASA girl. Her name was Jane Brookwood, and she worked in the logistics department of the Western Basin project. She knew exactly which materials were being dropped where, but it was obvious that Loorey's interest in her went beyond the merely professional.

Harald, Jerome, Moses, and Steve retired to Calahan's bungalow and got extremely drunk. Later, nobody could remember how they had managed to find their way home.

# CHAPTER THREE

# DROPPED

After ten weeks of theoretical training at the Cape and in Houston under the supervision of geologists, geophysicists, oil and pipeline specialists, experienced drillers and engineers, biologists, botanists, palaeontologists and anthropologists, the unit was moved to Arizona. There they were taught to use newly developed military equipment: 'the "cat", a light, crawler-type vehicle specially designed for moving about in desert and savannah, climbing steep hills and operating in swampy territory; and the 'fireflash', a medium-weight rocket-thrower developed by the Navy, which could also be used for propelling tactical atomic shells.

Over the weeks, they practised driving in steep and difficult territory, learnt how to get out of swamp holes and sand dunes, how to build shelters in loose ground, dig wells in dry soil, set traps for small animals and roast lizards on a spit.

In spite of the bright sun the thermometer rarely climbed above fifteen degrees centigrade. The year 1985 was coming to an end, and winter was early this year. In the mountains it had been snowing already.

Every weekend he could get leave, Steve flew from Tucson to Albuquerque to visit Lucy. He felt guilty for having volunteered for the project and made up for it by being particularly nice to her. She appreciated it, and made a fuss of him in return.

'Don't worry so much, Frankie boy,' she said. 'You're a true adventurer – that's why I love you. I'm more the settled type. Jesus, I've looked after old O'Nooly's business for almost twenty years now. In five years' time I'll probably be an ugly old hag – who knows? Anyway, if you still feel like it, drop in and see me. I'd be glad, if only to make you a cup of tea. Or write me a letter from wherever it is you're going.'

Steve felt distinctly uncomfortable. Yet he couldn't tell her that he wouldn't be able to write. At such times he felt rather like a half-hearted lover who disappears without a trace after a brief encounter.

Towards the end of March 1986, Steve and his colleagues were posted to an Air Force training camp south of Lake Utah where parachute units were instructed in how to cope with difficult or unusual conditions. They learnt to drop first from a height of two thousand, then fifteen hundred and finally one thousand metres, first in an empty glider, so as to get the feel of it, then with full equipment and crew. The 'dragon', as they called the twelve-metre-long glider, was a rake-like structure made of light metal and a plastic foil cover with a fuselage roomy enough to take a 'cat' and trailer, plus a considerable amount of equipment and weaponry. An old Sikorski S-64 Skycrane took them up to the height required and flew them into the landing area. From then on, the procedure was always the same: the distorted voice in the earphones squeaking orders – barely intelligible because of the rhythmic, whiplike jerks caused by the wings of the helicopter; the short litany of the countdown; then, suddenly – weightlessness. The rudders would gradually register resistance; the whipping of the rotors stop, giving way to a soft, whimpering sound: the air friction on the outer surface of the glider. Now there was time to gaze at the panoramic scene – dark, snowcapped mountains in the distance; underneath, the shimmering basin on which they would land. The sensation of flying. The singing of metal strings, stays, rudder cables; then more hoarse barks from ground staff over the earphones. Then moving the pedal to bring out the landing gear and valance the angle. The basin drops downwards, the sky falls forward; the nose is lifted higher with a strong pull of the control stick. Sunlight pours in. Touchdown. The sharp scratch of the landing gear, then the springy, pumping, chattering noise of the large spoked bow-wheel. A rush of dappled light; glimpses of branches and bushes rushing past; the rumble of the runner wheels, slowly dwindling.

Unfastening the seat belt. Waiting. Silence. Suddenly the ground staff are all around. Impatiently they chase away the pilots, who clamber out, stiff-limbed, and walk over to a waiting jeep in the noonday heat. The smell of hot oil and burnt rubber. Chilly spring breeze tearing at sparse bushes which were singed last summer. The crackle of hot metal cooling down.

Jerome Bannister and Steve Stanley were to form a two-person unit. Their equipment consisted of a fully-tanked 'cat' and trailer, fifteen cans of fuel, a radio set, a two-man tent with sleeping bags, first aid kit and camping toilet, laundry sack, water container, two additional light fatigue suits, food for ninety days and vitamin-rich dry food concentrates; they were armed with a heavy machine gun, two machine pistols, two automatic rifles which could be converted into hunting gear, and about ten thousand rounds of ammunition. These supplies were to be replenished if necessary at the depots, which for the past few months had been dropped by the Sixth Fleet along the western coast of Corsica and north of the Balearics. The remainder of the scientific equipment had been catapulted into the past and dropped by parachute into the border areas of the western basin.

Harald Olson, Moses Calahan and Paul Loorey were to form a mobile technical base unit, supplied with jeep and trailer. Their fourth man was captain Salomon Singer, a Harvard psychologist and anthropologist who had fought in Vietnam as a young man and was therefore one of the few men on the project with military experience. He was in his late thirties, with brown frizzy hair which did not quite match his dark complexion and the fleshy, permanently worried-looking Levantine features. He was of medium height and rather thin, though apt to gulp down enormous quantities of food and drink, particularly when somebody else was paying. Rumour had it that when these opportunities offered themselves he ate and drank double rations like a camel and could do without food for weeks afterwards.

Salomon Singer had been given a strange task, and Steve could hardly believe his ears when he first heard of it: Singer was to establish communication with the ape-men of the era, who belonged to the species *Australopithecus africanus*, and test their intelligence and their suitability for a kind of colonial force.

Jerome and Moses were vastly amused by this notion, imagining a horde of club-swinging ape-men in Navy uniforms, beating hairy chests decorated with tinkling medals.

Harald Olson laughed until the tears came to his eyes. 'What a crazy idea!' he giggled. 'I can't believe it!'

Salomon looked at them gravely in turn, and said reproachfully: 'Maybe it's not as farfetched as you might think.'

Whereupon they all burst into even merrier laughter, and Jerome called out: 'One thing's for sure – the Navy will have to change their shaving regulations!'

By mid-June of 1986 the preparations were complete. Disguised as a group of tourists, an advance unit of eighty men were flown to Madrid, arriving there late in the afternoon in pouring rain. Two officials of the Guardia Civil armed with machine pistols and wearing their strangely flat, black-lacquered box hats checked their passports.

From the airport they were taken to the Hotel Escorial in town. It was still pouring with rain. Steve had always imagined Madrid to be a large, dusty city under a silver sky and bathed in a gloomy light that swallowed all colours and wrapped a light veil of grey around everything, as in the pictures of El Greco. But even in the rain the venerable Spanish capital turned out to be full of bright colours, its dazzling city lights reflected in the wet pavements.

The next day Steve went to the Prado with Salomon Singer.

The famous picture gallery had a paralysing effect on Steve. He liked art and loved painting, yet he felt oppressed by the gloomy gallery of Catholic potentates and dressed-up hydro-cephalic cretins, clutching their sceptres like children's rattles and bearing all the signs of physical and psychological sickness. The portraits particularly disturbed him. Often the subjects had the air of imbeciles dressed in royal purple. And in the background, behind the lost-looking, over-fed faces, were always the same deserted ports, overhung by the same distant storms, darkening horizons and threatening cloud formations.

The paintings on religious themes were no better: canvas after canvas depicted the tortured bodies of saints, severed heads in starched white ruffs on platters of chased silver and grisly scenes of martyrdom and crucifixion. The ecstatic piety of some of the pictures made Steve shudder. He was repelled by their morbidity and their worship of pain and faintly sickened by their religious fervour. After gazing at them for some time it came as a great relief to move on to the Rubens and delight in his lively representations of nakedness and sensuality. What if human flesh *were* transitory? Wasn't that all the more reason to enjoy life while you could? To hell with Western Christianity, with its sin and guilt and promises of rewards in the afterlife. What was needed were positive steps to improve life *on earth* – to give this planet the bright serenity it seemed to possess when looked at from space; to make it an oasis, a refuge in the dusty reaches of infinite space.

Salomon seemed to share Steve's feelings. 'I often ask myself,' he said with a frown, 'what a visitor from outer space would think if he were faced with all those horrible pictures – crucifixions, beheadings, the sufferings of the Christian saints. He'd probably think we were cannibals.'

'Isn't that what we are?' Steve asked. 'In a certain sense we've always been cannibals – although we've refined our feeding habits, as civilised peoples tend to.'

Salomon paused, his brows furrowed in thought. 'But perhaps our visitor might have his gods and demons too, perhaps thousands of years old, persecuting him in his dreams. He might be hoping for salvation too – in which case he'd find all this only too familiar.'

Steve shrugged his shoulders and made for the exit. When they stepped out into the street, the sun was breaking through the clouds and the colours were even brighter than before. Steve felt as if a gloomy, densely crowded altar piece was shutting for good behind him. He had a sudden craving for a cup of hot spicy coffee, and invited Salomon to join him.

They found a street café which was open in spite of the chilly weather, and sat down. The colourful marquee was still dripping from the rain and there were puddles on the white-topped metal tables. The street in front of the café was covered in bottle tops, baked into the tarmac on hot summer days. Girls' laughter could be heard, and the evening was fresh and invigorating.

Late that night he wrote a long letter to Lucy in which he confessed that she would not hear from him during his five-year absence. And he added that he loved her very much.

Two days later they were divided up into two groups and late in the afternoon two large new tourist buses arrived to collect them, bearing the word *Malaga* in big letters on the windscreen. There was even a tourist guide who cracked a few feeble jokes in broken English, but he soon gave up when nobody seemed to respond. Most of the travellers slept during the journey. The tinted window panes of the coaches transformed the soft evening sky into a threatening stormscape. Between La Roda and Albacete, night fell, and the scenery became more mountainous. In Almansa they stopped for dinner at a deserted modern hotel, whose decor vainly attempted to recall the Moorish past.

Two hours later they arrived at Alicante. Here the road signs to Malaga pointed south; but the coaches took the road north instead and the destination on the windscreen was altered to *Barcelona*. Finally, after passing through San Juan de Alicante, then Campello and Villajoyopa, the coaches stopped at a tiny port. Everyone got out. Only a few lights were on. The coaches disappeared into the narrow streets and thundered up into the mountains, leaving silence behind.

Black, litter-strewn water lapped softly against the harbour wall. A warm breeze came off the now-invisible mountains with their covering of gnarled cork-trees, a breeze smelling of sunny fields and sage blossom. Though it was early summer, there was a mood of autumn in the air, of something final, irrevocable. Steve took a deep breath to steady his nerves, but it brought no relief. The others were also silent, as if they were under the same spell.

From a tourist bar across the harbour strains of music came floating over. Somewhere a donkey brayed, as if in the throes of a nightmare. A cock crowed, mistaking the time; there were still hours to go before morning and the night felt like a warm, dark cloth.

Sometime during the next few days they would disappear from this world without a trace, to reappear somewhere in a world utterly different from the world they had left behind. It was inconceivable – and yet even now the moment of farewell was drawing relentlessly closer.

Steve was looking into the water, trying to overcome his anxiety. At a distance he could see two motor launches tied to the harbour wall. Suddenly a few sailors appeared from nowhere to help them embark. A few mintutes later they had pushed off from the harbour and were chugging out to sea, with harbour lights gradually receding into the distance behind them.

Outside the harbour walls the waves were higher and the launch began to heave. Now and then a gust of foam splashed into Steve's face and the throbbing of the motor changed pitch according to the position of the screw in the water.

They sat huddled together on the white plastic-coated benches. All was silent except for the sound of the motor and the occasional squawk of a walkie-talkie. Fifteen minutes later they saw lights ahead. It was the *Fellow*, at anchor in the shadow of the island of Benidorm. Ten minutes later they were aboard and tucking into hot soup, sandwiches, beer, and coffee. Steve was amused to notice that the crew were fussing over them as if they had been saved from drowning. They were given blankets, then they sat in folding chairs on deck, talking, drinking beer, or trying to catch some sleep.

The *Fellow* had weighed anchor as soon as they had arrived and was now heading east. Towards dawn two giant helicopters approached. While one of them landed by searchlight and was made fast on deck, the other circled the ship, rippling the grey waters with its flailing rotor-blades.

Steve and Jerome boarded the first helicopter with eighteen other members of the commando unit and took off while the second helicopter landed. After a flight of about two hours they landed on the deck of the *Thomas Alva Edison*, which was cruising seventy nautical miles south of Mallorca.

Steve felt tired after the journey and was glad to be shown immediately to his cabin, where he lay for some time before the effects of the coffee wore off and he finally fell asleep. In his dreams he saw a row of altars whose pictures had been painted over with shining black paint so as to resemble newly cleaned slates. Somebody behind his back impatiently ordered him to 'start', but all Steve could do was stare blankly at the piece of chalk in his hand. Try as he might, he couldn't imagine what he was supposed to do with it. Nor did he know who was behind him, and he dared not turn round in case it was the man in the leather mask. He felt eyes drilling into the back of his neck and his desperation grew. His thoughts were going round and round in circles. Suddenly he heard raucous laughter as if a whole class of children were sitting behind him – except that instead of the high-pitched laughter of children, this was the malicious barking of grown-ups. Steve tried in vain to hold back his tears, but soon felt them rolling down his cheeks. Bracing himself with all the strength he could muster, he turned round with a jerk. Before him were row upon row of toothless, grinning old men,

Aristotle among them. At that moment he woke up.

Steve felt the anxiety and sadness which gripped him gradually recede and a sense of relief overcame him. He had said goodbye. Presently he sank back in to a deep and this time dreamless sleep.

Disguised as a supply ship, the *Edison* was in fact one of the most modern of the cage carrying vessels. Steve and Jerome, the technicians' base unit led by Calahan, and five other groups of twos and fours were to be dropped from it.

Since the reactor took about fifty hours to build up the artificial gravitational field of the cage and the technicians took about twenty-four hours to recover the empty cage, service the generator and reload the cage, it was only possible to make one drop every fourth day. This always took place in the early morning hours when it was light enough for the flash caused by the release of the gravitational bubble to be out-shone by the sun, and yet early enough for the morning mist to cover the clouds of steam given off during the operation.

In order to build up the Kafu field, the cage and its load were lowered through a trap in the hulk of the ship by cables. There the cage hung for two days and two nights, until the necessary field force had been reached and the computer of the chronotrone indicated *go*, accurate to a fraction of a billionth of a second. The cage was then pulled up again, serviced and reloaded. The entire ship was placed on alert throughout the operation, and the *Edison* was continually flanked by two destroyers to guard against enemy submarines. Other Navy units were usually standing by for protection, too.

Steve and Jerome were the third group to be dropped, followed by the Calahan-Olson-Loorey-Singer group. This meant that they had a wait of more than a week, which Steve spent mostly reading and playing cards. Against the usual strict custom obtaining in Navy units, they were allowed as much alcohol as they wanted; it was, Steve felt, rather as if they were awaiting a difficult landing operation involving heavy losses.

That thought reminded Steve of Norman Mailer and other books he had read on the Pacific War. While he was thinking of books, it suddenly occurred to him that he hadn't brought nearly enough reading matter to last him the full five years. He therefore used the remaining days to comb the ship and beg, steal and borrow any worthwhile book he could lay his hands on. His library eventually consisted of several Cassius Lows, Barry Rauhsacks and Billy Hammocks; a Saul Bellow, a Hemingway and a Henry Miller, a Silverberg, two Hesses, two Dostoievskys, one Tolstoy, one Flaubert, a Mark Twain anthology, Proust's *A la recherche* Volume 1, in a torn edition, *Les Misérables* by Victor Hugo, and a collection of Strindberg plays. Steve packed as many of these books as he could find room for in his holdall, which expedition participants were allowed to use for personal belongings.

During his search of the ship Steve noticed that the *Edison* crew consisted of many more scientists and technicians than military personnel. Wherever he looked, he saw white lab coats and light-blue overalls, rarely a uniform. But conversation with the technicians was unrewarding. They talked shop constantly when they were together, dropping phrases like 'field force equivalences', 'gravitational pulsations in the giga watt range', 'chronotronic scatter in the target time sector', 'temporal emissions' and 'matter-time-distance relation'. And they treated the members of the unit as if they were no more than guinea pigs – 'load' for the cages, whose weight and mass had to be calculated and balanced down to a thousandth of a gramme in order to place it as accurately as possible in the 'target time sector' and to get the 'chronotronic scatter' down to a minimum.

Steve also noticed that the *Edison* and its accompanying ships constantly moved around in a circle. While the cage was being charged, they followed an eastern course almost exactly along latitude 38 to longitude 8° 30′ east; they then turned south towards the African coast, left the islands of La Galite to starboard and took a westerly course, moving at a distance of about thirty nautical miles from the mainland, parallel to the Algerian coast. During this part of the circle, the field force of the cage reached the charge required and the contents of the cage were dropped. Usually this took place off Cape Roas, sometimes a little further west in the direction of Cape Bougaroun.

Looking at the map, Steve noticed that to the north of El Kala, Annaba, Chetaibi and Skikda, the bottom of the sea dropped to an almost level plateau of about twelve hundred metres depth. This was their landing area. Immediately after the load was dropped, the ships headed west-north-west, turned round at the longitude off the coast of Algiers and started the whole procedure again.

During the night the second group were due to be dropped, Steve woke up with a start. He thought he had heard a terrible scream coming from the depth of the ship's hull. He held his breath and listened in the darkness. A few moments later he heard a noise as if a heavy spanner were hammering against steel plate. For a while he had the horrifying thought that a dock worker might have got himself trapped in the hull while the ship was under construction and was now trying to make himself heard. It was nonsense, of course; the man would have been long dead by now – unless he fed on rats and licked the condensation off the steel plates. Yet Steve seemed to remember that every ship gets a thorough gassing while in dry dock in order to destroy vermin. He could be sleeping right next to a dead rat himself. He switched on the light and got up. Jerome was fast asleep in the bunk below. Steve got dressed and crept out of the cabin.

There was a fresh wind blowing on deck. It was dawn, and the sky to the east looked like a pale green lagoon with a few narrow rafts of cloud scudding across it. The *Edison* was cruising at full speed due west, and the water in its wake looked as if it were boiling. Steam was rising up, blanketing the sea with a low mist. Steve went over to the railing and peered down.

Suddenly he seemed to hear another cry of terror, like the one which had woken him. A moment later, a deep red flash of light appeared underneath the ship's stern, colouring the water, as if a harpooner had ignited a charge of dynamite in a whale's heart, exploding it in a burst of blood.

Evidently they had just made the drop. Steam rose astern, spiralling and twirling and blocking out the rising sun. Steve hurried below decks in order to watch the technicians recover the empty cage.

It seemed to take an eternity to winch it up. Steve was standing on the gallery opposite the mobile all-glass control centre, which was suspended above the transparent inner trap door. Inside, he could see the chronotrone technicians sitting watching their instrument panels. He could tell from the gestures and mouth movements that they were giving orders, but it was impossible to hear what was going on through the thick soundproof glass. Outside, the cranks were squeaking as dripping, greasy steel cables were wound back on to the drums. A waterproofed cable tree as thick as a man disappeared into the ceiling like some dark primeval snake, and finally a long dark shadow appeared underneath the trap. While the winching engines whined in protest, the mighty animal itself rose up from the dark waters, shimmering and gleaming under the arc lights. With a dull metallic click the thirty-metre-long cocoon of the transporter cage settled into its anchorage. A siren sounded. Water was pressed from the trap chamber, then the inner gates opened. Suddenly there was a strong smell of salt and burnt seaweed. Below appeared the black, honeycomb-structured top of the device, a slim ellipsoid with a bumplike appendix at its stern where the cable tree was rooted. This was the aggregate of the chronotrone, the gravitation generator.

The valves were opened, and air streamed into the evacuated cage cell. It took more than half an hour for the technicians to undo the screw, then the lid was hoisted up with a crane and swung aside.

Steve looked into the empty yawning interior which less than an hour ago had held four men and their equipment. Tomorrow night it would be his turn. He and Jerome would climb into the whale's body and wait for the technicians to close the lid, lower the cage through the trap door and twenty metres down into the sea. Then they would have to wait for a further fifty hours, while the generator fed by the enormous reactor on the ship built up the chronotronic field. Finally, that incredible moment would arrive; the moment when they would send the whale into the depths of time, to spit them out onto a distant shore . . .

Steve forced his thoughts back to the present, and watched while the crane lowered a new floor grille into the cage. Frequently fragments were torn off it and sucked into the past along with the 'load' when the critical field force was reached.

After watching for some time until the operation was completed, Steve began to feel hungry and went down to the canteen, where he found Jerome sitting in front of a double portion of bacon and eggs, and tucking in heartily.

'My last decent breakfast for the next five years,' he said, chewing with pleasure. He poured Steve a cup of steaming hot coffee. 'I wish they were giving us chicken and pigs instead of those crappy astronaut concentrates.'

Steve ordered scrambled eggs and bacon and picked at the food listlessly. He was still hungry, but somehow he couldn't face the idea of eating.

When they had finished, Jerome went down to watch the cage being prepared for the next drop. Steve hung around the deck for a while. It was warm in the sunshine and the *Edison* was rolling gently in the gusty west wind, every now and then washed over by a foamy wave which was thrown leeward. In the east, three more Navy ships could be seen, all heading in the same direction as the cage carrier.

It promised to be a beautiful day. Steve got himself a book, set up a deckchair in a corner out of the wind and tried to read; but he couldn't concentrate. Seagulls were sailing overhead, looking down on him with lifeless eyes. He stared back and tried to drive them away by sheer willpower, but they didn't seem to react to his brain impulses. He swore as he wiped a dollop of acid birdshit off his windcheater.

Late in the afternoon Steve and Jerome were given a last medical check-up, an unnecessary but strangely calming ritual. Then it suddenly looked as if their turn would come, a full twenty-four hours later than scheduled.

The Chinese atomic submarine *The East is Red*, which had been lying at anchor in the port of La Valetta, had left there heading for an unknown destination. The excitement spread from the bridge of the *Edison* through the entire ship. Coded radio messages suddenly started flying between the cage carrier and the flagship, the rocket cruiser *US Albany*, and between the Admiralty and the operational staff at the headquarters at Rota in the Bay of Cadiz. At 18.00 hours came word that the Chinese submarine had been sighted on its way to Tripoli. It took another hour for the message to be confirmed and for the *Edison* to receive a provisional '*go*'.

Steve and Jerome had been sitting in their underwear in the sick bay while the decision was awaited; they now donned their travel clothes: a specially-developed light fighting suit with several patch pockets, parachute boots, leather helmet and steel helmet, ammunition belt with pistol holster and parachute in case of some mishap during the drop. Then they were given their final instructions.

'In sixty hours we shall be positioned over the projected

landing area – the Red Zone,' said the first officer of the *Edison*, a squat, broad-shouldered man in his late forties who was in charge of the chronotrone operation. Although he kept chewing his gum with grim determination, he didn't entirely succeed in concealing his nervousness. With pointedly casual gestures he indicated the distances and the ship's position: 'The point of landing is about three miles ahead of you, depending on the force of wind and your speed of descent. The ground is flat, sloping gently from south to north. The salty soil allows hardly any growth, and if there *are* trees there, they ought to have been felled long since – unless you're the first unit to arrive. You'll probably find level territory where you can land safely, even in darkness.'

'How did you like it there?' asked Jerome.

'What do you mean?' the first officer asked irritably.

'Well, it sounds to me as if you've been there yourself,' Jerome said, shrugging his shoulders.

'These are factual descriptions, Major. They're almost certainly correct,' the Navy man answered fiercely.

'Calm down,' Jerome insisted. 'I didn't mean it like that.'

'I'd advise you to stay in the Red Zone until you've established radio contact with base – especially if you land at night. The chances of that are about fifty-fifty.'

'That sounds logical,' Steve sighed.

'Then try to make your way to base. That ought to be about here.' He pointed to the southern point of Sardinia. He looked at his watch. 'Time's running out. In about forty-five minutes you ought to be in your cage. Have yourself a last decent meal – you'll have time before the cage is closed. I wish you luck.' After this he seemed in a great hurry and disappeared in the direction of the bridge.

They were lowered into the cage with a hoist. The loaded glider, a high-backed vehicle securely blocked at the wheels, stood on the lattice grille of the loose floor, which would fall away at the moment of drop.

Shortly before the cage lid was put on and tightened, they were served their last meal. Steve had ordered a pile of sandwiches and two thermos flasks of tea so as to be well prepared for the following two days and nights; Jerome ate a double portion of beef stroganoff and a pile of sandwiches. His request for a bottle of rum and a case of beer was ignored, as were his protests, so he had to make do with one can of beer. He drank it grimly, then settled down in comfort on the back seat of the 'cat'. The lid was hardly closed before he fell asleep.

An enviable talent, Steve thought to himself, lying in the narrow cockpit of the glider with the seat tilted as far backwards as possible. Jerome had always been like that. Once, during their time at the Cape, a launch had been put off because of bad weather, and Jerome had slept calmly for hours until it had cleared up. Nothing seemed to disturb his calm – unlike Steve, who usually had to fight off attacks of claustrophobia after half an hour. For Steve, the next fifty hours would be the most arduous of his life, and the worst of it was that he knew he would be dog-tired when the decisive moment came.

While they waited, they remained in contact with the operational staff via the intercom, but as the energy in the Kafu field built up, reception would get weaker and weaker until it ceased altogether about five hours before the drop. Then they would be isolated, shut in behind a wall of time, unable to tell if they were still in the present or already falling into the abyss . . .

No, no, Steve told himself; while the wall of the cage is still visible, we must still be in the present. So long as we're hanging underneath the keel of the *Edison* like a baby monkey clinging to its mother's belly, we're safe enough. And yet . . . He switched on a glider searchlight to make sure, switched it off again and moved it around, thinking he had heard the sound of water. He climbed out and peered closely at the honeycomb wall of the cage. Not a drop of water to be seen.

For a moment he was seized by claustrophobia. Hastily he climbed back into the cockpit, pressed the breathing mask against his face and opened the oxygen supply. He took a few deep breaths until the anxiety abated, then leant back.

The voice of the first officer woke him. He looked at his watch: only six hours had passed. Still about forty-five to go before the drop. Whistling happily, Jerome was squatting on the camp toilet, which he had unloaded and put next to the nose of the glider on the grille.

The first officer wanted to know whether everything was all right.

'We're in excellent shape,' Steve assured him.

'Would you like us to play you some music?'

'Good idea.'

Two minutes later they were receiving late-night music from Radio Algiers over their earphones.

Once they had both settled comfortably into the 'cat', Jerome insisted on a few rounds of chess. Steve lost every game, finding it difficult to concentrate. Jerome ate almost without interruption. Steve guessed it was his way of mastering the situation.

After listening to Radio Italia's morning show, then Radio Palermo's afternoon programme, they finally moved far enough east to pick up AFN Southern Europe from the nuclear aircraft-carrier *Richard G. Colbert* and the old *Chester W. Nimitz*, but the reception got worse every hour. The voice of the first officer who called at regular intervals gradually got weaker, too, and was all but drowned by thin crackling noises like rustling tissue paper.

The next day passed with excruciating slowness.

Around them a mighty fist of energy closed which would soon thrust them five and a half million years into the past.

Jerome was sitting on the driver's seat, brooding over a map of the western Mediterranean which he had spread out over the dashboard, and trying to memorise the landmarks. Steve was sitting in the back seat, reading Proust again after a long time. Up *there* it might be dark now, but in his mind's eye he pictured the sunlit scenery of Combray: the bright, becalmed sky of Normandy; the deep silence, broken only by the whirring of insects; stagnant water in overgrown, rotting and neglected gardens; the gentle banks on either side of the cart-track, flaming with red poppies; the hedge-rose in its rural simplicity, and the bright, pale-pink-coloured, almost weightless splendour of the white thorn hedges . . . Steve suddenly stopped reading and closed his eyes. He saw everything clearly: the hedges forming a continuous row of chapels and offering their flowers as if on altars, the red-brown bark of the branches, cracked with age; the smooth, light grey of the thorn twigs, the young leaves in their fresh green, and the exploding abundance of delicate white blossoms . . . Yet something was wrong. He could not recover the memory of their smell in his mind. The sensation was obscured by some intangible barrier . . .

The chirpy voice of a technician which seemed to come from the other end of the world interrupted his train of thought to announce triumphantly that they had now calculated their mass: it was 5.38972833244 tons, precisely.

Jerome pointed down to the camp toilet.

'They're tremendous, our friends from NASA.' He un-wrapped a sandwich and bit into it. 'Nothing's overlooked.' They were listening to Radio Palermo, but somehow Sicily seemed further away than the planet Pluto. The chirping became more and more unintelligible, turned into a mushy noise and finally became excruciating on the ear. The roar caused by the increasing energy in the artificial gravitational field became louder. It sounded as if tons of tiny steel balls were raining on concrete.

Jerome lay down on the back seat of the 'cat' and Steve climbed back into the cockpit. He soon fell into a doze, but was startled several times by sounds of rending metal as the tension between the artificial gravity field and the earth's field of gravity increased.

Suddenly Steve noticed what it was that had been disturbing him. It was a sickly-sweet aromatic smell as of vanilla or cinnamon, and it was growing stronger. He remembered hearing about it during their theoretical training: it was a mysterious phenomenon associated with the Kafu field. The first groups to be sent into the past had reported noticing it shortly before they had been dropped.

Around midnight the first officer came over the radio once more. His voice seemed to come from a different galaxy. 'Everything OK?' The countdown, apparently, was going as planned. Calahan and Olson were with him, but their voices were hardly recognisable. They wished them 'a good fall'.

'Same to you,' Steve called into the microphone, but they did not seem to understand him, for he heard a voice distorted by interference, ask: 'Are they really still there?'

'Tell them to bring something to drink when they come,' Jerome was calling up from the loading area. 'Something to celebrate our reunion with. Tell them we'll look out for a comfortable spot for a party.'

Shortly afterwards all radio contact ceased and silence fell. The sweet cinnamon smell intensified and the temperature began to rise perceptibly. A little while later came a phenomenon Steve knew only too well from his time as an astronaut: an irregular gravity fluctuation, as if a rocket engine was defective. The energy bubble generated by the chronotrone began to tremble. Soon they would reach the critical field force.

Jerome closed all the hatches and joined Steve in the cockpit.

Together they checked their instruments. Everything was in perfect working order. They closed the cockpit, fastened their seat belts, switched off the lights and waited.

The temperature continued to rise. They began to sweat, and started inhaling oxygen at more frequent intervals. The cage walls gradually began to glow a deep red. Breathing hard, Steve fought off another fit of claustrophobia. In the corner of his vision patterns of coloured light appeared, and for a minute he thought they had got through and he was looking at the stars. But when he raised his head he saw only the distorted reflections of the instrument panel on the plexiglass of the cockpit over his head and behind it a diffuse gleam.

In the distance a roar could be heard. It was growing louder rapidly, threatening to burst the cage with its vibrations.

'This is it,' Jerome called out behind him.

The roaring grew louder still. Short periods of gravity alternated with periods of weightlessness which came in short spasms as the artificial gravity bubble battled with the pressure of incoming water.

*Jesus Christ!* Steve thought.

And once more the heart of the whale burst.

A moment of numbness.

*And then they were falling . . .*

. . . Falling through blood-red smoke and wisps of cloud, straight into the sun, a deep red sun which touched the rim of the western horizon.

Steve saw the floor of the cage whirl down into the abyss. Instinctively he pushed his control stick forward to stabilise the flight of the glider; the movement which the *Edison* had supplied was not sufficient.

They passed through a thin layer of cloud. Underneath them an incredible vista appeared: whiteish plains suffused by the pink evening light, flecked with vegetation and striped by long shadows, a few high mountain ranges, their peaks still in the sunlight, the steep flanks already covered by the darkness rising from the plains. Ahead stretched a vast sheet of water, extending towards the west as far as the eye could see, its shores much further to the south than the maps had suggested. By the light of the purple evening sky it glowed like a bowl of chased copper. In the south loomed a massive mountain range, soaring higher and higher. The African coast.

The sun was sinking rapidly behind the horizon, the shadows deepening. The glider was now pitching down into the gloom.

'We'll have to be quick if we want to get down before nightfall,' Jerome said. Just then they heard the echo of their materialisation explosion, rolling along the mountain on the coast like a mighty groan.

Steve pushed the nose of the glider down, feeling widely-splayed wings rocking in the turbulence. Ahead and to the right, the shore of the lake described a flat curve south-west into the landing area. Since the ground might be swampy, Steve let the glider drop further to the south in order to land far enough from the shore.

Meanwhile Jerome had started tapping out the agreed signal on the radio. 'Boy calling anchor, boy calling anchor. Come in please. Over.'

They listened intently.

*And do not forget that any group could be the first . . .*

Suddenly there was a crackle over the receiver, then a voice shouted: 'Switch off your transmitter. If you want to get down alive, shut up for God's sake. Stand by to receive . . .'

Jerome turned off the transmitter instantly and looked at Steve, astonished. 'Some welcome. What do they mean "If you want to get down alive"?'

'Maybe it's not as easy as the Navy figured. I had a hunch it might not be . . .' Steve stared into the growing darkness ahead, and noticed that there were a few isolated trees in the landing area after all. 'They must have some reason for breaking off transmission like that,' he grunted. Seeing a palm tree ahead, he pulled the control stick round; behind it were bushes, bare, flat ground. Cursing, he switched on the landing light. They were about twenty metres from touchdown now. The territory was quite flat, but marked by craters like those made by artillery shells. Here and there grass was burnt and bushes charred, with bright patches of sand in between. Steve pulled up the nose of the glider and put the runners out steeply. Still about five metres above ground. Then first one and then both runners scratched the ground. The nose jerked violently downwards, and the bow-wheel touched ground, bouncing. Now the runner wheels were rumbling and Steve was braking hard. Some branches hit the cockpit, the glider rocked violently to the side a few times, then it rushed into something that gave, and stuck fast.

Steve switched off the landing lights, undid the straps of his seat harness and opened the cockpit. The night air was unusually warm and smelt of salt. There was a loud noise of cicadas. Jerome, who had quickly climbed into the loading space through the hatch and inspected it by torchlight, called up that everything was OK. A few minutes later he came back into the cockpit armed with two machine pistols.

'Do you think they were having us on?' Jerome asked.

'That's not the impression I got,' Steve said emphatically. 'I wouldn't want to take a chance on it, anyway,' he added grimly.

'Who could be the enemy?'

'We'll probably know very soon.'

Steve listened in the darkness.

He heard a crackle of broken twigs, and somewhere in the far distance what sounded like the rumble of an engine, a heavy vehicle. It seemed to be moving away from them, and soon it could no longer be heard.

Were they really in the past now? Steve felt as he had always felt on test flights in jet fighters over the Atlantic; afterwards, back in the canteen, he could not help feeling that he had not *really* been in Europe at all; it was as if he had experienced everything in a kind of simulator. He had felt as if he had covered the distance only on a map. The *real* distance remained as abstract as distances given in the language of astronomy. His mind had not travelled along with him; it had simply reacted by conditioned reflex, just as it had been trained to. It was the same now. His limited sensory apparatus told him that the air smelt different, that the ground felt different, yet the distance between his former position and his present one seemed completely inconceivable.

Well, they were certainly in the Mediterranean basin – the landmarks proved that. And since it was not filled with water, they could no longer be in the present. About five and a half million years ago this basin had not held any water. *Ergo . . .*

Jerome climbed out and made a tour of the glider with his torch. 'Looks like we've been lucky. So there *are* trees here.' He pointed the torch forward. The glider had broken through light bushes and got stuck in a tangle of thorn thicket and dry leaves, which now half-covered it.

'I think it would be best if we stayed where we are, at least until the morning, or until we get new instructions,' Steve said. Jerome nodded. 'We can't do much at night. I wouldn't care to switch the lights on until we know what's going on round here.'

Steve hit out at a mosquito which had stung him on the forehead. 'These insects seem to have got wise to us pretty damn quickly,' he grumbled. 'I'll bet they can't wait to make a meal of their first human victims.'

'Incredible to think that everything is ready and only man is missing.'

Suddenly at a distance of about fifteen to twenty kilometres to the south an artillery shot rang out. They listened, holding their breath, then they heard the impact. It was about two kilometres to the north-west of them. A bright flash of light tore through the darkness.

'Looks like we didn't land in paradise after all,' Jerome said. 'Somebody's laying on a pretty hot reception for us.'

'If we hadn't come down rather steeply and if I hadn't steered the glider a little to the south, we'd have come down almost exactly where that shell hit,' Steve said. 'They must have heard our materialisation explosion and then calculated our most probable point of landing.'

They listened anxiously into the night, but the enemy seemed to have stopped firing.

Suddenly the radio crackled back to life again.

'Welcome to hell,' a voice said in immaculate English, with a barely noticeable accent. 'Had a good landing?'

'Don't answer!' another voice broke in. 'Don't let them fool you. They want to get your position in order to finish you off.'

Jerome's index finger had been hovering over the switch. Now he hesitated and turned to Steve questioningly.

'It would be much better if you surrendered as soon as possible, like most of your comrades. You are in extreme danger. The area where you have landed is highly radioactive. You haven't got a chance. You will be finished off in three or four hours. Speak up so that we can get you out as quickly as possible. Every minute is precious if you're to be saved.'

'Be reasonable,' another voice continued. 'You haven't got a chance. There *is* no enterprise Western Basin, it has never existed. We issued an ultimatum to your predecessors. A few hotheads tried to disregard it. They have long since been killed.

We have dynamited the Straits of Gibraltar. The waters are rising by the hour. The supplies dropped for you are at the bottom of the sea. You are cut off and without supplies. Speak up and tell us where you are. We'll get you out.'

'Don't answer, for God's sake,' another voice called. 'They'll have your position in a second.'

'You have been cheated. Not one of you will return to the future.'

'They want to demoralise you. Don't listen to them. Don't believe a word of what they're saying.'

'Who are "they"?' Jerome asked.

Steve shrugged his shoulders. 'Maybe the sheikhs haven't been quite as idle as the Navy hoped.'

The propaganda transmitter had fallen silent and now the second of the two voices was giving instructions. 'Unload before dawn and start out as soon as the light allows. No lights. Drive north, then north-east as fast as you can. Keep under cover wherever you can. Watch out for fresh camel tracks. If you meet a mounted troop, open fire without warning. The bandits are after your luggage. We'll get you out as soon as possible. Stay on "receive". Out.'

'Do you know what camel tracks look like?' Jerome asked.

'I haven't the slightest idea. I didn't even know camels existed in this age.'

'Our friends must have brought them along. Good idea. No fuel problem.'

'It must be the Arabs, then.'

'Most probably. And they must be damn good if they've managed to knock out enough of our men to secure the landing area.'

From the north-west where the shell had exploded, they now heard a few protesting trumpet noises. Mastodons? A few frightened birds were screeching. Then all was silent again.

Steve gazed up into the starry sky, but was unable to find any familiar constellations. So they really *had* landed in the past. The sun still had to go more than 4000 light years of its circular course around the centre of the Milky Way before the first Pyramids would be built.

Knowing that they had a difficult journey ahead of them, they took it in turns to try and get some sleep, but without much success.

CHAPTER FOUR

# THE PLACE OF THE SKULL

Steve took the first watch. Venus shone brightly in the western sky, and moving slowly, set on the horizon. A thin, fragile crescent moon seemed to float towards it like a glass barge. Looking south he saw a comet just over the African mountains, its tail pointing east and resembling a shower of sparks from a blacksmith's forge. It was a strange, threatening sky that spread out overhead: the sky of a world which was not yet ready for man, the sky of an unfinished creation. But gradually Steve adjusted to the reality of this world, accepted its physical substance. It took shape, was no longer the abstract past, but became the here-and-now, a present which he could breathe, smell, taste, and touch. It was as if a pore was opening up on the enormous body of time and he was invading it like a microbe. He felt he was being received again by the stream of life he had left at some other spot, and swept along in the direction of a future. His former 'present' seemed to him now like a distant galaxy, separated from him by eons, like an island whose shores one has glimpsed in dreams.

He was interrupted in his meditations by a noise. There was a breaking of twigs, then he heard a snort as if from a large animal. Not far away some monstrous creature was crashing through the undergrowth. Steve cocked his machine pistol, suddenly feeling acutely vulnerable. Was it a dinosaur? No – surely, to meet a dinosaur they would have had to be catapulted ten times further back into the past. It was probably a mastodon or some other giant mammal. Most species had developed to large sizes in the Miocene Age.

He woke Jerome. They listened together. They saw a giant shadow touch the glider, brush against it, then the nocturnal apparition disappeared.

Soon afterwards the voice came back on the air again.

'Looks as if we can't get you out for a while yet. But we'll help you as soon as we possibly can. Leave the Red Zone quickly.

Don't abandon your vehicle unless it's absolutely necessary. The landing area is partially radioactive. We shall make contact with you again. Out.'

Jerome cursed while he closed the cockpit and locked it. 'Those idiots should have told us earlier. Damn it. Leaving us to fry in the fat here without warning.'

Steve tried to sleep a little, but the narrow cabin soon became hot and sticky and he woke up covered in sweat. He put the oxygen mask on and took a couple of deep breaths. There were still about two hours to go to daybreak.

'Shall we start unloading?' Jerome asked.

They took out the equipment and instruments from the cockpit and loaded them into the 'cat'. Then they detached the stern of the glider, unfastened the 'cat' and trailer from their moorings, started the engine and drove out.

The stars had faded. Mist had risen during the night. Towards the east it was getting light and the contours of the surrounding area were beginning to emerge.

On landing, the glider had ploughed a narrow furrow into the undergrowth and had come to rest with its nose in a thicket of thorns and mimosas. They couldn't have found a better cover. Only the top of the cockpit and one side of the rudder were visible.

'We seem to be in luck so far,' Steve said. 'Perhaps we can slip away unseen.'

Jerome stepped on the accelerator. The terrain was quite level, savannah-like, overgrown by clumps of coarse grass, alternating with thick undergrowth and scattered groups of trees, mostly euphorbias with here and there a palm tree. The 'cat' moved along quite fast, but driving it was a hazardous business, with bushes constantly looming up out of nowhere; the mist seemed to be getting thicker.

They had not covered further than five hundred metres when they heard the impact of an explosion behind them. Steve looked back and saw that the area around their landing place was bathed in orange light. There was a flash and afterglow, and then a mushroom cloud rose eerily out of the mist.

'They're using atomic missiles!' he shouted.

Instinctively, Jerome stepped on the accelerator, then braked hard to avoid a thick thorn bush. The 'cat' lurched violently. Steve stared back over his shoulder as if spellbound, waiting for the flash that would blast them into radioactive dust. It never came.

'They must have located us by guided microphone,' Jerome said. 'They can't possibly have seen us in this pea-soup.'

'Then drive more slowly. Damn it – they can probably hear us for miles around,' Steve shouted furiously, and was sorry at once that he had lost control over himself. Jerome threw him an angry look, but said nothing. He was sweating hard now from the effort of driving and there were beads of moisture on his forehead and between the dark three-day-old stubble.

'Their supplies must be far better organised than ours if they can afford to squander atomic missiles like that,' Steve said after a while. 'I'm not surprised they've got the edge on our people. Looks to me like we'll be hard pushed to pump oil from underneath the sheikhs' bottoms if they sit on it as tightly as that.'

'Which means that the most imaginative and possibly also the most expensive coup in world history has turned out to be a miserable failure,' Jerome said.

'Do you think they've really dynamited the Straits of Gibraltar?'

'With the explosives they have, it's quite conceivable,' Jerome said, shrugging his shoulders. 'But the trough wouldn't fill up as quickly as that. They'd have to make a very big hole indeed. Remember, even rivers like the Nile and the Rhône and a hundred other quite respectable waterways couldn't stop it drying up.'

'But I seem to remember that the coastline of the Balearic Lake was quite a bit further south than the topographic reconstruction maps showed it.'

'What worries me is the thought that we might not be able to return to the future.'

'Do you seriously think we've been betrayed?' Steve asked, horrified. 'That would mean that . . .'

Suddenly Jerome stepped on the brakes with all his might and brought the 'cat' to an abrupt halt. Steve peered through the windscreen to see what the trouble was, and found himself staring into the most horrible face he had ever seen. Impaled on a steel pipe, which had been rammed firmly into the ground, was a severed human head. Evidently it was the head of a young man – his mouth, open as if to scream, showed a perfect set of teeth. He wore a tightly fitting leather airman's helmet like the ones worn by Russian cosmonauts. Fixed to its side by a strap was an oxygen mask; the man's neck and the ribbed hose-pipe of the mask had apparently been slashed open with the same blow.

Jerome stopped the engine and the two men stared at the horrible sight with fascination. Death must have taken place not long ago. The pale skin showed no traces of decay, and the blood on the steel pipe looked fresh. In spite of the mist the first flies had only recently settled on it. Steve looked around for signs of a corpse, but in vain. The silence all around them now assumed an air of threat. Somewhere in the distance a high-pitched, clucking laugh could be heard – monkeys babbling, or maybe the call of a large, unknown bird. Perhaps even the triumphant laughter of the beast that had perpetrated this horrible act.

Steve breathed a sigh of relief when Jerome started the engine up again, but as they drove on the sight remained fixed in his memory. Whenever he saw a shape in the mist, he tightened his grip on his weapon, imagining he saw the man in the leather mask blocking their road, his sword of judgment raised high. Usually the shape turned out to be the dark branches of a euphorbia tree.

Soon they came to a river, which they followed in a northerly direction, looking for a place to cross over to the eastern bank. They were moving at little more than walking pace now, as the bushes on the banks were almost impenetrable. Again and again fallen trees blocked the way and they were forced to make long detours. Finally they found a place where the water seemed shallow enough to drive across.

Seeing movement on the opposite side, Jerome turned off the engine. A herd of mastodons broke through the undergrowth and came shambling down to the watering-place. The enormous animals were up to six metres high, with short under-developed tusks and short tapir-like trunks which looked clumsy compared to the skilful grasping organ of the mammoth and elephant. They all seemed tired and listless, the dark tufted fur falling out by the handful. Wherever the bare grey skin showed on their lean flanks there were festering wounds and fresh gashes, from which bright-red blood was pouring. The typical symptoms of advanced radiation sickness. One of the young animals had a crippled trunk, which jerked to and fro between the short budding tusks like an amputated leg.

One of the older bulls had been wounded in the head by shell shrapnel. Blinded by the flowing blood, he lifted his trunk in their direction, sniffing suspiciously and uttering a thunderous trumpeting noise which petered out into a hoarse sob. The mighty bull's flanks trembled weakly. He looked pitiful. The animal must have been close to an exploding atomic shell and would not live much longer. The females surrounded the young animals as if in gloomy anticipation of disaster and pushed the bull away, sniffing in all directions.

The leader bull trotted reeling down to the river, and fell to his knees on the muddy bank. He dipped his trunk into the water and sprayed himself with it, then began to drink in deep gulps. The water began to turn red. Only when the bull had quenched his thirst and took over the watch again did the rest of the herd dare approach the watering-place.

'Terrible,' Jerome whispered.

'This is only the beginning,' Steve said with bitterness. 'Wherever man arrives he dominates ruthlessly at the expense of his environment.'

While they waited for the animals to stop drinking and withdraw from the bank, they finished the remains of their sandwiches and drank the last of their coffee from the thermos flasks. Finally they saw the mastodons move pathetically off into the swirling mist. Each one bore all the signs of impending radiation death.

Steve now took over the wheel and Jerome sat next to him, machine pistol cocked in his lap. On the other side of the river the country became savannah again. The trees grew more sparse, the bushes thinned out. They were now driving almost exactly due north-east and covering quite a bit of ground. Gradually the terrain began to rise and occasionally a timid and pale-looking sun managed to poke through the mist. The 'cat' was climbing, and suddenly, as if they were emerging from a lake, the sea of mist was beneath them, stretching right over to the horizon. To the south they recognised the cone-like stumps which would one day form the islands of La Galite, and behind them, like a dark jetty against the white breakers of the mist, the edge of the African coast. It was from there that the atomic shells were being fired. Jerome raised his binoculars to his eyes and scanned the forested mountain ranges. He could not make out anything in detail. There was no flash of gunfire to be seen.

Below them, the feathery tops of palm-trees stuck out like strange over-sized water plants from the blanket of cloud. Jerome pointed north to a wild and rocky plateau which would be the island of Sardinia in a few million years. 'That's where we should head for,' he said. 'But I'd prefer to wait until late afternoon before we start the ascent. We'll have the mist for cover by then.'

Steve remembered with a shudder the severed head of the pilot. 'I don't mind,' he said. 'We don't know the range of their guns, but I guess the further north we get, the safer we'll be.'

Jerome scanned the steep rocky slopes of Sardinia. 'Who knows?' he said with a shrug of his shoulders.

'The landing area is infected by radiation,' Steve pointed out. 'We could be as hot as the sun already. We ought to try and get help before it's too late.' Even now he felt the beginning of an unbearable itching on the unprotected parts of his skin, the clearest sign of a dangerous dose of radiation. 'They won't let us down,' he added hopefully. 'They promised to get us out.'

'If they can. Otherwise we'll go to the devil,' Jerome said, adding sarcastically: 'if he exists in this age. But I don't have the slightest doubt of that.'

In the early afternoon Jerome took over the wheel again. By now they were high above the sea of mist, but the Sardinian plateau seemed to be almost as far away as ever. The trees and vegetation were gradually changing, and dotted among the palm-trees and euphorbias were the odd umbrella acacia and pine-tree, sometimes even gingkos.

A little later they came to the burnt-out wreck of a jeep. The unit had consisted of four people and traces of their uniforms still clung to the skeletons. One of the men had managed to drag himself forward on the ground for about sixty metres before collapsing. The vultures had picked his corpse clean. Judging by the damage to the jeep they had been attacked from the air by rocket. The enemy must be in control of the air space too. Steve searched the sky with an uncomfortable look.

Further on, they came upon more traces of heavy fighting. The ground was dotted with bomb craters, the vegetation burnt down, with charred tree-trunks sticking up into the sky. Jerome drove more slowly, the caterpillar tracks whirling up clouds of dust and ashes as he picked his way between the craters. Soon the route began to climb again more steeply, along a dry riverbed which they followed northwards. The heat in the closed vehicle became unbearable.

'Seems to be pretty clean round here,' Jerome said, and steered the vehicle under a dark, shady roof of thickly woven pine-branches. Nearby, water had collected in a pool and the sun fell through the branches and glinted on the surface. Jerome wandered across to it, took off his boots and let his legs dangle in the water, while Steve climbed up the embankment to keep a look-out. They were now at the foot of the plateau; the sun was still shining with unmitigated intensity, but the steep slopes of the southern coast of Sardinia were already furrowed by shadows. Somewhere up there was the base they had to find. Only there would they have reached safety.

Suddenly Steve heard a hoarse growl. At first he thought Jerome was playing around with the engine, then he realised with horror that there must be a predator nearby – a big cat probably, a lion, or something similar. And he was unarmed. He dashed down the slope as fast as his legs would carry him, yelling at Jerome, who leaped out of the water in fright and grabbed his machine pistol.

'A lion, *a lion!*'

Jerome was waving the weapon fiercely, but he could not find a target. During their training they had been taught a lot of unnecessary things, but not how to behave if confronted with big cats.

'For Christ's sake – you must be more careful!' Jerome shouted at him. 'There could be sabre-toothed tigers round here. Jesus – they can kill *mastodons*. Take your gun next time, OK?'

Furious at his own carelessness, Steve threw his steel helmet on the back seat, sat down at the steering wheel and started the engine. He drove until it got dark and continued for a while with the help of the lights, until finally it seemed pointless to proceed any further in the trackless terrain.

It had started to rain. All afternoon there had been thunder clouds over the high plateau; now there were flashes of lightning over the peaks in the east and soon the storm broke out in earnest. Fearing floods, Steve steered the 'cat' away from the river bed which they had followed so far and up the steep incline. As soon as he reached a safe stopping place, he slammed on the brakes and sat back, exhausted. Raindrops the size of pebbles were bouncing off the roof, and water was flooding down the windscreen. Within seconds they could see no further than two metres. Lightning flashed and thunder crashed against the nearby rockface, rumbling down into the valley and the trees groaned under the force of the wind.

When the rain finally subsided, they set up their tent under the protection of some branches. They had just finished doing so when there was another crackle from the receiver. A voice apparently coming from nearby said: 'Anchor to boy. We shall try to establish direct contact with you during the night. Give us a signal so that we can locate your position. We are standing by. Out.'

'One moment,' Steve said to Jerome, whose finger was already hovering over the transmitter indecisively. 'This could be a trick.' Jerome nodded.

While they deliberated, the voice came again. 'You're right, boys. It's an old trick. If it succeeds our task is to send an instant warning and do everything we can to get you out safely. We have no common code, but our request is genuine. You have to be quite near by now. Please come in. Over.'

Jerome briefly switched to transmit. 'Understood. Over and out.'

'Excellent, thanks. That's enough. Stay on the air. Out.'

Steve took over the watch while Jerome tried to sleep. From time to time, a distant flash of lightning lit up the swirling banks of cloud and a shower of rain poured down on the roof of the tent. Shortly after midnight the noise of a helicopter could be heard. When the *whop-whop-whop* sound was almost above their heads Steve softly spoke into the microphone and said simply, 'Land.' He cocked his machine pistol. Jerome crawled from the tent with his weapon and took cover.

For a few tense seconds Steve expected to see a burst of machine gun fire or the ignition flash of a rocket, yet nothing like that happened. Instead the small two-seater plane switched on a searchlight and came down. Two figures climbed out. In the uncertain light Steve recognised two men wearing rather shabby and bleached fatigues and steel helmets.

'Murchinson,' announced the smaller of the two, and stretched out his hand. He was about fifty, as far as Steve could make out in the darkness.

'Ruiz.' The other man stepped forward, a medium-built squat figure in his mid-forties who aimed the light of his torch at them. 'From the other side of the Mississippi, but a hundred per cent one of the boys.' Neither Steve nor Jerome understood this remark. Since the new arrivals did not seem to care for military rank Jerome only gave their surnames. The two men nodded.

'I believe I saw your names on the list of those who are still on the way,' Ruiz said, smiling. 'You've been lucky.'

Steve nodded. 'It could have been worse.'

'When do you come from?' Murchinson asked.

'Nineteen eighty-six,' Steve said. 'What's going on here?'

'Hell,' Murchinson said. 'But you must have noticed that yourselves.'

'How many have arrived already?' Jerome asked.

'Oh, quite a few,' Murchinson said, after a pause. 'After all, the first ones arrived more than forty years ago. And some of them have : . . gone . . . already.'

'Back into the future?' Jerome asked.

Steve noticed the two men exchange a quick glance.

'Well, you know, that part of the project isn't really our responsibility,' Ruiz said, scratching on the wet ground uncomfortably with his boot. 'We'll just give you a few tips and a map to help you reach the fortress safely tomorrow. We don't want to anticipate what the commandant has to say. He'll answer all your questions to your satisfaction.'

'What about the pipeline?' Jerome asked. 'If they've been operating here for forty years, they ought to . . .'

'Listen,' Ruiz said with a weary expression which they were just able to make out by the light of his torch, 'you'd better forget all about that. That stupid idea has cost a lot of people their lives. And we've both wasted more than twenty years of our lives on this bloody project, with a damned slim chance of ever getting out of this mess!'

'You mean to say that in forty years *nothing* has been achieved? That our men have barricaded themselves into fortresses while all the material that's been transported here is rotting at the bottom of the sea?'

'Listen, mister . . .' Ruiz was getting worked up now.

'Major Jerome Bannister, Sir.'

'Don't get so hot under the collar,' said Murchinson. 'You'll have all your questions answered soon enough, Major – that's if the lessons you've learned so far aren't enough for you.'

So saying, he spread a hand-drawn map on the wet boot of the 'cat' and lit it with his torch. Murchinson marked their position with his index finger and pointed in a northerly direction. 'The exact position of the fortress isn't marked, for good reason,' he said. 'If you meet some rather small gentlemen with hairy bodies who speak a rather strange English, throw yourselves trustingly at them. You'll have reached safety then. But if you should meet a troop of camel riders – they rarely dare come up here, but there's just a chance – don't hesitate to open fire. They're mercenaries – they used to fight for the sheikhs, but they've long since broken away to fight for their own interests. The bastards feel cheated, too. Not all of them are bad by any means, but there's an unwritten law that they keep off new arrivals, even if they're dying to get at their luggage. Understand?'

'I don't understand a damn thing,' Jerome said angrily.

'I guess it'll take you time to get used to things round here, Major,' Ruiz said in an attempt to reassure.

'It certainly will.'

'Well, there'll be a few more surprises in store.'

'We came down here to correct a few things,' Jerome continued, unperturbed. 'If things didn't work out as planned, the project coordinators should have been told. Surely the Navy must have been informed by returning units that . . .'

'Excuse me, Major Bannister,' Murchinson interrupted,' but over there on the Bermudas there are men getting on for seventy years old, and they're *still* waiting for their return passage. And the reason they're sitting over there and waiting safely is because we have the lousy job of transporting them over there. Otherwise they'd have finished up like quite a few other guys we *couldn't* help.' He pointed into the darkness over towards the south-east. 'We don't stay out here for the fun of it, Major – we're literally risking our skins. Do you understand what I'm saying?'

'Sorry,' Jerome murmured. 'I didn't know . . .'

'It's not your fault, I guess,' Ruiz said, 'but I get pretty damn sick of seeing new guys come along and throw their weight about when they don't know the score. I've seen it happen too often . . .'

'And why haven't you returned into the future?' Jerome asked. 'If you're so fed up?'

'He really wants to know,' Murchinson sighed.

'Because we've been cheated, Major,' Ruiz said. 'There *is* no return to the future!'

Steve felt as if an icy hand gripped his heart. The simple thought formed behind his forehead, then seemed to detonate inside his skull.

*Everything is finished.*

He suddenly knew how a condemned man must feel when he faces the rifles of the firing squad and sees the sword of the officer in command raised high. He clutched at the wet metal of the bonnet for support.

'I knew it,' Jerome whispered. He was immensely calm, but the words came out as a tortured groan.

'There was no deliberate deception,' Ruiz said comfortingly, 'but something seems to have gone badly wrong.'

'Do you know of the Treaty of Miami between Castro and Maximilian the Fifth?' Murchinson asked warily.

Jerome looked at him uncomprehendingly.

Ruiz nodded emphatically and said: 'You see?'

As soon as the helicopter had taken off, Steve crawled into the tent. Jerome took over the second watch from the shelter of the trees, where he had found a dry spot for himself. A little while later he came back into the tent to fetch something. Steve pretended to be asleep. He thought he heard his friend suppress a sob, but he could have been mistaken. Jerome crawled out and fastened the zip from the outside.

Steve felt completely worn out, but he couldn't sleep. Every now and then raindrops fell on the roof of the tent like handfuls of ripe plums dropping from the branches. Steve had never known such despair. He knew now that freedom was completely unattainable, and that everything he loved and longed for lay in the distant future, millions of years out of reach.

Gripped by a primitive terror, Steve found himself praying to the Christ-figure of his childhood. And then he realised that the earth would have to wait for more than fifty thousand centuries for its saviour.

As he tossed and turned on his bed, he thought of the doomed herd of animals they had met in the landing area. Miserable

creatures, all alone with their nightmares. We have changed the
earth to please God, he thought grimly; have subjugated it in
His name. And now the earth has become timeless like its
creator. Man's meddlings have polluted the oceans, ploughed
up the earth, fouled the air, forcing migrant birds to look for new
routes in the confusion of flight paths and air corridors. Steve
recalled the young mastodon with the injured trunk; saw again
the faltering steps, the trembling, bloodstained flank. Man had
raped and ravaged the present. Now he was cruelly destroying
the past.

The following morning was sunny and clear and full of the
smell of resin. The sky was radiant and eagles were circling
overhead, testing the upward thermals which were beginning to
stir. From somewhere nearby came the call of a hawk. Then a
rifle-shot rang out, its echo rolling along the rocky crevices.

Jerome had prepared breakfast. He looked worn out and
there were deep shadows under his eyes.

They ate moodily, listening attentively, but there was
nothing to be heard apart from the singing of the birds. Trying
to make as little noise as possible, they took down the tent and
stowed it in the trailer.

Jerome, consulting his compass from time to time, pointed at
the hand-drawn map. 'That Ruiz mentioned a river valley.
This could be it. But I've a feeling we're too far east. If this
mountain range is what was called Cap Teulada we should
keep further to the left – the fortress is situated here, in Porto
Pino.'

They followed the river bed for a few hundred metres, but
soon found that it led further and further eastwards. Steve
turned round, drove back a little and headed up the west bank,
weaving through undergrowth until they reached an almost
treeless plateau which sloped gently south.

'It can't be more than four or five miles now . . .'

At that moment there was a loud boom as if a plane had
broken the sound barrier, closely followed by the screech of jet
engines. A low-flying fighter plane came racing along the
mountain flanks from the east, heading straight for them. Steve
opened the door, ran a few steps away from the 'cat' and hurled
himself flat on the ground. A few seconds later the plane had
passed overhead. It was a MIG 25.

For a minute Steve was tempted to leave the vehicle behind

and save his skin, then he climbed back behind the wheel hastily.

'Let's get out of here,' Jerome shouted. Steve steered off to the right in a narrow curve and made for the low rock face at full speed, while Jerome scanned the sky. Five minutes later the MIG returned. Steve donned his steel helmet, brought the 'cat' to a standstill alongside the rock face and dived out to take cover behind a couple of rocks, scratching his face on the brambles. He heard the characteristic *ffwosh-ffwosh* sound of two air-to-ground rockets being fired and at the same time the *tat-tat-tat* of a light anti-aircraft fire. It seemed the attack was not aimed at them after all.

Steve ran back to the 'cat' and saw Jerome sitting behind the wheel, motionless. His normally bright eyes were quite dark with fear and there were thick drops of sweat on his unshaven face..

'What's the matter with you?' Steve shouted at him.

'We're bloody fools,' Jerome shouted, hitting the wheel with his fist. 'Bloody stupid fools to have got ourselves into this mess.' He opened the door abruptly and dashed out. Steve heard him run behind the trailer and vomit. Everyone had his own way of facing the shock, he told himself. For Jerome it was a physical thing. His own response was less obvious – but just as real.

Suddenly, the MIG returned. Again they heard two rockets being fired, followed almost instantly by the detonation of the warheads and the renewed chatter of anti-aircraft fire. The MIG came up screeching and darted away overhead, leaving a thin line of smoke in the blue sky. The pilot was evidently trying to pull his damaged plane high enough to bale out. Suddenly a parachute opened up in the sky and floated down, lit from behind by the sun. An orange flash lit the sky, where the plane had hit and without a sound, a cloud of smoke rose over the point of impact. Silently the bunched white cloud floated upward in the blue noonday sky, gay, before it was torn up by the boom of the explosion.

Steve was suddenly overcome by an immense calmness. It was as if Jerome's moment of weakness had taken the horror out of the situation. He had a sudden feeling that here and now he was needed to help his own kind. And this feeling gave him satisfaction. The nightmare which had weighed down his heart the night before had left him.

Steve got out and lit the calor gas cooker. When the coffee was ready he filled two mugs and went back to Jerome. Sitting together in the shadow of the rock face they drank the hot brew without looking at each other.

'Thank you,' Jerome said, wiping the sweat from his forehead and eyes and letting the steel helmet fall into the grass in front of him.

Every now and then they heard throaty, cackling shouts which were answered in the distance and repeated. They sounded cheerful, as if a satyr were bursting into laughter during his amorous noonday play, and the cheerfulness communicated itself from mountain to mountain as if there were invisible love nests all around them. Steve lifted his head, listening with astonishment, but he could not interpret the calls. An extinct species of birds? Maybe – yet somehow in spite of their strangeness, they sounded vaguely familiar and he almost answered them with a clumsy imitation.

# CHAPTER FIVE

## THE FORTRESS

They had rested for about an hour when they heard the noise of a car engine in the south-west. Steve and Jerome instantly grabbed their machine pistols and took cover. The noises approached quickly, and presently, a little further down between the rocks and bushes, a jeep appeared, an ancient vehicle without a roof, dented and muddy, its windscreen broken. The man who steered it was of small build and was barely visible behind the steering wheel. It drove up at full speed and stopped with squeaking brakes about ten metres away from them. The engine was switched off immediately.

They could hardly believe their eyes when a strange creature jumped nimbly out. It was short and hunched, with disproportionately long arms which reached to the ground because of his stooping posture. It wore a steel helmet which was far too big, and a pair of ragged and faded khaki shorts which might at one time have belonged to an English colonial officer. The bare parts of its body were hairy all over – even the face. The shaggy legs which stuck out from the khaki shorts were thin, but astonishingly muscular, and the toes, which were almost as long as fingers, ended in strong, dangerous-looking claws. The strange creature had one fist clenched and was using it to support itself on the ground, while in the other hand it held an American automatic rifle.

An ape, Steve thought immediately. We have to take the gun away from the beast before it can do us harm.

The creature lifted its head and a threatening growl came from its throat; then it bared a set of dangerous-looking teeth, sharp and immaculately white in pink gums. Steve hesitated. Was this a warning? Or was it meant to be a welcoming smile? The next moment all doubts were removed; with its free hand the creature made a gesture which could only mean 'Come out; I won't harm you.'

Steve and Jerome came cautiously out from their cover and

lowered their machine pistols. The creature jerked his chin forward and formed his fleshy lips as if about to speak. '*Goodluck*,' he finally announced in a deep throaty voice. Then he wiped his face with a sinewy hand, overgrown with sand-coloured hair, before stretching it out in welcome with the fingers bent casually down. It was a narrow, strong hand and it felt hard and cool. Steve felt a pang of revulsion as his fingers touched the dense fur, but a glance into the dark-brown, attentive, almost twinkling eyes told him that he was face to face with a clever, thinking being which resembled the apes he knew from former times only in appearance. Here was a creature that was no longer an animal; already he had begun to develop towards an intelligent being, but without having relinquished his instincts. Steve was fascinated. He was strange, and yet the nearest thing to a human being he had ever met in the animal kingdom. He was attractive in his nimble and natural grace and yet repulsive in his animality, obscene in his shamelessness and dangerous in his wildness. All these impressions seemed to be concentrated in the predatory smell which surrounded the creature, a sour, indefinable, fascinating smell which affected even Steve's faded senses. Steve realised that he was a carnivore, a dangerous and merciless hunter – perhaps the most terrible predator earth has ever produced. And that he was being robbed of his paradise.

'Good luck,' Steve said mistaking the ape-man's word for a greeting, but the creature burst into happy laughter, moved his ears and replied with pointed lips: 'Goodluck is my name.' He scratched his hairy chest, baring his teeth. 'And you are the two new men.' Then he nodded in the direction of the jeep, adding: 'I've got him.'

Now Steve saw on the back seat of the jeep a body, a wiry youth of barely twenty years, with dark skin and a fuzzy crew-cut. He must be the pilot of the MIG that was shot down. He was tied up with parachute string like a parcel and his forehead was bleeding. His olive-coloured skin had turned waxen with fear, and he was trembling like a leaf. Steve felt for him, imagining what it must have been like to be taken prisoner Faced with this nimble, muscular dwarf even a fully grown man wouldn't have a chance. This bundle of concentrated energy would probably be able to jump over the jeep from a standing position.

126 The Last Day of Creation

'Mosquito,' Goodluck said cheerfully, and clapped his flat hand on the hairy lower arm. He was apparently making a disparaging reference to the MIG 25. Then he added, 'Money,' and made a gesture with thumb and forefinger which even in the twentieth century everybody all over the world would have understood.

There must be a premium on the heads of captured pilots, Steve thought. But then he realised what the ape-man had meant.

'He's been lucky,' Goodluck said. 'His legs aren't broken. I can sell him. Otherwise . . .' He put his index finger on his throat and made an unmistakable gesture.

Steve remembered the head on the iron pipe. Obviously they didn't take prisoners unless they could be sold into slavery. But who kept the slaves?

Goodluck lifted his hands to his mouth and produced a cackling, satyr-like call – the sound which Steve had heard the night before. He was promptly answered by two voices from the mountain slopes overhead.

'Follow me,' Goodluck said in his awkward English, and climbed into his vehicle. Jerome and Steve clambered into the 'cat', and the two vehicles set off.

Goodluck drove like a madman over the inhospitable terrain, and was obviously familiar with the area. After about half an hour they crossed a dried-out river bed. Goodluck stopped. On a hill further up river stood a strange structure formed out of plastic pipes about thirty metres long and three metres in diameter; these had been anchored between the rock face and piled up to form a kind of pyramid. The area around was covered in craters and torn up by shell holes, and much of the surrounding vegetation had been burnt down.

Goodluck switched off the engine and gestured to them to do the same. He called up into the mountains, but no answer came.

'This seems to be the fortress,' Jerome said, but Goodluck didn't seem to be taking any notice of the pyramid.

'It's a mock-up,' Goodluck shouted, pointing to the structure. 'Many mock-ups.' He pointed over his shoulder. 'Fell into the trap,' he laughed happily. Then all of a sudden the smile died on his dark lips. 'Much death,' he said sadly, and made a sweeping gesture all around. 'Much death.' He scratched himself on the lower arms, with an expression of disgust, then slapped the prisoner abruptly in the face with the flat of his hand. 'Much death,' he growled, and gave a sigh. Suddenly he seemed to be overcome by an unspeakable sadness, and all his former cheerfulness deserted him.

Goodluck continued driving slowly east. After skirting some wooded promontories, they turned north and eventually reached a maze of gorges with steeply falling sides. Below them wound a fast-flowing stream, and between the dense trees a dirt road had been cleared, scored with tyre-marks and caterpillar tracks. From time to time Goodluck stopped, switched off the engine and produced one of his strange calls, each of which was now answered although none of the callers showed themselves. They were always high above, their heads hidden in the upper reaches of trees or on protruding cliffs.

'Guards,' Goodluck explained. The system seemed to function very efficiently.

'This must be the maze of gorges underneath the Porto Pino in the Gulf of Palmas,' Jerome said. 'We've arrived.'

It was not until now that Steve noticed that the narrow valley in front of them was covered with an artificial roof. Into the rock face on both sides niches had been carved and lengths of pipe had been piled close together to make a roof as if of straw. On top of these was a layer of soil in which bushes and trees were growing.

They drove into the gaping mouth of the cavern and found themselves in a spacious vault in the middle of which flowed the stream they had seen earlier. Everywhere lay heavy equipment: steam-rollers, excavators, cranes, tractors and tip-trucks. On both sides of the track there were prefabs and wooden huts, and here and there fuel tanks made of plastic. But there was not a soul in sight.

Suddenly a shaft of sunlight broke through a gap in the roof, revealing a barrier of sand bags and behind it an armed guard consisting of two elderly men in khaki shorts, one of them naked to the waist and deeply tanned, the other wearing a ragged T-shirt and a broad-brimmed hat. They were sitting on the wreck of a vehicle that must once have been a 'cat', and were playing cards. One of them greeted the new arrivals by lifting his hand and casually waving them through.

'We certainly aren't the first ones here,' Jerome said, with a hint of disappointment. Steve felt the same way; it was like turning up to see a play, only to find the stage hands already clearing away the sets. They stopped in front of a prefab which seemed badly in need of repainting and Goodluck brought them before the commandant.

'Welcome to Fortress Future One,' said the commandant. 'We call this place Maledetta. I'm Howard Harness.' He stepped forward and shook hands with them. He was a broad-shouldered man of about sixty-five, with energetic dark eyes and thin, snow-white hair. His naked chest was tanned and he was dressed in a pair of faded shorts and home-made sandals, whose soles had been cut from old car tyres. Jerome registered all these signs of decline with growing horror.

'I was the highest-ranking officer here in the Western Basin,' the commandant continued, gesturing them to a seat on a roughly constructed bench. 'We long since abolished all military ranks, but I retained the position of commandant.'

Steve couldn't help staring at the commandant's left arm. It had been amputated below the elbow joint and the stump looked dreadful – as if it had been severed with an axe and stitched up by an amateur. The wound must have taken months to heal; even now it was covered with unsightly grey scabs which looked like badly mixed cement.

'When we first arrived, medical care was indeed inadequate,' said Harness, who had noticed Steve's look of disgust. 'You'll be better off in that respect.'

Embarrassed, Steve stared at his boots and murmured: 'I'm sorry, Sir. I didn't mean –'

Harness took no notice. 'Unless you get malaria, of course. We're badly off for medical supplies.'

Just then they were interrupted by a squawk from an inter-com in the room next door. The commandant excused himself and turned in the direction of the noise. 'Under no circum-stances is the container to be opened by dynamite,' he shouted through the half-open door. 'As long as we don't know what's in it, under *no* circumstances . . . How old? Two hundred years? Then it must have been one of the first to have come down. Excuse me,' he apologised, turning back to them. 'It's always a bit of an event when we dig out a container somewhere in the basin which hasn't already been rifled by the trader mer-cenaries.'

'Did you say two hundred years, Sir?' Jerome asked.

'That's right.'

'We were told the scatter would be between six and eight years.'

'That may have held true with those beautiful round test eggs. Here it's been raining material for two hundred years. When the first troops landed, a large proportion of the stuff was hopelessly decayed and unusable.' He took up a list, held it far away from his eyes and read off the names. ' "Major Steve B. Stanley and Major Jerome Bannister, dropped from *USS Thomas Alva Edison* on June 30th, 1986." My God, how long ago was that?'

'Only two days ago,' Jerome said.

Harness let out a bitter little laugh, then, using his stump to hold the list on the table, struck their names off carefully with a pencil stub and wrote some numbers after them.

'Can either of you grind lenses?' he asked.

Steve and Jerome looked blankly at each other.

'No, Sir,' Steve said.

'I was afraid of that. You'd have had to make me a pair of glasses – my eyes are failing fast these days. I hope you have some useful knowledge or skill of a non-military kind. It would make you very sought after here. There's no shortage of petro-chemists, pipeline specialists and geologists, though,' he added. 'By the way, the date I put after your names isn't as fictitious as it may seem. It's certainly more realistic than any other kind of chronology. You'll find that out for yourselves, I expect – the hard way. You're now in the year forty-seven after the first registered landing. Our enemies arrived a few decades earlier and were better equipped, worst luck; otherwise we would have achieved more. We should have foreseen that. Perhaps we would have done if Francis hadn't been so damned confident.'

'So everything's in vain?' Jerome asked. 'And millions of dollars and hundreds of lives have been wasted?'

'More than that. I'd say a few hundred thousand million dollars, and about three thousand men, of whom two hundred and eighty have died so far, either in battle or from radiation sickness.'

'And where are all these people?' Steve asked.

'Most of them have been shipped over to the Bermudas, especially women and children. There's quite a flourishing colony over there by now. The inhabitants call it Atlantis, after the legendary continent. There are now more than four thousand of them, all waiting to return to the future.'

'So it's true then? There *is* no return to the future?' Jerome asked.

'I wouldn't be too sure,' the commandant said. He opened a drawer in his desk, looked in briefly and shut it again. He nodded. 'Muiz and Murchinson got you out, right?'

'Got us out is good,' Jerome said. 'They gave us a few tips, that was all.'

'Their orders are to preserve the helicopter at all costs. It's our last one. And we've only managed to keep it going because good old Harry patches it up again and again. If it were shot down there'd be damn little we could do for anybody. But it was wrong of them to break the news to you like that. The shock can be pretty devastating. We've had a few tragic cases of new arrivals who, when told, immediately reacted by turning on the transmitter and revealing their position to the enemy. They were finished off in minutes – either an atomic missile, a marsh missile with a nuclear warhead or a MIG sent over from Africa.'

'But who are our enemies?' Steve asked. 'Arabs or Soviets?'

'A motley collection. Mainly mercenaries – French, Italian, German; a few so-called military advisers from the Eastern bloc. Originally they were all in the service of the sheikhs, but they soon began fighting their own battles – and also trading in slaves. We call them trader mercenaries. There are some nasty types among them, men who see no value in human life, but as far as we're concerned, they're still the lesser of two evils. Some of them have cooperated with us in order to buy themselves a passage to Atlantis. The fanatics are worse, particularly the Palestinians. They arrive here as kamikaze pilots. It's like this: the Soviets sell their old MIG 25s to the sheikhs; they train up pilots and send them into the past by means of their chronotrones – against an adequate payment in crude oil, of course. Those pilots are suspended for fifty hours all alone under the *Kiev* or some other chronotrone disguised as a helicopter carrier; they get into a panic and start feeling murderous. By the time they're dropped, with fuel for four to five flying hours plus rockets, they're practically screaming for blood. They tear madly all over the basin and shoot at everything that moves – even their own fellow-countrymen – until someone finally persuades them to land over on the African plateau. Either that, or they run out of fuel and crash, or else they deliberately dive on what they presume to be a pipeline. There are still a good half-dozen planes over there in their hangars, but thanks to our anti-aircraft guns they get fewer and fewer and they fly less and less often. They also seem to have supply problems. Like us, they've discovered that things don't always turn out the way you plan.'

'But how was it possible to be defeated like this?'

'Defeated? We have been defeated, you're right; but not in the way you mean,' the commandant said. 'Major Bannister, I've had a lot of time to think about it. You've just arrived fresh from the future – you think in quite different categories. I've been here too long; I've seen too much. I'd put it like this: the belief in the dollar and in the infinite realisation of possibilities is as much of a chimera as the hollow world concept. Speculating about the future on the basis of yesterday's interest rate is like drawing conclusions about the universe from the holes in the toes of somebody's shoes. It's folly to believe that reality has to adapt to *your* ideas. Either you go to pieces, or reality does – or both.'

A woman in her mid-forties in a simple, gaily embroidered dress entered, carrying a wooden tray and three glasses with narrow, prettily carved wooden spoons and a glass jug filled with a yellowy liquid. She set the glasses in front of Steve, Jerome and the commandant, and placed the glass jug in the centre.

'This is Nina,' Harness said. 'She stays here and looks after us.'

The woman nodded at Steve and Jerome in a friendly way and left the room without saying a word. Harness poured the drink.

'What is it?' Steve asked curiously, and pointed to his glass.

'Molasses with lemon juice and water,' the commandant said. 'We try to manage on native products.' He smiled. 'Have I answered your most urgent questions now?'

'Yes,' Steve said, sipping his glass. The drink tasted sweet and sour and very refreshing. 'But what did you mean when you said reality could go to pieces?'

The commandant hesitated, rubbing his stump on his chin. 'Undoubtedly, there was gross negligence. Nobody should have been sent into the past without first making sure that they could be brought back again. But it was done in good faith. It wouldn't make sense otherwise. There would have been no point in it all, unless the oil and the people working on the project could have been brought into the future. All objections were answered with the argument that at some time in the future *that* problem would be solved, just like all the others. It was a blank cheque for the future – except that at some stage the cheque must have bounced. The technicians here have an explanation, of course. They maintain that the procedure involved in returning to the future must also entail some kind of scatter, and that the energy used for the retrieval can't be concentrated on a specific point in time. Instead it gets diffused over a wide period of time and discharges itself in storms which constantly rage over the retrieval zone. The material in the retrieval zone itself doesn't move. Now the experts say that this problem *is* soluble in principle – I've no idea why. But the fact that it *hasn't* been solved can only mean one thing: that the US simply didn't have enough time to solve the problem.'

'And what does that mean?' Jerome asked irritably.

'Now that's just the point. That's what I mean when I talk about reality going to pieces. Back in the future they constantly change history by action and counteraction without even noticing it. But here in the past, we discovered that we come from quite different futures.'

'The Treaty of Miami,' Steve said, remembering Murchinson's parting words.

'That's Murchinson's future,' the commandant nodded. 'You see, in his version, the United States never acquired Florida from the Spaniards; Fidel Castro sold it to the Emperor of Mexico in July 1969 under the Treaty of Miami – or rather, he sold it to PEMEX, the biggest oil empire between the Mississippi and the Rio de la Plata. Maximilian the Fifth was only a figurehead. It's fascinating to talk to Murchinson about it. In the same way, there's a Jerome Bannister future which is identical to the Steve Stanley future; but there's quite a different Howard Harness future as I know it and *experienced* it.'

'And what's that?' Jerome asked suspiciously.

'In your future the state of Israel probably controlled the area between the Nile and the Euphrates?'

'That's exaggerated,' Steve said. 'They controlled the area

between Mitla Pass and the Golan Heights.'

'Well, before I came here from the year 1989 I'd never even heard of a state of Israel. I heard about it for the first time from people like you, who had been dropped early. When I was at school I remember reading about the sensational and mysterious Zionist murders around the turn of the century – the murder of Leo Pinker in 1882 in Odessa, of Theodor Herzl in 1896 in Paris and Baron von Hirsch-Gereuth in 1897. Then there was the fire started during the Zionist congress in Basel on the same date; the terrible Palestinian massacre during the Second World War by Arab terrorists, who were fighting on the German side in Africa and in the Middle East. In my version the Holy Treaty of Medina established one of the most powerful states in the world: the United Pan-Arab Republic.'

'That's crazy,' Jerome said, feeling his chest tighten and his throat suddenly go dry.

'No, it's a historical reality. One of many. I was even more astonished when a contingent of highly equipped élite troops arrived here from the year 1992. They maintained that the state of Israel was in possession of the Sixth Fleet, as well as being the main protector of the southern section of NATO. That was twenty years ago. After a fierce battle with the Arabs, the Israelis finally put their threats into action and dynamited the Straits of Gibraltar.'

'So it's true,' Steve said.

'Yes, they made a big hole which is growing slowly. They also created one of the most impressive natural spectacles I've ever seen: a waterfall four hundred metres high. It carries a hundred times more water than the Niagara Falls, but in spite of that, the level of the sea rises barely a metre a year. It could be a thousand years before the Mediterranean fills up. I don't suppose we'll get our feet wet.'

'Will the fortress be abandoned?' Jeome asked.

'Not for the time being. But there can't be all that many groups still to come. At most one or two of the very first groups, from the 1986 units. They had the biggest scatter. The later drops – the last ones were in autumn 1996 – arrived almost exactly in the middle of the target time-period. By that time accuracy had improved.'

Steve suddenly remembered Moses and his group. Were they still coming?

'In autumn 1996 the supply drops stopped, too. We never found a container that was sent down later than that.'

'I suppose the project was declared a failure and called off,' Jerome said and finished his drink.

He still won't accept it, thought Steve. The reason they never noticed that it was a failure was because there was no feedback. Only *we* could tell them. Only we know the truth: that there are now not one, but several futures, all variations on each other. But why did nobody ever think of that, predict that? They broke reality into pieces. Now the futures are flying away from each other like galaxies. Even if it was possible to return to the future, how would they ever know which of those galaxies was their home? Maybe this was why the chronotrone functioned only in one direction – a difficulty the experts had overlooked.

'Of course, it's quite possible,' the commandant said, looking gravely at Jerome, 'that after the autumn of 1998 the United States of America ceased to exist.'

'That's mere speculation,' Steve interrupted angrily. Suddenly very thirsty, he gulped down the contents of his glass.

'I agree,' the commandant continued as he refilled the glasses. 'But it's overwhelmingly likely, even so. The US took a gamble on the future and lost. We approached the matter with too much self-confidence; that made us careless. Now we're paying the price.'

Jerome stared ahead in silence, his eyes wide open with horror. Steve followed his gaze. On the wall was a rather yellow, fly-spotted PEMEX calendar for 1992, showing a map of North America. The area of the United States stretched from Maine in the north to Georgia, Alabama and Mississippi in the south. The other side of the river was a giant area in flaking gold reaching to the Pacific and far into the south: the Empire of Mexico. In the upper left-hand corner was printed the pompous coat of arms of the Hapsburgs, to the right the even more pompous coat of arms of the oil company.

Steve found himself grasping the roughly carpentered wooden armrests of his chair as if he were sitting in the ejector seat of a plane, due to be catapulted out any second. Breathing out carefully, he let his shoulders slump.

'Let's return to our common present,' the commandant said. 'Today is the twenty-sixth of July. Our amateur astronomers have calculated the date. It is now . . . ,' he looked at his wristwatch, 'Sixteen hundred hours and twelve minutes. Would you please set your watches by mine? This is necessary in order to maintain order; we couldn't survive without that, nor would we want to.' Jerome and Steve obediently set their wristwatch, 'sixteen hundred hours and twelve minutes. night at two minutes to midnight. Our day is about two minutes shorter than in the usual chronology. The earth is still turning a little faster. Tidal friction, you understand.'

From somewhere came the distant *put-putting* of a diesel engine, its metallic heartbeat seeming to set the rhythm for the afternoon. Now and then there was a hoarse crackle from the radio.

'Since we can't be called a military organisation any longer, I don't want to give you orders. We're about thirty people here, plus about fifty natives commanded by their two chiefs. Goodluck you've already met, Blizzard you'll meet soon. Some of our men like Murchinson and Ruiz ought to be relieved from their guard duties as a matter of priority. They've both been on the listening post for more than six years, which means being constantly on the alert, even if it's months before the next group arrives. When a materialisation explosion goes off, they have to establish contact with the new arrivals instantly, warn them, and get them out of the landing area before the Arabs get them. They're both suffering from radiation sickness because they have been to the hot spots too often. Unfortunately we can give them only limited protection.

'You have both signed up for five years. In view of the changed circumstances, you are of course relieved of this obligation. But I'd like to ask you to support us in our efforts to get new arrivals out of the danger zone. Things don't always turn out as well as they did in your case – I have to emphasise that. Often men arrive in desperate need of medical help, of which we are already desperately short. Sometimes we reach them too late and risk our lives in vain. Think it over, anyway. Alternatively, each year before the autumn storms start, we send a ship over to the Bermudas. You're free to make use of it and to help build Atlantis. Life there is certainly easier and much more pleasant than here.'

'I'll stay,' Jerome said.

'You don't have to decide immediately,' Harness replied.

'There's nothing to decide,' Steve said.

'I'm afraid I have to requisition your jeep, fuel supply, weapons, and ammunition. The foodstuffs are yours to dispose of as you please. We always have a kind of a ... ah ... welcoming party when somebody arrives safe and sound. We even open a few tins of food to remind us of the future, so to speak. Not that we eat badly here, on the contrary; but it's become a custom.

'Your clothes and personal belongings you're allowed to keep, of course. Your boots are worth their weight in gold. Don't let anyone persuade you to part with them. Get yourself some more comfortable clothes, something better suited to the climate. Most people wear shorts like me, or a turban. There are a few traders who sell cloth from Atlantis. It's of quite remarkable quality already.

'We have no money. We barter. This method of trading forces people to rely on their manual skills and encourages them to develop them, to use their brains and think up useful objects You're also allowed to trade with the mercenaries and buy Navy goods pinched by them from our supply containers, but it's forbidden on pain of death to sell them arms and ammunition. The best thing would be if you –'

'Hey,' shouted a voice from the door. 'Don't believe a word he says. Howard sells borrowed futures – and he's in love with the sound of his own voice.'

Steve turned round, startled. On the threshold stood a small man, about seventy years old. He was completely bald and his wrinkled face was deeply tanned and dappled with brown age spots. He opened his toothless mouth wide and gave a senile laugh that revealed his pale-pink gums. 'I couldn't believe it when Ruiz told me who'd arrived,' he cackled with enthusiasm and came running up to them. 'Jerome!' he shouted and embraced him. Tears came to his light blue eyes and rolled down his cheeks. Jerome stood bolt upright and looked embarrassed. 'Don't you remember your old friend Harald Olson?'

'Hal?!'

*Merciful God!* Steve thought and stood like a bull who has just been hit by the slaughterer's axe. Only four days ago the two of them had been sitting together and Harald had been barely thirty. Steve had not yet overcome his shock when he felt the haggard old man's arms around him and the touch of the lean, wet cheek on his, and heard the whiny voice say: 'I never thought I'd live to see it. How I waited for you! My God, how I waited for you all these years!' Suddenly Steven understood what had so far escaped him. Now he knew what *time* meant.

'We kept looking for you. We started out in all weathers, no matter how many of the oil guys were around the landing area. We thought you would have arrived much earlier – after all, you started out before us. You sure took your time! We were among the first people to arrive here – apart from the sheikhs, of course, but they weren't so bad in those days. Every now and then a few camel riders, every now and then a MIG, nothing very exciting. They didn't throw atomic shells then; want to keep us alive to face some kind of tribunal in the future. Of course, in the end they understood that they had been betrayed too. Then they let their anger out on us and things hotted up. Those were the bad times, until Salomon had trained the Chaps and we felt a little safer.'

They had shaved and showered and changed, and were now sitting outside underneath the dense foliage of a chestnut tree on the edge of a section of roofing. The sun had set and the smell of a wood fire was drifting down into the valley. All the others had eaten canned food, while Jerome and Steve had enjoyed a hot meal in the company of the commandant, about ten other men from the fortress, and half a dozen of Goodluck's warriors. The 'Chaps', as they called the sand-coloured ape-men, were very keen on canned food and pâté. 'They have a special preference for the livers of the enemies they kill,' Harness explained. Steve almost choked on a piece of goat's meat he was about to swallow. 'Don't be astonished. They're all cannibals. We've tried everything to make them stop, but without success. The only thing we managed to make them understand is the fact that it's more lucrative to let an enemy keep his life and then to sell him.'

'So you support the slave trade?' Jerome asked, aghast.

'You can call it what you want,' the commandant said. 'But it's the only way we have of exchanging prisoners. Our enemies are against any direct contact.'

'You mustn't think that they drag their enemies' corpses in here to have them cooked in the canteen,' Old Harald said with a giggle. 'They settle the matter between them. Just stay away for a few days. And somewhere a skull tree will go up, a new head on the banks of one of their holy rivers. I guess you're right, Jerome, the customs are a little primitive round here.'

After the meal they sat in the open air and Hal and another old man, who had a smashed foot and walked with the help of a crutch, brought a jug full of some mysterious brew that tasted vaguely of fermented honey and herbs. 'Mead,' Harald told them, 'the most delicious drink we produce here.' Jerome threw him a sad look and thought with longing of the can of beer he had poured down his throat only four days ago. Gradually, however, the two of them took to the mildly intoxicating brew.

It was almost dark now and old Trucy, or Elmer with the smashed leg, as he was called, stuck a thick candle of beeswax on the top of the roughly-made table. 'It's safe here,' he said, noticing Steve's questioning look. 'As safe as Abraham's bosom.'

'And what happened to the others?' Jerome asked. 'To Paul and Salomon? And where's Moses?'

'Where do you want me to start?' Harald asked. 'There's so much to tell. It's more than forty years now. Moses is up north, roughly where Switzerland will be. He breeds camels. He used to come down every year to sell animals and skins, but now he sends his son. He must be over eighty now. He took a woman when he was still a hunter and she went with him. He trained a few Boisei to work for him. He always got on well with them; got to know them on his expeditions to the Gorge of the Rhône and the Alpes Maritimes where they hide out.'

'Boisei?'

'Yes. They're the big brothers of the Chaps, the Anthropus Africanus Boisei. They're shaggy creatures with red or black fur, up to two and a half metres high. They look wild with their flat, square heads, but they're as gentle as lambs really – wouldn't harm a fly. They're vegetarians, live off bananas and berries and stuff like that. The Chaps will soon push them out, and one day they'll wipe them out completely; they can't stand them. The mere smell of a Boisei makes a Chap see red, even though they're completely harmless. They're a little slow on the uptake, but I've always liked them very much.'

'And what about Paul Loorey?'

'He went to Atlantis a few years ago. He's still quite active for his age. Wanted to take a good look at the place before deciding whether or not to retire for good, but it seems he liked it over there. For a long time the people on the Bermudas were a wet, miserable lot; spent all their time staring at the test matter in the retrieval zone and writing claims for damages against the Navy. But about fifteen years ago a few clever guys over there took charge and tried to get people interested. They coined this slogan 'We shall build Atlantis', and since then they've been trying to become civilised, build a new town, train artisans; they've minted their own money and started to send us stuff; cloth, glass, paper, domestic utensils, tools, all sorts of things. That's what Paul wanted to inspect before he made his decision. We don't want to go there though, do we, Elmer? We're glad to have put civilisation behind us. We've lived here like a tribe of savages and we've got used to it, so what would be the point?'

The candle was flickering now, painting ghostly shadows on the faces of the two old men, who for a moment looked like deaths-heads. Steve felt chilly. The water of the brook had been icy and the cold had spread all over him within seconds. He gripped his wooden mug and emptied it. Elmer filled it up again.

'What about Salomon Singer?' Jerome asked.

'That's the saddest and also the funniest tale of all,' Harald said. 'He really succeeded in establishing good relations with the Chaps. In the beginning we all laughed at him, but he didn't let that bother him. Soon we stopped laughing.'

'He was the first who screwed one of their females,' Elmer giggled. 'From behind, of course, the way they do it. They start to bite when they get turned on. And the smell they produce, it can be quite overwhelming, don't you think, Hal?'

'Yes. You see, he thought it was necessary in order to be accepted into the clan. And he had observed the Chaps for months, knew every one of their gestures, wouldn't let them shake him off; he stuck to them like a burr. A few times he got so badly hurt that we thought we wouldn't manage to keep him alive. But as he said, people learn from their mistakes. He started out again. One day he got what he wanted. He was accepted into the clan by Goodluck's father, whom we called Lazarus.'

'If you can call him a father,' Elmer interrupted. 'They're used to taking turns with the females.'

Jerome was laughing his head off, while Steve tried in vain to imagine Singer copulating with a female ape – from purely scientific motives, no doubt.

'Somehow in the course of all that he discovered a real source of pleasure. Couldn't leave them alone. And the females were enthusiastic too; they were very keen on him; they sat all night on the threshold of the dormitory hut and made a grab for anybody's private parts when they went for a pee. The men had no objections, of course. Often we had real orgies. Oh boy!' Harald giggled.

'Eventually, of course, the male warriors objected, and there was friction. The females often showed up with bloody noses. But Salomon had the chief just where he wanted him. The old hairy devil soon knew that if he kept the right side of us, we could give him know-how, regular meals, equipment and weapons – which gave him a long lead over the other clans between the Atlas mountains and the swamps of the Rhône delta. If Salomon had asked him, he would have cut off his own son's head with his own hand.

'Lazarus had ordered the young males of the tribe to obey Salomon – so Salomon immediately put them into khaki shorts and made them undergo regular army drill. "*Erectus, erectus!*" he kept shouting, and he flogged them with his bamboo cane whenever they went down on all fours or looked sloppy on parade. "You want to represent the pithecanthropus erectus, and yet you go on all fours?" The guys soon learnt what it was all about. They're very bright – they imitate every movement you make, even the ones you'd prefer them not to learn. They're ideally suited for guard duties, too, because of their sharp senses. Every time a sheikh coughs over there in Africa, they have him on target straight away. But if you ask me, those oil guys only have themselves to blame. In the beginning they were stupid enough to hunt the Chaps and drive them from their traditional hunting grounds with incendiary bombs. But soon the tide turned, and the skull trees sprouted more and more brown and white heads.

'Our main task in the beginning was to make the Chaps understand that we and those people over there were on similar terms with each other as they were with the Boisei. They already knew the others were the baddies, so all we had to do was try hard to be the goodies.

'But one day there was a kind of palace revolution. Old Lazarus appeared one day, dying of an ugly shot wound in his guts and suddenly Goodluck was in command of the tribe. Somebody must have believed he could settle an old account with Salomon and get away with it. He was probably jealous of him because his favourite female was hanging around the dormitory hut too much and rejected his advances. Anyway, whoever it was, he bit Salomon's throat off in the confusion.

'Of course, that old ass-hole Six-Star-Walton wanted to know exactly what had happened.'

'What? Captain Walton's here too?' Steve asked in astonishment.

'Was here. Is no longer, thank God. We had a difficult time while he was the commandant,' Harald said. 'He decided to have a court martial at the very moment when relations with the natives were at their most tense. He found the Chap who killed Salomon, arrested him and put him up before a court martial. The Chap admitted his action honestly and innocently, because for him it had been a simple case of single combat from which he had emerged victorious. Walton confiscated all weapons, but of course nobody knew how many rifles the Chaps had accumulated by then. Then he tried to form a firing squad. When some of the guys from the fortress refused to participate, he started to abuse them for their lack of discipline and threatened to shoot everybody who disobeyed him. Eventually he found that he had no choice but to take his automatic and shoot the convicted 'murderer' with his own hand, though he had never understood a word he had said. The next night all the Chaps had disappeared from the fortress – and Six-Star-Walton, too. I don't believe anybody in Goodluck's tribe had a single bite from that filthy fellow's flesh, but he disappeared without a trace. Nobody was bothered. A few weeks later a new head appeared on a skull tree high up on the plateau. It looked like the head of our gallant Navy officer, but nobody could be completely sure because the vultures had had a go at it already. Whatever happened he can't have had an easy death.'

The night air had turned chilly. A Chap who had returned from guard duty had sat down with them and was listening silently and attentively. The flickering candle flame was reflected in his eyes. His broad nose flared as he sampled the scent of the new arrivals.

'It took us a lot of persuasion and presents before we patched it up with Goodluck.'

The pithecanthropus stuck his right index finger into the candle flame. The hair on its upper side began to glow and there was a smell of scorched fur. He pulled back his finger and sniffed at it, then stuck it in his mouth.

'Believe it or not, under Walton, about twenty kilometres of pipeline were built into the Tunisian shelf. Seventy lives were lost in three months, but he didn't care; he wanted to force the project through, even though he could see that most of the materials were unusable – either corroded by decades of lying around, or spoilt by the mercenaries. They called the pipeline "Walton's Folly". Later the sheikhs had it bombed off the face of the earth.'

The stars were twinkling through the foliage of the chestnut tree. The jug was empty.

'I mustn't get carried away,' Harald said, yawning. 'Tomorrow before daybreak I have to saddle the camels and load them up for market. If you want to come with me, you're welcome. I'll be heading back in twelve or fourteen days.'

'We promised the commandant we'd relieve Ruiz and Murchinson from their look-out post and help get the landing parties out.'

'Yeah? Well, don't imagine they drop out of the sky like ripe apples. It'll probably be weeks or months before the next lot arrives. Even at the best of times there were two or three a month at the most. There are only a few still to come.'

'I'd rather stay here,' Jerome said.

'I'll come with you, then.' Steve said.

'I'll wake you in time,' Harald said.

Elmer with the smashed leg collected the wooden mugs, put them into the jug, picked up his crutch and said goodnight. The pithecanthropus followed him, touching his forehead with the fingertips of his right hand before disappearing into the darkness.

'Where does he sleep?' Jerome asked.

'He has his place in the trees,' Harald said, and pointed vaguely upwards. 'That's what he's used to.'

Later that night, when Steve snuggled down under his blankets, the *USS Thomas Alva Edison* was already light years further away from him than Sirius. He thought of the smart officer who had waited for him in Miami at the airport, and was ashamed to find that the picture of his head stuck on a skull tree gave him a certain sense of satisfaction.

# CHAPTER SIX

# THE DARK BARGE

The morning light was dawning in the sky above. Under the roofs of the fortress it was still pitchdark, and Steve was stumbling sleepily along by Harald's side.

They heard soft voices and the snorting of animals; smelt the dung and scent sensed shadows in the twilight, the squeak of leather straps, comforting calls, the stamping of hooves on hard ground. There was the sound of water sloshing as water bags made of skin were loaded onto saddles and fastened in position; there was the metallic clanging of weapons. Somebody gave Steve an earthenware bowl of hot peppermint tea which brought him to life immediately with its strong smell. He breathed in deeply and drank down the liquid in small sips.

By the time they left the fortress, it was daylight and the sky was covered in thin salmon-coloured flecks. As they zigzagged up a mule-track to the plateau, they could see to the west the wooded hills of San Antioco and San Pietro – saints yet to burst forth from the womb of history – and behind them, in the misty depths of the Balearic basin, the slowly swelling ocean.

The twelve camels were loaded up with water bags, weapons and ammunition. Apart from Steve and Harald, there were six other men and four Chaps, two from Blizzard's clan and two from Goodluck's, all walking on foot through the cork-tree forest. The morning air was heavy with the scent of myrtle and oleander, which up here was a blaze of white, red, and pink. The camels swayed rhythmically in their strangely stiff-legged, graceful gait, picking their way effortlessly over the rocky ground veined with gnarled tree-roots.

Steve was hungry, but it was some time before they had their first rest. He ate a strip of dried meat, a handful of dried dates and drank the bitter, unsugared peppermint tea.

While the sun was directly overhead, they rested again, unsaddling the animals and putting them out to graze. Then they continued northwards past Monte Linas, setting up camp

for the night at its foot. Two evenings later they reached a river
which would one day bear the name of Tirso, and rested by its
banks, eating trout grilled over the fire on sticks.

On the sixth day they reached the promontory of Asinara and
started their descent into the basin. Down below they saw the
growing ocean, and by the evening they had reached its shore
and could now hear the waves lapping against it. As they
neared the water they found themselves in half-drowned forest
terrain, and in the crystal-clear depths the water-washed
promontory could be seen, its trees already covered by the
ghostly white of death, while sea birds screamed and squabbled
on the topmost branches, which still protruded out of the water.
They travelled northwards along the shore into the darkness of
the night, then camped in a bay and listened out to sea for
sounds of the barge which would ferry them across the water.

During the day some of the men had collected snails by the
wayside. Now they cooked them in boiling water, dug out the
tender, almost tasteless entrails with a thorn twig, and ate them,
accompanied by lamponi, a sweet wild onion which grew in
profusion on the rocky ground.

In the middle of the night Steve suddenly woke up, thinking
he had heard noises. Perhaps the water level was rising faster
and the camp would have to be moved to higher ground. But no
– everybody was asleep, apart from two Chaps who were sitting
by the burnt-out fire which still glowed between the heaped-up
stones. They looked back at him in silence.

The water was pitch black, the shallow surf petering out
among ferns and low bushes. There was a cool, salty breeze and
the smell of wide open spaces, and a crescent moon hung just
above the horizon, a narrow trembling band in the mist.

Later Steve dreamt that he was a many-coloured flaming
firebird, racing through the forests, setting fire to the pale tree
skeletons with a beat of his hot wings and showering a trail of
sparks behind him. Then he realised that his cry echoed
unheard, that the salty water quenched all his heat, and that the
fire had died all around.

Shortly before daybreak they heard shouts. Steve woke up
and looking out over the water, saw a light blink at irregular
intervals. Harald answered by briefly shading the light of a
lantern with his broad-brimmed leather hat, then exposing it
again. After a while he put the hat back on his head and turned

to Steve. 'I told them that the coast is clear.' Steve noticed that the other men had deployed themselves and were securing the landing place against an attack by land.

Gradually it grew lighter, but however hard Steve strained his eyes he was still unable to see a ship on the water, though he could hear the bleating of goats at a distance out to sea. Then, suddenly, he made out the silhouette of the boat against the morning mist. No wonder he had not seen it earlier; the hull, deck structures, mast and yard were painted dark blue, almost black, and even the sail had been dyed indigo. He had never seen a boat as sad-looking as this; it was a flat, clumsy sailing boat with little draught and a primitive Latin sail on its short mast. The sail was just being reefed and the yard brought in; slowly the boat glided towards the shore. Shouts were exchanged.

It was like the boat of Acheron, thought Steve. But why paint it in such disgusting colours?

'It may not be beautiful,' Harald said, as if he had heard his unvoiced question, 'but it's practical. Even at daylight it's invisible from the air. And it escapes the radar, too, because it's made entirely of wood. The sheikhs have managed to destroy two of them, but we've learnt our lesson.' He nodded grimly. 'You'd have thought Navy men would have known how to build a ship, wouldn't you? Not a bit of it. We had to get a couple of carpenters to hammer the thing together. We don't want it destroyed after all that effort. That's why it's camouflaged.'

Ropes were now thrown ashore and tied to trees, and planks pushed over the ship's side. The crew wore dark, burnous-type robes, with headscarves and turbans in black and dark blue. Passengers and freight were hidden under an indigo-coloured sunsail.

'It goes out regularly and arrives here about every ninety days – our communication link with the bases in Spain. They send us food and animals for slaughter, mainly. Otherwise we'd have to drive them overland through the swamps of the Rhône delta. It also carries passengers from Atlantis and takes people who want to go over there in autumn.'

Petrol barrels rumbled down the plank. About two dozen tame goats followed, dragged off singly and tied together again on land. Then came baskets with dried dates and bundles of dried fish. Finally the water bags they had filled from a stream the evening before were taken on board to fit the ship out for its long journey of a thousand kilometres to the mouth of the Almanzora. When the winds were against them the barge could take up to thirty-five days to cover the distance – a full month under a merciless sky, with a strong west wind and treacherous currents to contend with.

A few sinister figures disembarked, former mercenaries. They had been hunting in the Rhône valley and were carrying packs of Boisei skins on their shoulders. The Chaps instantly noticed the scent of the skins and became restless.

'I'd leave them down here if I were you,' Harald called out, pointing to the skins. 'If one of Moses' sons is in the market, you'll be in trouble. And he's the only one who'll sell you decent animals. Be sensible . . .'

The three huntsmen exchanged glances, then they threw their packs of skins on the ground.

'Why can't you sell us animals?' one of them asked.

'What do you want with those things?' Harald asked, pointing contemptuously at the shaggy red skins.

'The sheikhs pay a high price for them.'

'And how do you intend to pay for camels?'

'We have tiger skins and teeth, too. Every year you get more for them in Atlantis.'

'That might be an attractive proposition,' Harald grumbled. Steve had realised by now that not much could be expected from the Bermudas. The link across the Atlantic alone cost valuable fuel, and although the supplies sent into the past were vast, they were not inexhaustible. In the Western Basin diesel oil had already become a rarity because most of the containers had been captured and squandered by the mercenaries, or else dropped to the bottom of the sea. The vehicles were used only in emergencies, when it was a question of saving lives or defending the fortress. When they got fuel from Atlantis they had to pay for it like any other goods. The young colony could not afford to give anything away.

'Watch out,' Steve heard someone call. He turned round and saw Blizzard, who had come from the north on the barge. He could hardly be called a Chap. He was an unusually large example of his race and his fur was silky, almost white. His imposing appearance and his measured movements gave him an aristocratic air. He radiated dignity. If Goodluck was a proud warrior, a chief who had proved himself in battle, then Blizzard was a prince. His pale grey eyes looked shrewd and unyielding, and he dominated with them silently and imperiously. He also dominated the humans, who found themselves obeying him unconsciously. In fact, as far as Steve could gather, nobody in the fortress would have been surprised if he was found one day behind Harness' desk, calmly supervising operations. His females – there were five or six always in attendance – pandered to his every physical and emotional whim, vying with each other as to who would be allowed to groom his beautiful fur, to feed him with delicacies or gratify his sexual needs.

He disembarked like a pasha with his entourage and greeted the assembled crowd with a gracious bow of his head.

Unintentionally Steve bent his head too.

The 'market' was half a day's journey away to the east of the landing stage, on a mountain top which afforded a magnificent view over the plain. Here, on 'neutral' ground, were gathered people from the fortress, mercenary soldiers, huntsmen, and former members of landing parties who had quitted service in the fortress and tried like Moses to build up an existence of their own somewhere in the wilderness of southern Europe. Here they bartered their products: skins, leather goods, consumer goods from Atlantis, materials looted from Navy containers and animals from the wilderness which they had tried to tame or breed. The goods on offer were miserable and touching at the same time, and reminded Steve of jumble sales where children sell home-made objects for a charitable cause – with the difference that the cause here was survival.

Steve was astonished at the variety of skins and hides offered by the huntsmen.

'Who needs all that fur?' he asked Harald.

'We trade it in for all the things we need from over there.'

'But isn't the weather in the Bermudas warm all year round?'

'That doesn't matter. It's a question of prestige and fashion. We help it on occasionally by letting our tradesmen dress up in fur coats like Russian potentates. They keep the prices up literally by the sweat of their brows.'

Steve was suddenly struck by a young man who looked just like the Moses he had known just ten days ago.

'That's Ruben, one of Moses' sons. His second. He brought the stallions down to be sold. Moses is too old to attempt the long ride from the Ticino. And the creature over there with the animals is a fully grown Boisei.'

Now for the first time in his life, Steve set eyes on one of the shy, harmless ape-men about whom he had heard so much. He was male and well over two metres high, broad-shouldered like an orang-utan with receding forehead, rusty-red shaggy fur, a parting on his head and large, dark, anxious-looking eyes. He had come along as driver with young Ruben Calahan, and was squatting by the tethered young camel, peacefully eating a handful of wild onions. Fascinated, Steve watched him peel them with careful, almost tender movements of his giant paws before putting them into his mouth.

At that moment a warrior from Blizzard's entourage discovered him. The Chap bared his teeth, dropped down on all fours and crept closer noiselessly, his hunting instinct aroused. By the time the Boisei noticed him, it was too late. Realising that he was trapped, he gave a howl and tried in vain to escape between the camel's legs, but the Chap grabbed him by his ears with both hands, pulled his head down with brutal force and treated him to a number of rapid kicks into the ribs with his claw-studded hind legs. Blood began to flow. The camels shied and moved about excitedly, while the Boisei screeched in mortal terror and urinated in a thin, golden-brown stream.

Steve was rigid with fright and did not know what to do. The reason for this wild fight escaped him, since the shaggy giant could hardly be accused of provoking the Chap.

But now Ruben was on the scene and was pulling the Chap back by his ears in an effort to free the Boisei's neck from the creature's teeth. In the course of this, the Chap was drenched by the Boisei's pee and gave a howl as if he had been wounded. Ruben let go of him and stepped back a little, leaving the Chap free to wipe his chest violently as if to erase the pee stains from his sand-coloured fur. Now he was beside himself with fury. Crouching down, he took a two-metre-high leap into the air and would have caught Ruben in the abdomen with his razor-sharp claws if Ruben had not thown himself forward and dealt him a murderous blow on the nose with his fist. The Chap rolled back in a somersault and fell backwards onto the ground, his ribs cracking. The blow would have felled a bull, yet the Chap shot up from the dust as nimbly as a cat, landing in a crouching position, with blood running from his mouth and nose. Ruben took up the stance of a boxer. The Chap expected another fist blow and tried to trick Ruben. This time he jumped higher to get the claws of his hind leg round the neck of his opponent, but Ruben made an unexpected step back and when the tensed load of muscles came flying at him with raised arms and legs spread out, he gave him a fierce kick in the testicles. The Chap dropped to the ground, doubled up in pain and lost consciousness. But within an astonishingly short time, he came round and before Ruben had time to catch his breath he was back on his feet again.

Ruben, who had been grazed on his upper arm by one of the Chap's claws, was bleeding heavily and had turned his back on him in order to calm down the frightened Boisei and the camels. Steve gave a cry of warning, but Ruben seemed not to hear him in the confusion. Steve was about to throw himself on the vicious beast from behind to prevent a treacherous attack, when a strange thing happened. Instead of launching himself on his opponent, the Chap went up to Ruben calmly and said: 'Is that yours?' pointing at the Boisei, who was rolling his eyes in fear.

When Ruben nodded, he said, 'Sorry', tapping a finger on to the blood-soaked shirt above Ruben's shoulder wound, licked him and trotted off as if nothing had happened.

'Why are the two races at each others' throats like that?' Steve later asked young Calahan, when they were sitting in the shade of the straw roof, grilling some goat meat over a small fire.

Ruben, whose dense mop of hair made him look as if he had a bird's nest on his head, shrugged his freshly bandaged shoulder.

'They have a mysterious relationship. Normally the Boisei can make out a Chap by his scent a mile away. They literally wet themselves with fear. They can't be calmed down. And when you lock them in for their own protection, they go berserk with panic. The Chaps get a kick out of seeing their fear; they can usually trick them, because they're much more cunning – then they torture the poor devils to death and eat them, as is their custom with their enemies. But I've also seen them lay out a Boisei solemnly, scattering flowers over his body and piling stones on top, as they do with their most popular tribal leaders.

In the mountains near us you can see some of these burial places. Somehow they seem to venerate them in spite of their hatred; they feel that they're more closely related to them than to any other living creature, that they're their ancestors. But at the same time they despise them for their shortcomings, their lack of survival instincts. That's what seems to provoke them the most. And the charming idiots haven't the slightest chance against the Chaps, even though they're superior to them in physical strength. They stumble straight into every trap the Chaps set for them. One day they'll be wiped out altogether. We've tried everything in our power to prop them up and bolster their self-esteem, but the moment they come face to face with a Chap, they crumple up. That seems to be their fate. Perhaps it's because of their food – it's almost certainly got something to do with it. They don't eat meat; they have an almost holy fear of it.'

'The species Man couldn't have developed from them,' Steve said. 'We must have followed on from the killer ape – cold-blooded, unpredictable and merciless.'

'They haven't been here for very long yet,' Ruben said. 'We've got the future ahead of us. Everything still depends on *us*.'

Steve shook his head wearily. We're no more than a mouthful of water spat out into the sea, he thought; it's no use. But he did not say this aloud.

On the ride back, the weather changed. The mountain tops became shrouded in cloud and the air began to turn chilly. Soon it started to rain, thin, incessant rain which fell noiselessly and soaked everything through and through.

The camp fires smoked, but no longer warmed them. The nights were clammy, the days misty. The forest, airy and streaked with light on the journey out, was now gloomy and foggy. The tree tops seemed to brush the low-hanging clouds, and droplets of moisture hung from every branch. The shining fur of the animals turned dull and dishevelled and their flanks looked haggard. The hoof-beats thudded on the wet moss and fallen pine-needles. The mood of dejection affected man and beast.

Mountain streams which a few days ago had been little more than a trickle were now rushing down into the valley, plunging down steep, winding gorges towards the Western Basin, tearing along stones and uprooting trees as they went. Time after time the animals lost their foothold while crossing the gushing waters or were pushed under a fallen tree trunk and threatened with drowning. The men were forced to wade into the water up to their hips, secure them with ropes and haul them ashore.

The Chaps were least affected. They bounded lightly over the fords, using fallen trees as stepping stones, or swung from branch to branch, carrying their rifles and equipment slung across their chests. The wet fur on their faces made their expressions sad, almost as if they had been weeping, but their eyes twinkled with merriment and occasionally with a glint of mockery, as they watched the clumsy efforts of their descendants.

The men themselves were dog-tired but unable to sleep at night. Harald was coughing his heart out after catching cold in an icy mountain stream. Once they crossed a fresh camel track, and a few times they saw the tracks of wild goats, but they met nobody. The country was empty and wide open. It belonged to the trees and the birds.

They reached the fortress late one afternoon. Under the planted pipeline roofs it was darker than ever. Somebody had thoughtfully lit a fire for them and put out dry clothes. The returning travellers were grateful; they were chilled to the bone and had been wearing the same wet clothes for days.

Steve dried his hair and face with a warm towel which somebody had offered him and drank a bowl of hot aromatic tea made of fresh peppermint. Then he helped with the unloading and rubbing down of the animals, who were so tired they could hardly stand. He took an armful of dry oakleaves which smelt of the sunny warmth of a mild autumn day and rubbed a young male camel's back with them, while the beast stood with trembling flanks, sniffing listlessly at the hay.

The river was roaring down into the valley, but further down the engine of a steam roller could be heard.

The major task was to unload the packs and carry them down to the store. Steve heaved one of the slippery leather sacks of dry meat onto his shoulders, digging his fingers into the crude seams in order to stop the load from slipping, and staggered down the footpath to the huts in the middle area of the fortress.

The warm tea and the physical effort made him feel light-headed, almost dizzy. All around, men were hard at work with excavators and shovels, building banks of earth to stop the stream from overflowing and flooding the huts. The roar of the torrent was so loud that they had to communicate by shouting.

'We've never had rains like this since we arrived here,' the commandant said. 'The weather seems to change more rapidly now.' He gestured to where a mechanical digger was manoeuvring in the riverbed, its tracks submerged in the fast-flowing waters, lifting a shovelful of gravel into the air and dumping it on the embankment. Steve took a shovel to help the men distribute the heaped-up gravel and form it into a low dam. At least the effort would get his circulation going again, he thought.

'How was it?' Jerome shouted across to him, without stopping in his work.

'Interesting', Steve shouted back. 'I met one of Moses' sons in the market. Nice guy. Moses is supposed to have quite a number of sons like him and a hacienda in the Ticino.'

'Moses – in the Ticino?' Jerome laughed out loud. 'Unbelievable.'

'He owns practically the whole of Switzerland and the rest of Europe, too. North of the Alps there are only a few tribes of Boisei. Always on the run from the Chaps.'

Jerome nodded. 'So I've heard. Looks like it's still dog eat dog, even though there's room enough for everyone in this wilderness, God knows.'

Suddenly Jerome threw down his shovel and ran off. Steve looked up and saw that two men who had been with them on the trip north were dragging Harald along. He had collapsed under the weight of one of the sacks and was unconscious. Rushing up, Jerome and Steve helped carry him to the sick bay behind the canteen.

'Take his clothes off,' Nina said, putting fresh sheets on one of the four beds. Then she brought hot water from the kitchen and poured it into a camping bath made of rubberised nylon material. They lowered Harald gently into it and he came round almost immediately.

'Hey, what's up?' he croaked, still a little dazed and puzzled to find Nina soaping his back and head. 'Have you no respect for an old man?' He shut his eyes as the soapy water trickled down his face. 'You're the last person I would have suspected, Nina. I always thought you were a decent type.' His bright red face appeared over the edge of the tub, and he gazed at the people who surrounded him. To Steve, he looked like a baptist who had almost drowned in the Jordan while officiating at his sacred duty. 'Hey – I'm not ill,' he growled. 'Leave me alone. I've got work to do.'

'Take it easy, Hal and get some rest,' Jerome soothed. 'You're feverish.'

Harald looked at him unhappily. 'Do you think so?'

'We'll see in a minute,' Nina said. 'I'll look after you. In a few days you'll be back to normal again.'

He looked around suspiciously and they all nodded encouragement. He was dried and put to bed, and seemed to accept his fate. They all came and visited him, even the commandant, Blizzard, and Goodluck, but soon he was fast asleep, totally exhausted.

After the meal that evening they sat huddled together around the fire, but even this did not dispel the clammy, all-pervasive cold. They spoke in short questions and answers, discussing who was going to Atlantis next spring; what they had heard in the market; how many Arab mercenaries might have joined the traders and were now waging war on their own; and how many of them might be prepared to make peace and find some common solution.

Even the Chaps looked out of sorts, their faces propped up on their dark, hairy fists. They, too, seemed to feel that somehow time was coming to an end. The tallow candles and oil lamps on the tables painted bizarre shadows on the crumbling, peeling walls of the hut.

One by one the men murmured good night and disappeared into the darkness, creeping off to their clammy bedding and their meagre dreams.

Harald was poorly. Steve guessed that he had got pneumonia. Jerome went to the commandant to ask for antibiotics, but Harness shook his head sadly.

'We haven't found medical supplies in the basin for eight years. Nor has anybody else, or else we'd have had a few items re-surface in the market. I guess the Navy must think we're in the best of health. Francis was always optimistic, and transporting supplies costs money. I'm sorry, Major. We can't help him. We have to hope that he pulls through on his own.'

They took turns at keeping Harald company, in between spells in the listening post, patrolling the basin, or working in the fortress. Steve sat up all night on one of the hospital beds listening patiently to the old man's confused stories and his rattling breath, wiping the sweat from his freckled forehead. At times it seemed to him as if Harald were not alseep at all, but listening, amused, to some conversation from the distant past which touched his fading consciousness like the ripples of waves lapping the shore.

Steve was struck by the disturbing thought that death itself might be some kind of ultimate forgetfulness; a mere extension of senile disorientation, in which the mind, no longer capable of groping its way back into the present, wanders about in the corridors of the past, listening to ghostly remembered conversations, while the body yields to the laws of matter and rots away in the catacombs of time.

Steve pushed aside his black thoughts. He had dozed off for a moment, and was now looking up.

Harald was awake and looking at him attentively.

'I didn't want to wake you, Steve,' he said. 'But since you're awake, I can ask you. Have you ever seen this sign? It's of a flag with a cross on it, and it's held by a lamb.'

Steve shook his head without understanding.

'Agnus Dei,' Harald said, raising his index finger emphatically and baring his toothless gum in a smile. 'The lamb of Christ, which saves us.'

Steve tried to overcome his sleepiness.

'I can remember how I felt when I saw the sign for the first time.' Harald chuckled, took a couple of rattling breaths and continued: 'I was a small boy then, in first or second grade. It was during the Easter vacations, and my father had taken me with him to Germany on a business trip. We were in Munich and it was an incredibly warm day in early spring with a blue sky such as I'd never seen in Denmark, not even in July. People were sitting out of doors, drinking beer from enormous glass mugs. Anyway, in a baker's shop I saw a whole flock of these lambs like the one I told you about – the Agnus Dei. Big ones, medium ones, small ones, all covered with icing, rows and rows of them, all very sheepish-looking and winding their legs around the flagstaff. And on the flagstaff was this flag bearing the Danish colours.

'I asked my father what these cakes were supposed to mean, and he looked very serious and said: "They're laughing at us, Harald. That's the Germans saying that we Danes are ruled by sheep. And perhaps they're right." He gave me a wink. I remembered later that I had seen the amusement in my father's eyes, but I didn't know what it meant. I never doubted his words. I was deeply angry, and for years I took a very poor view of the Germans.' Harald giggled and suddenly broke into another fit of coughing. His face was hot and tears came into his eyes from the strain.

He's hallucinating, thought Steve.

'And you know where I saw this sign again?' Harald asked, looking at Steve intently. '*Here!*'

'Here?' Steve asked, not knowing how far to play along with the old man's fantasies. Harald seemed to be wide awake and quite lucid, in spite of his age and failing memory. He had closed his eyes to form narrow slits and with his mischievous grin he reminded Steve of the aged Henry Miller being interviewed about his life in Clichy.

'Yes, here!' Harald said. 'I had gone by jeep far to the south east, towards the mountain ranges of Sicily, and I'd stopped on top of a mountain which gave a panoramic view over the Tyrrhenic basin. Suddenly I heard a materialisation explosion further towards the east and a few minutes later I saw what I would once have called a flying saucer. It was a beautiful cobalt blue, with a dangerous-looking gun on board that looked like a short-wave aerial and was mounted on the roof of the saucer. And on its nose I saw the sign. It was splendid – gold on cobalt blue, the little lamb with the flag. I drove the jeep out from its cover and straight up to the object. Steve, I couldn't believe my eyes! A guy as tall as a house came climbing out, wearing a cobalt-blue spacesuit and a helmet like an astronaut, with a gold-covered visor. I could barely make out the guy's face behind the mask, but on his sleeve there was that sign again. Looks like we've got another partner in this poker game, I thought. I got out and walked towards him, deliberately leaving my automatic in the jeep.

' "Hi," I said, but the guy didn't speak a word of English, let alone Danish. He spoke a language that reminded me vaguely of my Latin lessons at school, but it wasn't Latin or Italian – more like something in between the two. I couldn't figure the guy out, but I soon realised that the gun on the roof of his vehicle was automatically following every movement of his hand. Of course, I made sure I didn't give him a chance to point at me.

' "Laser?" I asked, all innocence.

'He pointed to a clump of trees, perhaps six or seven hundred metres away. The gun jerked up, spat fire. The moment it hit them, the trees literally jumped into the air, burst into flames and crashed down to earth.

'I nodded with admiration, but secretly I was shit-scared, Steve, I don't mind telling you. As he rambled on in his comic-book Latin, I prayed to God he wasn't on the side of the sheikhs. I needn't have worried. When I finally managed to dig out some of my long-forgotten Latin and try it out on him, I found out what it was all about. He was a member of the Pope's Mediterranean Fleet, whatever that might be; his mission was to prepare the way for the Lord.

'Well, the sheikhs located the crusader in no time. It was soon after the battle of Gibraltar, and our friends were particularly trigger-happy at the time. They started to shell us both, so I escaped as quickly as I could. What good would I have been to him? The battle continued for days. The man in cobalt blue put up quite a fight, though. He blasted away with his laser gun until the whole of Africa was in flames. The MIGs flared up like moths and fell from the sky like dust, but somehow in the end they must have got him, because the shooting stopped. Matter of fact, they attacked him with such ferocity that I was scared to leave my hiding place. I caught a lot of radiation – was sick to death for weeks. I was so luminous I could have read a book in the dark, if I'd felt like reading.

'Well, Steve, that's the story of the guy from the Papal Fleet. Somehow he impressed me. He stood all alone against their superior force, and he never flinched. Suddenly I felt that that sign wasn't quite as silly as I'd thought, if you know what I mean.'

'Yes, I do,' Steve said. 'Have any more of these crusaders been sighted?'

But Harald gave no answer. He had sunk back on his pillow,

fast asleep.

Later, Jerome came to release Steve. He had already sat up on listening duty with Ruiz half the night, but although he was exhausted, nothing Steve said could dissuade him from watching over Harald. Steve went over to the dormitory hut, crept into bed and fell asleep at once.

A short time later – to him it seemed only a few minutes – somebody grabbed his ankle and shook him.

'Harald's dead,' Jerome whispered.

'Oh, my God,' Steve said. For a moment he lay back, waiting for the shock to sink in; then he realised that Jerome was sobbing. 'Why don't you rest a little,' he said to him. 'I'll see to everything.'

He got up. He suddenly felt cold though it was warm in the hut. It was still dark outside.

'Damn it, I only nodded off for a minute,' Jerome said, 'and when I looked up I saw he'd stopped breathing. I left him alone in his last minutes.'

'Don't worry, Jerome. He wouldn't have noticed.'

Steve walked out into the night. In the sick bay he met Nina and Goodluck. Had he been brought here by the smell of death?

'He passed away,' Goodluck said in his throaty voice.

Harness looked in through the door. 'I've just been told . . .'

'Yes,' Nina said. 'We'd better wash him. He soiled himself.'

'Let me do it,' Steve said softly. He wrapped the dead man in the sheet and took him in his arms. He seemed to weigh no more than a child.

'Let Alfaro make a coffin for him,' Nina said to the commandant. 'It would be best if we laid him out here.'

Steve carried Harald's body over to the stream, lowered it gently into the shallow water and unwound the sheet. Harald's mouth was wide open as if he had been singing in a choir only he could hear. Steve tore off a strip of the material and bound up his jaw before the serene expression could freeze into a tortured scream; then he washed the corpse. The body seemed to change consistency in the icy water; under his hands the bluish skin suddenly felt like metal: smooth, rounded and rigid.

'Let's bury him up there in the sun.'

Steve looked up and saw Elmer standing over him. He hadn't heard him approach.

'Up there, where the Chaps bury their warriors – that's

where he liked it best. It's a much nicer place than that war cemetery of Walton's below the fortress.'

Steve gave no answer. He wrapped the corpse into the dripping wet sheet and carried it back to the sick bay. The rain had stopped now, and bright shafts of light broke through the gaps in the roof. Over the mountains to the east, the sun had risen.

A few days later they buried Harald on the mountain top above the fortress, where from time immemorial, great chiefs and warriors had been laid to rest under their skull trees, in the shade of the big oaks, the stately cinnamon trees and acacias. The sunlight danced among the rustling leaves, dappling the freshly dug soil and the faces of the mourners, as Harald's body was lowered deep into the ground.

The commandant read a few words; the rest remained silent. Blizzard stood bowed, propping himself up by his mighty fists, gazing into the sun.

The plain coffin was heaped high with flowers so that the soil which was thrown on it fell into the grave almost without making a sound.

The wind whispered in the foliage and somewhere quite nearby a cicada was singing, incessantly and with almost mechanical precision. The sun had almost reached its zenith.

CHAPTER SEVEN

# A LOST LOT

The listening post was a rocky peak to the west of the fortress commanding a wide view south and south-west. It consisted of a ledge overgrown by low undergrowth which made it invisible both from below and from the neighbouring mountain ranges. Behind it was a dry cave into which the men on guard were able to retreat when the weather was bad, or when an enemy plane appeared. There was also a transmitter and a set of batteries which could be charged up with solar cells, as well as telephone contact with the commandant in the fortress.

In the weeks that followed Harald's death, Steve spent a great deal of time on the post, with Charles Murchinson. He liked guard duty in the morning best, because of the spectacular views. The comet they had seen on the evening of their arrival had since wandered all over the sky during the day and had begun to move away from the sun towards the morning. Shortly before daybreak a great fountain of light shot up over the eastern mountains, as if the rising sun were spouting air like a whale; then, while the stars were fading, the brilliant head of the star appeared with its brightly flaming tail, before it, too, faded and the morning light filled the whole sky. Each day it rose a little earlier and burned a little less brightly, its tail getting shorter and shorter until gradually it disappeared into the wide, dark robes of the universe.

Months passed, yet still there was no sign of another landing party. Again and again materialisation explosions could be heard in the west, but each time they turned out to be caused by sections of pipe or excavators being dropped. Charles was able to identify shipments by their explosions and Steve soon learnt to do the same, but he always stared nervously through his binoculars at the mist over the landing area to make sure. Charles, however, did not even bother to look up from his reading. He was an avid reader, and Steve was happy to lend him the books he had brought along.

One thing they noticed was that there seemed to be many more explosions over Africa than over their own landing area.

'They're getting supplies again,' Murchinson grumbled. 'I wish there was a future in which the Navy had the sense to drop some atom bombs into their laps. That would save us a lot of trouble. Unfortunately, our Navy scientists don't care any more than your NASA.'

'What do you mean, "your" NASA?'

Murchinson laughed drily. 'In our time there was no NASA, let alone space travel; the United States was too poor a country for that kind of thing. But it was a courageous country. It was our soldiers who won the war against Germany and Japan when Hitler occupied the Hapsburg homelands and challenged the Panamanian colossus. The promises we got from the Emperor's emissaries! He *begged* us to enter the Panamerican alliance – said we could help him recover occupied France and Spain, and the Lenin Republics and Great Britain. Thanks to us, they smashed the Axis powers and drove the Japanese into the sea when they were outside Los Angeles and bombing Mexico City and Pueblo!

'And what happened after the war? All the promises were forgotten. The Emperor even refused to pay war pensions to the cripples who had risked their lives for PEMEX in Okinawa and the Algarve. Suddenly the unity of all oil-producing countries had become the battle-cry, and Maximilian took the side of the Shah and the sheikhs. The price of oil rocketed – and so did the unemployment figures. And it went on like that until Carter brought in his energy law and forced every American who wanted to buy a hundred watt bulb to produce proof that he needed it for commercial purposes.

'No wonder we all had such high hopes for Fleissiger's fabulous time machine! It was our only chance of bleeding the sheikhs, of getting a slice of the big cake and stopping ourselves being encircled by the Empire. That's why we put all the money we had into this crazy project. We wanted to get Florida and an outlet to the sea in the Gulf of Mexico. Of course, the United States would have liked to buy the peninsula from Castro. A hundred years ago they could still have had that stretch of swamp from the Spaniards for a song, but Castro wanted a little more for it – naturally; he wanted to industrialise his island – and Washington was unable to bid against PEMEX.

'Nobody had ever wanted our dollars, bur after the Treaty of Miami, the exchange rate fell disastrously. Wherever you went, if you produced dollars, people turned up their noses. Sorry Mister, all seats sold, all rooms taken. You couldn't even get your shoes blacked any more. But if you flashed pesos or dirhans under their noses, it was Open Sesame. All over the world they ran after you, kowtowing; you could buy all the tarts and gigolos you wanted.

'I know what I'm talking about, man. I went over there, to the other side of the Mississippi, to Texas, as a foreign labourer, like many people from the States. I was a cotton-picker and also tried my hand as a driller for PEMEX. They paid me piece-work wages: no oil, no pesos. We lived in filthy prefabs, and when a man got ill he was sacked, and that was that. And once a man had been sacked, nobody bothered about him any more – except for the Imperial police, of course. They emptied our pockets and threw us into the Mississippi.

'You know how they pronounced the word "Yankee" over there? As if they were spitting into your face. That's how it was.'

In my world it was the other way round, Steve thought. But the facts were exactly the same. He remained silent.

'Then this Admiral Francis came along, from some kind of experimental weapons institute run by the Navy in Boston. He reckoned it couldn't go on like this. Quite a few people agreed with him, including me. But in Fleissiger's outfit there was a Japanese by name of Nobodaddy's Coffee or something like that who helped develop the miracle weapon. His father had escaped from a Mexican prison and swum across the Mississippi like Tom Sawyer and Huckleberry Finn in Mark Twain's book. And this wonder weapon, the chronotrone, really worked – though only in one direction. But nobody could have known that then.

'This guy Francis said we had to call a halt. We couldn't go on kissing the sheikhs' boots for every barrel of oil and letting the Empire pump off Mississippi water to irrigate their lands. Francis planned to turn the tables, and snatch the oil from underneath the sheikhs' arses before they could even sit down on it. He reckoned we should pump it across the dried-out Mediterranean and all through Europe into the British Sea . . .'

'The *North* Sea,' Steve corrected him.

Charles looked at him blankly, then went on: 'For some years natural gas and oil had been found there, but it had all been mightily exaggerated. Sullom Voe had been turned into a giant oil port, and huge refineries were built on the Shetlands and Orkneys to receive, process and ship the richly flowing oil from the British Sea. Francis planned to turn every second oil rig between Ekofisk and the Scottish coast into a camouflaged time machine and use them to pump the stuff up from the past. In a few years he said we could forget PEMEX and its decadent figurehead of an Emperor. We'd never need to buy another barrel of oil from them again. Together with BP and the other Europeans who weren't allied to the Hapsburgs, we would open up undreamt-of resources.' Charles shrugged his shoulders. 'That's what Francis thought and I thought so too – until I learned my lesson. That's why I volunteered for this project – to help our country get out of its hopeless mess. But when I got here and saw the truth, I felt like howling, Steve. It was all so *amateurish*. I saw then that failure had been inevitable from the start.'

They were silent for a while. Steve liked the small agile man in spite of his irritability and quick temper. With all his intolerance he was loyal, and Steve felt he had made a friend of him. He made an attempt to distract him from the subject that had made him so heated.

'You said that in Mark Twain's book Huck Finn and Tom Sawyer swam across the Mississippi.'

'Yes, I did. They did.'

'I believe I know Mark Twain quite well. They never swam *across* the river. They swam out to this island . . .'

'Listen, Steve. I know Mark Twain *very* well. I've read all his books. I know his novels, his autobiography, his travel books; I've read his *A Gringo across the Empire* in which he mocks Maximilian the Second, and his *A Yankee at King Arthur's Court*, in which he ridicules the monarchist clique and the sycophantic clergy of the Hapsburg Empire . . .'

Steve stared at Charles, aghast. Suddenly he knew the terrible truth.

'Where was Mark Twain born?' he asked.

'But every school child knows that,' Charles said. 'In Thebes, Illinois.'

'Have you ever heard of the town of Hannibal?'

Charles thought for a moment, then he shook his head.

'Never. Perhaps the place is on the other side of the river.'

Steve nodded. 'I don't know *your* Mark Twain,' he said. 'But if you want to know *my* Mark Twain, I have an anthology of his most important works in my bag.'

That evening he gave him a well-thumbed copy of a pocket book edition of Mark Twain's works. Murchinson disappeared with it and for the whole of the next day he was not seen in the camp. The morning later he reappeared on the rock where Ricardo Ruiz and Steve were on duty. He returned the book without a word. He looked pale, completely exhausted and visibly disturbed.

He must feel as if he had suddenly looked into an abyss, thought Steve.

Murchinson stared silently into the Western Basin. There was a strong wind blowing, strong enough to bring tears to the eyes. Charles wiped them off and said in a hoarse voice: 'Incredible.' And a little later: 'I never knew so much had got lost.' Then he turned round abruptly and looked Steve in the eye with a mixture of curiosity and anxiety, and perhaps even a hint of fear.

'I *see* you, Steve,' he said. 'I see your tanned face, the small, dry wrinkles around your hazel eyes from too much laughing and too much looking into the sun. I see your lips, your greying temples, your small, slightly protruding ears. I know you. You're *real* and close to me. And yet you're further away from me than another galaxy – you're some kind of monster, just like your strange Mark Twain. I'd never have met you if I'd stayed in my world. In my world you'd probably never have been born. Where *were* you born, Steve?'

'In Los Angeles.'

'In Los Angeles,' Charles said, pronouncing the city's name in the hard, throaty way of the Spaniards. 'Not many Yankees were born in the Los Angeles I knew. Los Angeles is a town of monasteries and saints. Right up to the twenties, books and people were still being burnt there in the name of God. Los Angeles is the seat of the Inquisition, where cardinals in red robes sit in judgment over the living and the dead. Suppose you had been born in the Los Angeles of my world. What would you have been? A pilot of the Diablos de los Aereos, who drop napalm on the jungles of Zamboanga and Basilan? Perhaps you would have been among those who slay the infidel Moors, or bomb the bases of Brazilian Indians who obstruct the PEMEX drillers and read revolutionary Leninist literature from Castro's printing presses.' He turned round brusquely. 'I'm sorry, Steve! I didn't want to hurt you. I've been through a terrible experience.'

'But why are you so bitter?' Steve asked. 'Do you mourn for your world? It was worth just as little as mine.'

'I wish I'd grown up in your world. It sounds far better than the world Admiral Francis promised us. It maddens me to think that that self-important idiot gambled it all away and didn't even realise it.'

'That's in the nature of chronotronic fractions,' Steve said. 'He would only have realised it if he'd come here.'

'I'd have shot him,' Charles Murchinson assured him. 'I'd have sent him to hell.'

'He's probably long since got there under his own steam.'

'I've often asked myself,' Ruiz interjected, 'whether one future wipes out another, or whether they somehow co-exist.'

'Somehow they must do,' Steve said, 'at least in our memories. But I doubt whether they exist in reality. We don't know enough about it, though.'

'That would mean that the future which I remember will die with me,' Ruiz said.

Steve nodded.

'I ought to write it down, then.'

'Who for?' Charles asked.

'For the Goodlucks and Blizzards of the next five million years. For the descendants of the Atlantids.'

Charles laughed. 'Forget it, Ricardo. Our world wasn't as desirable as all that. They'll find a better one.'

'Our reports could help them do that.'

'You underestimate the length of time involved,' Steve said. 'Between today and the epoch called 'human culture' there are unimaginable wastes in which the dust of history will be disturbed again and again. Even the pyramids couldn't last that long. How could a few pieces of paper? And besides, we could only describe a distant future which we already find unreal. Teach them a few dirty tricks and show them how to survive. That's the best you can do for them in the long run.'

A few weeks later, when Steve was riding north to inspect the coast he saw his first materialisation. It was a bundle of about a dozen fifty-metre-long lengths of pipe. Just as the echo of the explosion rolled along the western mountain slopes, clusters of parachutes opened at each end of the shipment, and the whole creation floated downwards majestically and hit the surface of the sea as if in slow motion. Fountains of water shot up higher and higher, then fell back soundlessly. The parachutes wilted and spread out and while the pipes sank slowly into the water, colonies of pale grey jelly-fish gathered at both ends before following the pipes hesitantly into the depths.

Next spring, Steve and Charles were goat-hunting in the mountains to the east of the fortress. They were wearing boots and battledress to protect against snakes, and sleeveless jackets made of kid skin over torn, faded T-shirts. Each had on a broad-brimmed woven hat made of reeds to ward off the sun. They hunted with bow and arrow to save ammunition and avoid attracting uninvited guests.

Charles had hit a young kid, but not fatally. It was escaping into the mountains and they were pursuing it up stony slopes, through cactus thickets and dry thorny bushes, following the clearly visible trail of blood. Finally they discovered the wounded animal entangled in thick bramble; it had collapsed and was struggling in vain to get up, and as they approached it uttered a miserable, thin bleat. Charles jumped on the kid and cut its throat with his knife. Bright-red blood poured from the wound and ran down his right arm in a thick stream, and as he held on to the dying animal's neck he felt it gradually go limp. He looked up and sunlight fell on his narrow sun-tanned face under the broad brim of his hat. There were bloodstains on his cheeks and forehead. He winked at Steve, smiling happily, wiped the knife and got up. Steve helped him pull the animal from the thicket.

At that moment there was a materialisation explosion to the south of them. Charles jumped up as if stung by a tarantula and searched the sky. Then his eyes fell on his bloody hands and arms. He looked at them and turned to Steve in dismay. 'That's a bad omen,' he groaned. 'Oh damn.' With hasty movements he tried to clean himself on the thin grass between the stones, but already the blood was beginning to dry.

Steve gave him his bow and quiver and slung the dead animal

over his shoulder. The body was still warm and started to bleed again. Quickly they began their descent and ran in the direction of the fortress.

'The fireworks will start any minute,' Charles called out.

Ten minutes later two MIG fighters appeared in the south-east and came screeching over the basin.

'Damn bad luck,' Charles shouted breathlessly, 'and not a cloud in the sky. The poor devils.'

When they reached the fortress at last, Steve's throat felt like sandpaper. Carelessly he dropped the goat onto the dusty ground somewhere near the huts, pulled his hat off, grabbed a helmet and reached for his machine pistol.

'Are you wounded?' Harness shouted.

Steve looked at him for a second without understanding; then he realised that his shoulder was covered in blood. He shook his head, but was unable to produce a sound.

'Take the helicopter. The others have gone, so take Blizzard's and Goodluck's men and anybody else who can be spared. Be careful in the south-west near the water – at least a dozen trader mercenaries have been sighted this morning. Keep to the south as far as possible.'

'Where did they land?' Charles asked.

'I don't know yet. As soon as I've located them I'll tell you by radio. Off you go.'

They ran through the camp down to the landing strip, where Elmer had already started removing the camouflage from the helicopter. Steve turned on the engine. Two minutes later they took off flying in a southerly direction and keeping close to the tree-tops. A few miles away the two MIGs were racing each other, heading in an easterly direction.

'Stay well down,' Charles said. 'They're going too fast. By the time they've seen us we'll be out of range. But we'll have to do a double take and disappear before they head back after us!'

Steve steered the helicopter south east into the landing area. Ahead, three columns of smoke were rising from the basin. Bombs, probably. Charles peered over Steve's shoulder attentively.

'Keep the terrain scanned. I'll warn you when the MIGs come back again.'

The commandant's voice came over the radio. 'They must have come down quite far over to the north-west, even nearer to

the water than the last lot. Can you hear me, Stanley?'
'I hear you. Over and out.' Steve corrected his course.
'Watch out and stay above light ground; then the whirr of the
rotor is less noticeable. They'll be back any minute.'
Two minutes later the two supersonic fighters thundered
east, close to the ground. This time they flew further south.
'We're having all the luck today,' Charles said, breathing a
sigh of relief. 'They can't be far off now.'
Just then, several things happened simultaneously. There
was a flash like a gun shot; a split-second later Steve heard a
high, shattering *ping*, and a hole the size of a thumbnail
appeared in the cockpit glass. At the same time the light falling
into the cockpit from the left assumed a purple colour, increasing in intensity within seconds.
Instinctively, Steve hauled the machine over to the right,
banking steeply just above the tree tops.
'What's the matter?' he asked, once he had steadied the
steering. Charles gave no answer. Looking round, Steve
suddenly became aware that the cockpit was covered in blood.
Charles had fallen forward in his straps with his eyes wide open,
and from his neck a stream of blood gushed forth rhythmically
in a thin red spray, spattering the cockpit windows with
millions of sparkling drops.
Steve began to scream and almost lost control over the
engine. For a moment he closed his eyes and saw Charles
wiping the goat's blood off his arms and hands on the dry grass.
He grounded the helicopter at breakneck speed, stopped the
engine, climbed from the cockpit, stumbled forward a few steps,
doubled up and was sick. He crouched on the ground for a few
minutes without moving, not daring to open his eyes and look
around. Over to the west he heard heavy firing. He listened
attentively.
Then he got up and went back to the helicopter, unfastened
Charles's straps, lifted him from his seat, carried him a few steps
and laid him on the ground. The terrible stream under his left
ear had stopped flowing.
Steve pulled off a few branches and camouflaged the helicopter as best he could. Then he took his machine gun and crept
forward in a westerly direction. The sea was not far off and he
could smell its cool water. About two hundred metres further he
came on a dead Chap, one of Blizzard's tribesmen, and soon

after that he saw the glider. It had cut down a few trees in landing and had been damaged quite badly. But it was open and the jeep had been driven out.

Steve saw a trader mercenary run across the clearing. At the same moment a machine gun started up from somewhere and the man fell.

Hiding behind a tree trunk, Steve tried to make out the scene. The shots must have come from the right; either the new arrivals or the men from the fortress must have dug in there. He worked his way from cover to cover until he reached the edge of another clearing. Then he saw the jeep. It had fallen over and was lying on its right side. The windscreen was shattered and a bleeding figure hung from the driver's seat, half flung out. About five steps from the vehicle lay another body; both were apparently from the landing party. Judging by the equipment it must have been a four-person unit, so where were the other two men? Steve crouched and tried to work his way forward under cover of the low bushes.

'Get under cover, man,' a voice was shouting, and as if to emphasise the words, Steve felt a blow on his shoulder. Then he was pulled around and flat onto his face and dragged into the bushes. He found himself lying next to a man in battledress who grabbed him by the head and hauled him roughly deeper into the bushes. A dirt-spattered face turned to him.

'Bailey,' the face said, 'Rick Bailey.' The mouth pulled into a broad rectangle, baring a remarkable set of teeth. 'Let's have a look at you.'

Only now Steve noticed a burning pain in his left shoulder. He groped for it clumsily.

'Hands off,' Bailey ordered, and started to investigate the wound. 'Only a scratch. Must have been the guy over there on the tree. We can't get him with the machine gun, it would take a rifle.'

Steve rolled over on his belly and pressed his teeth together.

'Who are these people?' Bailey asked.

'They're after our equipment. Particularly the ammunition.'

'I can believe it. But who are they? Russians or what?'

Steve shook his head. 'If I tried to explain to you now, it would take too long. But there must be about a dozen or so.'

'You can reckon without four or five; they got finished off. Good thing you warned us over the radio. None of this would have happened if we'd managed to get the jeep out of the damned glider. Because of that they were able to ambush us. Lucky the MIGs didn't get us either.'

Steve nodded. 'Where's your fourth man?'

Bailey pointed in the other direction. Steve turned round and saw the shape of a woman two steps away, doubled up under cover of some bushes. She was crying softly. Next to her a dead Chap lay on his back, another one of Blizzard's tribesmen. He had been shot in the right temple.

'I couldn't believe my eyes when this chimpanzee suddenly turned up next to me in his helmet and told me to cover him. He only managed a few steps, then he got hit by the sharpshooter over there. I pulled him back at once, but I couldn't help him any more.'

Steve had to fight down another fit of nausea. Then he said: 'I'll try. I . . .'

'To hell with you trying. We'll never do it if there are as many as you say. Where are our people?'

'They can't be far. If Blizzard's warriors are here . . .'

'*Whose* warriors?'

'Blizzard's. He's the boss of these men.' He pointed to the dead Chap.

'Of the apes?'

'They're not apes.'

'Listen. I can tell a human being from an ape.'

'No, you can't,' Steve said angrily.

Bailey looked at him in dismay. Then he shook his head as if to rouse himself from a bad dream. 'OK, and you're the goatsherd here.'

'Goatsherd?'

'You smell as if you were, man. Keep your eye on the right section. I'll secure the left side. Let's see who's faster, your people or those men over there. Perhaps we'll be lucky.'

Twice the fighter planes thundered overhead, then they turned off and disappeared. Once they heard voices to the north and four or five rifle shots, but otherwise everything was calm. Insects were humming. Steve stared into the bushes. Every now and then he thought he saw a movement. But he couldn't make out a target. The pain in his shoulder was steadily getting worse. A few times he heard the woman sob quietly.

'Pull yourself together, Jane,' Bailey said, surprisingly

gently. 'Don't make things more difficult for us.'

A few minutes later she came creeping over to them and lay down between them. Steve threw her a quick look from the corner of his eye. She was small and fragile-looking, and her snub nose was sun-tanned and freckled under her over-large helmet. The face looked familiar to him. How long ago was it since he had last seen it? One year, ten years? A thousand years? It was in Madrid he had last seen her. Jane . . . Jane Brookwood. Loorey had been with her. Of course – *my God!* She'd been a member of the landing troops too. She'd been earmarked for the second wave which was to follow immediately after the advance party.

When seeing the dead men lying by the jeep, she covered her face with her hands.

Suddenly there was a movement on the other side of the clearing. Shouts could be heard; shots rang out, and they pressed their faces into the grass. Then Bailey's machine pistol started up again.

'Damn,' he said. 'I'd love to have killed the bastard. Now he's managed to get down from his hideout.'

'I can smell fire,' Steve said, and raised his head. In the north he could see thick clouds of smoke; he could hear shouts and a strange growling roar. Then the earth began to shake.

'What's that?' Bailey asked. 'Some kind of devilry?'

'No,' Steve said, looking at the approaching cloud of dust. 'It's our people.'

'God help us,' Bailey said when he saw the first grey-brown monsters appear. 'You guys seem to have summoned up a zoo against your enemies.'

A herd of six or eight baluchitherias was approaching from the north, rhino-like creatures with necks like giraffes and gigantic horse heads – the biggest mammals that ever lived on earth. Their heads bent down for the attack, they ploughed through the undergrowth like living excavators, snorting and roaring. On the mighty haunches of the leader bull, Blizzard was standing, holding on to the monster's tail with one hand and driving the frightened animal on with a spear which he stuck into the anus and abdomen of the tormented creature. Blizzard's white fur was dishevelled, his teeth bared, and he was throwing his head from side to side ecstatically and uttering shrill, joyful shouts. His men and Goodluck's were crouching on the animals behind, driving them on like a herd of demons.

When the apparition had passed, Steve and Bailey ran over to the jeep, but the men were long past help.

The trader mercenaries had disappeared without a trace. They left behind six dead, four of whom had been shot by Bailey; two had not escaped in time and had been crushed by the Baluchitherias.

They unloaded the jeep and stood it up, bound the corpses on to the trailer and drove over to the helicopter. A few minutes later Ruiz turned up in the jeep with Goodluck.

Steve reported what had happened. Ruiz went pale when he saw Murchinson's body.

'Bastards,' he sobbed, kicking the front tyre of his jeep with his boot in impotent rage.

'Take the helicopter and fly Miss Brookwood into the fortress,' Steve said to him. 'I'll take the jeep.'

The Mexican shook his head without saying a word, carried the dead body over to his car and sat cradling his friend's head in his lap. He looked straight ahead into space and cried without shedding tears, his shoulders bent.

The others stood around in silence for a few minutes, exhausted and dejected. Steve pulled out an armful of grass and began to clean the helicopter's cockpit. The blood had clotted into thick lumps and in trying to wipe it off, Steve merely smeared it all over the window and the shabby plastic seat so that the cockpit looked worse than before. Bailey was helping him. He wetted the dry grass with water from his canteen.

'They must have been good friends,' he said.

'We're all friends here really,' Steve said. 'They arrived here together twelve years ago, from the same future.'

'I'll stay here for five years, not a day longer. Nobody told me I'd have to fight for my life here.'

Steve looked firmly at the new arrival. 'You'll have to do what we all have to do – that means waiting here a bit longer. I'm afraid we've been cheated.'

Bailey's lively dark-brown eyes looked at him as if to test him out.

'What do you mean?'

Steve explained the situation to him. Bailey's jaw muscles were twitching. He shook his head softly as if he were giddy, sat down on the landing skid of the helicopter and stared at his

bloodstained hands. Then he pushed his helmet off his head
and rubbed his forehead and short-cropped head with his lower
arm.

'Aren't you well, Bailey?'

'I'm trying to wake up, man. *To wake up!*'

'Unfortunately this isn't a dream.'

Blizzard appeared from the south with about twenty of his
and Goodluck's warriors. They had dispersed the trader
mercenaries and captured a few of their riding camels. They
were in a victorious mood and looked surprised to find everyone
looking so glum.

'Charles is dead,' Goodluck said.

Blizzard, his normally snow-white fur dirty and bloodstained, pushed his men aside and came forward. In his dark
eyes there burned a dangerous fire. He was still highly excited
from the hunt and his massive penis was erect. He went over to
the jeep where Ruiz was sitting and stared at the dead man.
Raising his hands, he touched Charles's forehead and cheeks as
if he were blind and were trying to make out his features. Then
he turned round, straightened himself up to his full height as if
about to beat his breast, fell forward onto his clenched fists and
uttered a tortured growl which seemed to come from deep down
in his chest.

'We have to get away from here before the fire cuts us off from
our route,' Steve warned.

'Take the woman in the helicopter,' Goodluck said. 'We'll
bring the vehicles home. And the dead.'

Bailey looked at him in astonishment. 'Hey,' he said, 'is he in
command here? Who in the devil's . . .'

A questioning look from Goodluck silenced him.

'Come along, Miss Brookwood,' Steve said. 'I'll take you to
safety.' He helped her into the cockpit, bolted the door and
climbed into the pilot's seat. When he started the engine he saw
that the radio was still switched on. He heard Jerome's voice.
Together with Leonard he had been searching further east.
Steve told him briefly what had happened. Jerome cursed.

As he started up the engine he noticed that four or five Chaps
were sitting on the landing skids, hoping to save themselves a
walk home. As a result he barely managed to get the helicopter
up into the air. Suddenly he felt unjustifiably enraged with his
passengers and only calmed down when he realised that these

Chaps had probably saved his life by stampeding the Baluchitherias with fire and shouts and driving them like living
tanks into the enemy's positions.

He took his right hand off the steering and looked at it. It was
trembling like a leaf.

'Shit,' he said. 'Excuse me, Miss Brookwood.'

But she was taking no notice of him, sitting crouched on her
seat next to him, her hands held in front of her eyes. His
shoulder was suddenly hurting badly and the wound was
starting to bleed again. Below, he saw the jeep with Jerome and
Leonard come up from the east. He gave them the others'
position over the radio and saw the vehicle change direction in
order to intercept the convoy.

It was a sad homecoming. It had been the bloodiest day for
many years.

Nina took the girl under her wing. Then she bandaged up
his shoulder while he reported to Harness.

It was hot that summer. Once more, several people decided to
leave the camp and take the autumn ship to Atlantis. Alfaro
was one of them; he was a carpenter by profession and a kind of
jack of all trades in the fortress. He wanted to try his luck in
Atlantis, open a workshop, or so he said. The fortress crew had
now shrunk to a handful of men and two women.

All through July they were plagued by a feverish infection
and suffered from diarrhoea and other maladies.

In the west, swarms of supply shipments fell from the sky and
drowned in the rising waters.

Steve's shoulder wound gradually healed. For weeks he, too,
had been laid low with a fever, dozing fitfully and lost in blurred
memories of the past and future. When he was finally strong
enough to walk about the camp again, he occasionally visited
Jane Brookwood for a chat, because he had the vague feeling
that she might help him remember a world which was growing
increasingly unreal to him. He felt as if she still wore the scent of
that remote reality in which Lucy had lived, as if she were the
trail he had to follow in order to find his way back to the land
from which he had been banished. Sometimes his memory
failed him and he called her Lucy by mistake. She would put her
arm round his shoulders and his narrow freckled hand would
settle on hers. These moments stayed clearly in his memory

because they filled him with strong emotions.

One day shortly before Nina was due to leave the fortress, she came into his room unannounced and mistaking his intentions, told him to leave Jane alone, warning that she had suffered a severe shock after the landing which she would probably never get over. It would be best for her to go to Atlantis on the next boat where she could live in the illusion that she had escaped hell and had returned to civilisation.

Steve looked into Nina's aged face without understanding her meaning; then he saw the deep lines which were beginning to form around her eyes and mouth, and he nodded silently.

'You're still very ill, Steve,' she said, sobbing, turning hastily and running away.

'Why did she cry?' Steve asked himself aloud and lifted his hand in a helpless gesture. He stared blankly into the mirror which hung over the scratched plastic wash bowl. The man who looked back at him reminded him remotely of his father. The top of his head was almost bald; a thin, greying beard framed the haggard cheeks. The eyes were unnaturally bright, as if under the influence of some drug.

He pushed up the torn, faded T-shirt to his shoulders. His chest was emaciated, the skin taut over the ribcage, showing thumbnail-size wet, whitish patches between dark red spots under the collar bone and on the hips.

'Radiation rash,' he murmured. He had seen the same symptoms on Harald and Harness. 'I guess I've been exposed a few times too often.' With slow movements he pulled his T-shirt down again, stuck his index fingers into two holes and pulled. The worn material gave without so much as a tearing noise.

Steve stepped up close to the mirror and looked with fascination at the silvery web behind the glass. He thought he could see patterns in it forming a spacious landscape. For days he became obsessed by the idea that the mirror might be magic and that it opened onto another reality. Perhaps he could get there if he shattered it; perhaps beyond it lay a sunny landscape, towns, highways, immense wheat fields, dams, rivers with tourist steamers, a runway on which he could land . . .

He gazed down at the pieces of mirror which lay shattered at his feet. A few grey earwigs were crawling back to seek refuge in the cracks of the rotten wood frame. With trembling hands, Steve collected the bits into the plastic bowl.

As soon as he had got his strength back, he climbed up to the spot where Harald and Charles lay buried. Up there he often sat for hours without moving, staring over to the promontories of the mountains in the south. He had been told by men who had been there that the Sahara desert did not yet exist, but was still a vast savannah in which unimaginably vast herds of animals grazed; that the mountain ranges were densely over-grown with larches and holm oaks, and that the lowlands were criss-crossed by river-beds and fringed with birch trees and alders. The Chaps had come from there, from the heart of Africa; they had extended their habitat into the Mediterranean and right up to the Alps.

As he lay there, Steve felt as if he were drifting aimlessly in the mouth of a river, surrounded by the rotten stench of dead time. The land around him shimmered in a heat haze, and dark vultures wheeled overhead, gliding on the powerful upward winds over the salt basins. One time he saw heavy mushroom clouds, puddles of light on the steely-grey water. At other times, when the evening was clear, he could see the peaks of the Italian plateau right over in the north-east, the other side of the Tyrrhenian Sea. Narrow ridges glowing red in the evening light, eaten into by rivers tumbling down more than three thousand metres into the basin. Occasionally he thought he saw strange lights over there, like the signals of a light tower flashing out at irregular intervals and disappearing again. He smiled as he thought of Harald's archangel with the laser gun and the Agnus Dei on his sleeve.

From down below where the darkness had set in already, he would sit and listen to the roar of the mastodons, the endless herds of prehistoric animals moving south through the basin. What prompted the migration? Steve wondered. Could they feel some imperceptible change of air pressure, perhaps? Of magnetic field?

Africa, the great bone deposit of earth's antiquity, fell into a silence like the silence of death. No more supplies were dropped, and the people on the fortress waited in vain for the arrival of another landing party.

Winter came early and the weather got cold. They wrapped themselves up in greasy animal skins at night and were plagued by fleas carried by Goodluck's and Blizzard's men.

One morning they found Harness dead in the armchair in his office. He had laid down his command silently and passed away without causing a stir. When they opened the desk they discovered dozens of alternative futures mapped out on metres and metres of paper and waiting to be processed by computer. Unfortunately the computer had never arrived and was probably lost in time. Night after night the commandant had worked with incredible patience at his desk, holding the paper down with the stump of his arm, sketching out the synchronoptic linear patterns of alternative movements of time in his tiny printed handwriting, determining the significant intersections and plotting points where historically important interventions could have been made. Tiny crosses marked the death of Columbus, of Cortez and Pizarro, of Napoleon, Maximilian of Mexico, and Hitler; the crosses of Lincoln, Kennedy and Martin Luther King had also been carefully marked in, and arrows indicated the battle of the Catalan fields and the battles of Gettysburg, Cannae, Stalingrad, Little Big Horn, Liegnitz, Tours, Poitiers, Guadalquivir, Waterloo and Chikamauga.

'He often had pain in the stump of his arm. It kept him from sleeping at night,' Nina said. She had lived with him for more than twenty years.

'Years ago I saw an interaction matrix analysis by the Institute for the Future in Middletown, Connecticut,' said Jerome. 'That had a similar structure to this analysis of Harness's. They ought to have applied his method to their project, but they were too sure of themselves and therefore negligent and careless. They had the means to do it, though. It would have been easy with the computers NASA possessed to trace the causal connection of alternative possibilities with other realities into their smallest ramifications. He tried to do it without technology, just by using his memory and a few reference books.'

Steve stared at the immense map of mankind's realised and unrealised possibilities, victories and defeats. 'One ought to build a gigantic palace and carve these time-lines on it for posterity. It could be a kind of history of the realisable futures of this world.'

'You'd do better to throw the whole load of nonsense in the fire,' Leonard said in his soft voice. 'Do any of you seriously believe that mankind has a future after what *we've* done?'

'Never,' Elmer said firmly. 'It's God's will that the spirit will overcome time until all the matter in the universe will be transformed into spirit which cannot be destroyed by entropy.'

Leonard peered at him over his spectacles. Jerome tapped the side of his head with his index finger.

'Before Moses climbs Sinai in another time-line to receive the ten commandments, long before the foundation stone of the Egyptian pyramids is laid, we shall have colonised the galaxy and pushed far into the past,' Elmer declared eagerly. 'That is our mission.'

'Excuse me, gentlemen, if I retire from this metaphysical debating club,' Bailey said. 'I'm going to sit with Blizzard and Goodluck. I need the company of sensible human beings.'

Elmer clenched his left fist indignantly and lifted up his crutch with his right hand. 'What do you know?' he shouted. 'You know *nothing!*'

He would have fallen to the ground if Jerome had not caught him in time.

'How long have you been here, Elmer?' Steve asked him.

'Thirty-three years,' Elmer said. 'And believe me, I've had enough time to think about it. Do you think you can live for thirty-three years without a cause?'

'All right, Elmer,' Jerome said.

'You'll all die in vain if you don't believe in a cause,' Elmer said. 'Do you want our lives and the lives of countless good men to be sacrificed for nothing? We have to accept our challenge. The future of the world belongs to us if we go about it the right way. With God's help . . .'

'It's all right, Elmer,' Jerome said.

'Leave me alone,' Elmer hissed at him angrily and limped away.

Next night Steve dreamt Harald's dream, except that he did not encounter the archangel but was the archangel himself, dressed tightly in a terribly uncomfortable space suit in which he was hardly able to move. But he was full of energy and initiative; it was his mission to point out the black spots in human history and burn them off. Again and again he tried to lift his arm to direct the scorching beam of his laser gun at the target, but his arm hung lifelessly from his side like a stump, like a scarred piece of rough concrete which refused to move.

A day later they took a vote on who should be the next commandant of the fortress. Jerome proposed Bailey. There were seven Yes votes, including the votes of Blizzard and Goodluck, and one No vote from Elmer. There were also two abstentions: Nina and Bailey.

On a sunny winter's day Snowball, Blizzard's son, came to Steve and told him that in the valley above the camp a wild goat had got caught in one of his traps. They set out immediately to make sure no wild animals or vultures got there first. During the climb upstream on the well-worn muletrack, Snowball stopped to fish for trout, which lay like spearpoints of darkened silver in the shady pools. Every now and then he overturned a stone in the wet soil on the bank and found it teeming with crabs underneath. He caught a few in a flash, cracked them open with his immensely strong teeth and pulled the flesh from the carapace with his quick tongue, while the animals were still waving their claws in the air.

When they arrived at the trap, the goat was still alive. It looked more like a short-haired sheep, because the two species were just on the point of splitting up into two separate lines of development. It was very young and was bleating miserably. A few vultures had already arrived and were circling overhead, ugly undertakers with unkempt feathers and cruel, indifferent eyes. Snowball's white neck-hair bristled and he bared his teeth and growled at them, but they did not seem impressed. A marabou retreated a few steps as if insulted, opened its wings and examined him accusingly.

The little goat seemed to be grateful to escape the vultures' beaks and did not put up any resistance as they led it down to the stream. But its amber eyes filled with unbelieving horror when Steve stuck his knife into its throat. Immediately the bright bleating changed into a rattling sigh. The body doubled up as if in a noiseless fit of coughing, and bright red blood gushed out over the light-coloured pebbles on the bank. Snowball watched him, staring at Steve's hand in a mixture of horror and admiration as he withdrew the knife from the fatal wound. He never missed the slaughtering of animals; killing seemed to exert an immense fascination for him.

Steve tied the animal by its hind legs to two strong branches, placed the sharp blade on the back and pulled it vertically from the abdomen to the neck. Then he pushed his strong fingers under the skin until his arm had disappeared up to the elbow and it looked as if he held the goat's naked body in an obscene embrace. Finally he cut the skin off at the legs and spread it out on the pebbles to dry.

Snowball was crouching a few steps behind Steve, the hair on his neck still bristling, registering every movement attentively. As Steve once more placed the knife on the body and opened it up with a strong, cracking sound, the Chap began to growl menacingly. Steve turned round.

'What's the matter with you?'

Snowball tried to speak, but his jaws seemed paralysed, as if he had sunk them into a victim. He only managed an inarticulate growl.

'We seem to be getting more and more alike, you and me,' Steve said, as he gutted the goat with short, quick cuts, severing the intestines, which finally fell to the ground. 'I was trained in the art of killing members of my own species – it was very different from this sort of killing. Now I've had to learn what my ancestors practised daily hundreds of thousands of years ago, and I still shudder. And I teach you how to destroy all living creatures with a piece of metal or a stone, and turn them into food, even if they're superior to you in teeth and claws, power and speed. And that makes me shudder, too.'

Snowball looked at the grey-blue tangle of guts now hanging in the stream, moving slowly like a snake and releasing yellow-green excrement into the water. He examined the intestines with interest and shyly touched the liver and spleen with his index finger. When he noticed that Steve was watching him he quickly withdrew his hand, as if he had been found out while doing something forbidden. Steve put his hand on the dense hair on his neck and stroked him.

'One day you'll learn to read your future in this.' The boy looked at him questioningly. Am I about to initiate him in metaphysics? Steve suddenly wondered. 'Let's wash the meat,' he added quickly.

'Meat,' Snowball said.

Just then Steve saw that on the other bank of the stream they were being watched by a giant newt, a grey-black monster more than a metre long, with a flat, shark-like head and mysterious-looking far-apart eyes which seemed to move independently.

How could that tiny brain make the two perceptions match and fit together into a world? Steve asked himself. But it seemed to function with precision when Snowball threw up his arms in a threatening gesture. The animal disappeared like a dark flash of lightning into the bushes on the bank.

In spring a rumour began to circulate that Paul Loorey had returned from Atlantis. He had been seen in Cadiz in autumn, had travelled on the barge, but nobody knew anything definite about his whereabouts.

'Paul was very sceptical when he went over,' Elmer said. 'He was chosen as a kind of emissary to gather information about the life over there. And since he didn't believe that the Atlantis project had a chance, we chose him. He was a critical fellow.'

Steve was lying on the rock outpost in the dry grass, enjoying the Spring sunshine and only half-listening. They still took turns at the listening post, although nobody seriously believed that any more landing parties would arrive. According to Walton's and Harness's list, everybody working on the Western Basin project had arrived from their respective future. But that did not, of course, mean that in some other future, someone might not have undertaken a similar project aiming at the same target time.

'Paul maintained that far more people were needed to build a civilisation to a standard above that of stone-age hunters. In order to achieve the division of labour which is the precondition for a high culture, there would need to be a community of at least twenty or thirty thousand individuals, plus all the conditions that make agriculture and animal husbandry possible.'

'But they have technical equipment.'

'Paul maintains that it's of no value whatsoever. It'll be scrapped in a generation, and forgotten within three.'

'But they have the know-how.'

'Not the know-how they really need: scythe-makers, shoe-makers, ships' carpenters, wheelwrights, rope-makers, tanners, saddlers, millers, blacksmiths.'

'They'll have to learn the trades. We, too, are trying to learn old techniques again, however unsatisfactory the results may be.'

'But there's another major problem over there. A large part of the population is either indifferent or actively opposed to the

movement to build Atlantis; many of them are still waiting
eagerly for salvation in form of a time machine as promised by
the Navy – particularly the former NASA technicians and the
higher officers. They're not prepared to put their intelligence to
the service of the cause.'

'I doubt whether *their* kind of intelligence is necessary to build
up a civilisation. What's needed is imagination and inventive-
ness, daring and initiative – virtues rare among specialists,
logisticians, officials, or military personnel.'

Elmer shrugged his shoulders. 'You may be right. But they
can't even see what a great opportunity they're missing.
Mankind could save six million years. This leap . . .'

'Don't let's start on that again, Elmer. Remember what that
means – six million years! Even if Atlantis *did* have a chance, at
some stage in that gigantic desert of time our genes would
disappear. We're nothing more than an artificial appendix of
evolution – we'll dry up like all those other shoots on Darwin's
tree. You must get rid of your illusions. Even if Atlantis survived
for a few thousand years, it wouldn't even live on as a legend
because it'll be followed by dark ages.'

'I don't believe you.'

'Around the year 1,000, Leif Erikson's dragon boats landed
in the New World. The Normans pushed far inland on the
continent and colonised the shores of the Big Lakes and the area
round the sources of the Mississippi. Not all of them were
murdered by Indians, that's nonsense; they were simply
assimilated. In 1738 and in 1840, less than a thousand years
later, when Sieur de la Verandrye and Maximilian Prince
Wied-Neuwied visited the so-called white Indians, they found
it difficult to say precisely in what they differed from the original
inhabitants of America. The descendants of the Vikings had
become Indians – a few of them perhaps a little lighter of skin,
with blue eyes and slightly taller – but they'd completely
adopted the Indians' language, customs and methods of
survival. It's a process which can be shown to be at work here in
the Mediterranean.'

'So you believe we shall degenerate to the level of the Chaps?'

'Elmer, you've lived here long enough to know that that's the
wrong word to use.'

Elmer bit into a blade of grass and gave no answer. Suddenly
the telephone rang. It was Bailey.

'Something's brewing,' he said. 'I haven't seen any of Goodluck or Blizzard's people all morning. They've disappeared without a trace. Keep your eyes open. I sent Jerome and Ricardo off in the jeep to find out what's happened. I think it'd be best if you came down and got the helicopter ready to start with Leonard. Just in case. Over and Out.'

'Message received,' Steve said. He put up his binoculars and scanned the basin. The south and south-west were hazy in the noon light. He saw no movement.

As he ran down to the fortress he thought he heard shots in the east, quite far away towards Cape Malfatano, where Goodluck and Blizzard's tribes had their sleep-trees. Probably the Chaps and the trader mercenaries had clashed as so often before when they could not agree on the price of something or tried to snatch back what they had sold.

Leonard was waiting near the helicopter. They were about to take off when a jeep raced up the path to the fortress at breakneck speed. It was driven by Ricardo, and Blizzard was sitting next to him. The chief looked at them with blank eyes, he was bleeding from several wounds and held his chest with his big paws. The Mexican was driving like a madman, his vehicle skidding and jolting all over the track. Leonard and Steve ran after him to the camp.

Bailey, Nina, and Jane tried to help the wounded warrior, but there was little they could do for him. As if from nowhere, two females appeared and started to wail. Blizzard looked at them reproachfully and chased them away with a movement of his hand. He sat up, groaning as his life blood ebbed away. People stood around, not knowing what to do and trying to give him relief with silent gestures. He looked at them one by one with his dark eyes, dominating them silently right up to the end.

Slowly they all started to move again. Ricardo reported softly what had happened. The Chaps had come into contact with some trader mercenaries the day before at an appointed place in the east in order to barter goods. In the course of this, a few survivors from the battle in the landing area must have recognised Blizzard and decided to take revenge for their defeat. They succeeded in finding one of the sleep-trees, ambushed it at night and took two females and their three young prisoner. Blizzard offered to pay ransoms in the form of skins but the kidnappers asked instead for weapons and ammunition. When these were refused they strung up one of the females and put pressure on Blizzard. They felt strong enough to lay down the cònditions because there were twenty-two of them, armed to the teeth and mostly experienced and seasoned mercenaries.

Blizzard tried to hold them off while he organised his own and Goodluck's men, but the kidnappers realised what he was up to, massacred their prisoners and opened fire. Blizzard, beside himself with rage, tried to overrun the enemy before he had built up his army to its full strength and was wounded in the process. At that moment Ricardo and Jerome reached the battlefield. While Jerome joined Goodluck in leading the warriors of the two tribes, Ricardo tried to save Blizzard's life by taking him back to the fortress as fast as possible.

'Why didn't you call for the helicopter? We could have got to you in a few minutes,' Steve said.

The Mexican pointed to the bullet holes in his vehicle. 'The radio's smashed. We were lucky they didn't hit the tank.'

Late that afternoon Jerome came back with six Chaps, all of whom had been wounded, though none of them fatally. They had captured eighteen camels loaded with weapons, equipment, and commercial goods. The Chaps had completely wiped out their opponents.

Jerome looked pale. 'I've never seen anything like it,' he said softly, and threw a shy look at the wounded men sitting in front of the medical hut where they were being attended to. 'They fought like mad, regardless of losses. It was terrible. They attacked their enemies furiously and killed them. They tore their throats out when they could get near enough.'

'Are there many casualties?'

'All of the mercenaries died, and at least ten or twelve Chaps.'

At dusk Goodluck arrived with twelve more camels – carrying the dead warriors of the two tribes and the females and young. After Bailey had fed them all, Goodluck and his men and the survivors of Blizzard's tribe walked through the fortress and up the mountain to camp near the burial place on the plateau. The wailing of females and the crying of children could be heard all night.

Late in the afternoon of the next day Bailey, Jerome, Ricardo and Steve climbed up to the burial place. They met a ghostly spectacle. The warriors had dyed their furry faces white and were sitting on their haunches in a semicircle around the corpses, which had been laid out beside a long, flat grave. In the middle there was the mighty form of Blizzard, raised up a little; to the left and to the right of him, five dead warriors. The bodies were covered in green twigs and flowers. While the females and children kept silently in the background, the warriors began the ritual for the dead. Breathing rhythmically, they all threw their chests forward together, hands on their backs and lowering their foreheads jerkily until they almost touched the ground. The rhythm accelerated, the breathing turned into groaning, the dyed faces, almost indistinguishable, were distorted in pain, teeth bared. The foreheads moved up and down faster, the groaning increased and turned into a sharp, tortured screaming, which stopped as suddenly as the movement. Silence. Only heavy breathing could be heard and the rustling of leaves in the wind. Suddenly the females set up a piercing howling, while the young anxiously sought refuge and clung to the fur on their breasts, bursting into loud cries.

After a long spell of silent immobility, the warriors rose, standing like ghosts in the noon light, and started to collect stones which they piled over the dead bodies.

'Have you ever seen a skull-tree?' Elmer asked Steve the next morning.

Steve shook his head.

'Come up with me then . . .'

They climbed upstream past the saddling place to where the warriors were buried, and Charles and Harald with them. The place looked frightening. On top of the pile of stones heaped over the bodies of Blizzard and his men stood a bare tree-trunk bleached by the sea and sun, sticking up like a bony hand. At the forked ends of its branches there were twenty-two severed heads. Steve thought he recognised one of them as the pilot whom Goodluck had taken prisoner when they had landed, but he was not quite sure. There were many young, dark-skinned faces among them, still frozen in agony. No doubt their souls accompanied Blizzard on his long journey and would serve him in the country on the other side of the Great Water.

Flies were buzzing all around them and a vulture came floating down and looked at them, wings still half open, cold-eyed. The first whiff of decay was mixing in with the fresh smell of the morning. Soon it would be stifling.

They avoided the terrible spot after that.

# CHAPTER EIGHT

# JOURNEY TO ATLANTIS AND OTHER PLACES

Later that Spring they rode to market – Ricardo, Jerome, and Steve. They were also taking Jane to meet the barge. The ship that was to come over from the Bermudas in early summer was to take her to Atlantis.

The anchoring point was now a little further south. The waters were rising. The forests were sinking further into the deep.

They camped beside a stream not far from the anchoring point and spent the time hunting while they waited for the barge to appear. When, after four days, the boat finally arrived and tied up in the bay, there were crowds of people on board. Judging by their baggage, they were all bound for Atlantis.

'There's Paul Loorey,' Ricardo said, waving. 'So he's back after all.'

Steve peered through the throng of passengers, to where a small figure was waving back at them. He would never have recognised Loorey. The rather sullen young man he had met at the Cape seemed to bear no resemblance to the eccentric old gentleman who stood by the rail, raising his cane to greet them. He looked like a wandering preacher, dressed in a knee-length toga-like robe of brown material braided in leather, and wide black pyjama trousers tied at the ankles with ribbons. On his head he wore a saffron-yellow turban from which dense white hair fell to his shoulders, and a white trimmed beard framed the tanned face. On his equally tanned feet were comfortable leather sandals, at his side an enormous bag of roughly woven material, and next to him on the ground a travelling basket of wickerwork.

'Paul Loorey – the same as ever!' Ricardo said, laughing.' A shopping bag full of goodies and a basketful of proverbs. I bet he only came back because he ran out of listeners over there. Looks like he's bursting with news.'

Steve held his breath.

Jane stood next to Jerome at the end of the gangplank. As Paul passed her and set foot ashore he stopped briefly, thunderstruck. Then he walked on without turning round, shaking his head slightly, startled by this encounter with a reality he had long believed lost in the past. For a moment he paused, appearing to hesitate; then he tapped the ground with his stick as if to emphasise his decision to break with the past, and came walking over to them.

'Paul!' Ricardo called.

Paul hastily put a finger to his mouth. Jane turned around briefly and smiled and waved to them, but then she turned her attention back to the men carrying baskets and packs ashore and loading them on the animals. She had not recognised him.

Paul looked squat and broad-shouldered, almost a little stout, with the face of an ancient shrewd peasant in the best of health, with fat, red little cheeks and merry, twinkling eyes.

'Unless my eyes are deceiving me,' he puffed, putting down his travelling basket, 'I've just seen the lovely Jane Brookwood from the Department of Mathematics and Logistics at NASA. And looking crisp as a croissant, too.' He smacked his lips like a gourmet and stroked his well-groomed white beard.

'You weren't mistaken,' said Ricardo, embracing the new arrival and kissing him on both cheeks.

'Then let's get out of here, for heaven's sake, Ricardo. I'm too old to be chasing the girls. What memories, though! After all these years I still remember her fondly. It was in Madrid. We'd been . . .' He stopped and threw her a stealthy look over his shoulder. 'Let's go before she recognises me and suffers a shock from which she might never recover.'

'You exaggerate.'

"Who's that over there?' he asked, pointing at Jerome, who was about to carry Jane's baggage on board. 'I'm sure I've met him somewhere. And him too, damn it.' He pointed at Steve with his stick. 'I seem to remember a time when I swapped some delicious whisky for an even more delicious night in the arms of that beautiful young lady.' He closed his eyes and put his hand on his chest. Then he pointed discreetly over his shoulder with his thumb and said: 'If I remember right, this ageing Western star is Jerome Bannister and you . . .' he tapped Steve on the chest with his index finger '. . . you are our retired astronaut, Steve Stanley. Am I right? Tell me; how have you

stayed so young? Where have you *been* all this time?'
'We've been here for almost three years,' Steve said.
'Three years!' Paul snorted disdainfully. 'And where's old
slouch-hat? Haven't you brought Hal along? He always used to
be around when the barge arrived.'
'Hal's dead,' Ricardo said. 'And Charles, and Howard, and
Blizzard.'
'Dead, dead,' Paul said, and tapped the ground with his stick
as if in reproach. 'I've visited Moses.'
'We heard you came back from Atlantis some time ago. You
were spotted.'
'It's a small world. Everybody knows everybody. I've so
much news for you – all about Moses and his family. I spent the
winter with him. We had so much to talk about, somehow we
never had time before.'
'*You* had so much to talk about,' Ricardo corrected him.
'I guess you're right,' Paul admitted. 'But he did some
talking, too.'
Meanwhile the passengers had come off the boat, and kidskin
bags filled with fresh drinking water had been piled on deck, a
black, glittering heap looking like bloated and dismembered
animal cadavers.
The ropes were thrown off, the heavy yard hoisted. There
was the creak of timbers of wood, the screech of winches, then
the huge dark sail unfolded, and slowly the barge slid away into
the silvery, glittering water.
They stood for a long time, waving, while in the background
the animal drivers started up their loaded animals with shouts
and cracking whips, eager to get their goods to market.
'There goes my youth,' Paul said, and blew his nose noisily
into an enormous, not exactly clean red handkerchief which he
had fished out from the bottom of his bag. Steve gave him a brief
look and noticed that he was surreptitiously wiping his eyes. He
was just about to pick up the travelling basket and carry it over
to the camels, when it gave out a dangerous-sounding growl.
'Quiet, Davy,' Paul said. 'Nobody wants to steal you. We're
among friends here.' He opened the lid of the wicker basket and
took out a young dog by the scruff of his neck, a rust-red ball
with bushy tail, black nose and short blunt ears. The animal
sniffed at each of them before retreating between Paul's legs,
where he apparently felt safest.

'He comes from America,' Paul said. 'Some hunters caught some on the mainland and domesticated them. In Atlantis they're becoming a bit of a nuisance. I brought some of them with me to pass on to Moses. In fact originally I brought a whole pack of them, thinking that very few would survive the journey. But by the time I came off the boat at Cadiz they'd trebled in number. That captain was pleased to get rid of us, wasn't he, Davy? Strange, isn't it? For ages scientists puzzled over how the dog got from the New World to the Old World. Who'd have thought that I would be the solution to the mystery?'

'How's Moses?' Jerome asked.

'Not very well. Last summer he had a fight with a sabre-toothed tiger. They just managed to save his life, but he owes a lot to the Boisei. They brought him herbs from the mountains which seem to have worked miracles, so his wife told me. He walks on crutches now and sits on his porch most of the time. The sons and daughters do all the work.

'He built a house of stone – it was as if he wanted it to stand forever. And he's built himself a forge, too. I'm no anthropologist, but I wouldn't be suprised if Moses' descendants managed to breed with the Boisei and to survive five million years. They might create a race that could stand up to the Chaps without suffering the fate of the Neanderthal.'

'I hear he has a dozen children,' Jerome said.

'He has eight sons and four daughters, some of them as black as he is, the others more like their mother. His eldest, Algis, has travelled all over Europe, right up to the Baltic, where he discovered some very curious things I wouldn't mind taking a look at myself. But I suppose I'm too old for such difficult journeys.'

'I suppose he hasn't by any chance found the other end of Francis's pipeline?' Steve said.

'No. He said he found something looking rather like a gigantic bunker system. He thinks it might be some kind of fortification. It's situated on the coast and half covered by water, and further inland it's totally overgrown. The structures must be thousands of years old. He also found tracks made by some kind of material that doesn't get worn down by time. He said he rode along the tracks for hours until they led into the sea. And far down in the water he saw more of the bunkers, battered by breakers and encrusted with oyster-shells and other forms of sea-life.'

'What could it be?' Steve asked.

Paul shrugged his shoulders. 'You're young. Go and take a look. Judging by his descriptions I'd say they must be launching pads for space ships – perhaps some enormous complex from which they started out for the stars. Perhaps they were human beings who went to another galaxy, perhaps visitors from the stars who had a base there. Who knows? The boy also mentioned inscriptions carved into the concrete, but they were barely recognisable. The region has many storms.'

'And what do the inscriptions say?'

'Only the gods know. Moses' brats may be good at handling bows and arrows and knives, but nobody ever taught them to read and write. What for? But if the bastard had been brighter he would have sat down and copied out the signs. It's a real pity, because Moses and I could have deciphered them.' Paul sighed, took a gulp from the water bag which Ricardo handed him, and wiped his beard. 'I can guess what they *might* have said, though.' With his cane he drew a rectangle on the ground next to the burnt-out camp fire. ' "Whoever enters this world, leave all hope behind. It has no future".'

They looked at him questioningly.

'*Lasciate ogni speranze . . .*'

'I've heard that somewhere before,' said Steve.

'That, or something like it, will one day be said by a poet somewhere in this region, mark my words,' Paul said, with an ironic twinkle in his eyes.

'You always were a joker,' Ricardo said, laughing.

Paul shrugged his shoulders. 'Well, yes. But am I right or not?'

'You should know better than us,' Jerome said.

'You've been to Atlantis,' Ricardo said. 'Are things bad there?'

'I'll tell you about Atlantis,' Paul said.

'Atlantis is a strange continent,' said Paul. They were sitting round the camp fire in the evening after the market, now on their way south. The cicadas were chirping all around them in the darkness. 'Nowhere will you find such courage or such despair. There are two clear factions there – you can tell them apart by their clothes. The Atlantids wear turbans and woven togas, the others wear faded shabby uniforms. The first lot strike you as the real natives, settled and self-assured, the others look like tourists, impatient and a little suspicious. Everybody keeps half an eye‚on the so-called retrieval zone in the southwest; the Atlantids with amusement and a hint of boredom, the others nervously, grumbling like air passengers who have been waiting for days for their plane and are being put off from hour to hour.

'They've filled in the bay of Castle Harbour now, and a large part of the lagoon to the west of St George towards the northern reef – levelled it all out with excavators and steamrollers. The total area's about eight kilometres long and five kilometres wide. In its centre there's a platform on which the test matter is piled up, and for decades grabs have been made for it – in vain. Nobody really knows what the problem is. There are lots of experts, and as many theories. To me, the most credible explanation is that it's difficult to determine the retrieval field precisely in spatial and temporal terms. The field has a scatter of hundreds of square kilometres and of long time-spans. Do you remember the fuss that was made in the mid-seventies about the so-called Bermuda triangle? Well, it wasn't quite the humbug the scientists put out at the time. Someone quite high up ordered the rumours to be spread around, so as to obscure the truth. If you ask me, they were beginning to get scared at what might happen in that region once mighty time machines started work at the Navy base, sending gigantic amounts of energy uncontrolled into the past. Even at open gravitational fields, enormous masses could be transported through time; and God help the ship or plane that happened to get swept into the turbulence of an artificial gravitational bubble, drifting against the course of time in order to retrieve matter from the remote past.

'It makes an exciting spectacle when the remains of such chronotronic stormfronts reach Atlantis. People stare at the gigantic artificial plane of concrete as if spellbound. The light suddenly dims; the air is charged with electricity. From the test matter, flames of St Elmo fire flicker like tongues against the dark sky. Thunderclaps, lightning . . . Over the sea, waterspouts rise up, and far away inland, a shoal of fish is lifted high into the atmosphere and rains down from the sky. Sometimes the sky goes black, and a hot, dry breath of hellfire scorches the city. And sometimes in mid-summer, there's a sudden snow shower with hailstones weighing hundreds of pounds . . .

'A couple of times I went out to the retrieval zone after a storm like that. You feel suffocated, but people avoid that area. It feels as if you could be grabbed any minute and thrown into a dark abyss. Now it's covered with dust and sand and the strangest objects can be found there.'

Paul was fingering a leather pouch which he was wearing round his neck on a ribbon, and emptied its contents into the hollow of his hand.

'Here's a wedding ring. R.F. 16.1.1873. The strange thing is that the flat side is outside, the rounded surface inside, as if distorted by a mighty force. Here's part of an aluminium sign; on the top you can just make out ". . . RAY" – probably the last syllable of a name. Above that, "773" and underneath, ". . . ORCE". It must be the registration disc of an air force pilot by name of Murray, or something like that. Here – two gold-crowned canine teeth with a double bridge in between. And this here is undoubtedly a human thumb, completely dehydrated and mummified. This is a screw, a quarter-inch, twisted out of shape by an incredible force. This piece of brass must have come from a ship fixture, because engraved on its side is a nonius scale and the figures 7 and 8.

'Sometimes one finds quite different things. Bits of smashed machinery, distorted into unrecognisable shapes; fragments of aluminium and steel panels; charred plastic material; granulated metal which has been melted and hardened again; sometimes bits of bodies, torn-off human limbs, often completely dehydrated, with dark patches on them like blood or oilstains.'

Paul dropped the objects back into his leather pouch.

'The driftwood of time. The waves generated by the machinery of the eighties have swept them into the past and washed them up on our shores.

'Some things don't seem to have worked out the way they imagined,' he said, shrugging his shoulders. 'The Atlantids have had plenty of ideas as to how to send advice into the future: anachronisms, indestructible time-boxes – chronological messages in bottles, if you like; but nothing seems to have ever arrived. Perhaps they've all been washed up on uninhabited beaches or buried too deeply in the womb of the earth.'

When they reached the fortress and the daily round of duties was resumed, Paul Loorey's presence there was like a refreshing summer rain. They all felt revived, and plucked up courage again to face the future.

Paul reported that the Atlantis project was finding more and more support and that there was some hope it might succeed if the bases on the American mainland continued to develop well, thus guaranteeing a supply of necessary goods and later of raw materials. He himself was determined to return over the Atlantic.

After seven months without a materialisation and fifteen months since the last landing, they decided unanimously to abandon the fortress.

And so, on the 18th of August in the year 50 after the first registered landing, they recorded their decision, their names and the date in the logbook, which was then soldered into a lead box, melted into a time-probe of indestructible plastic material and buried on top of Monte Lapany.

Thus the most ambitious and most expensive project of human history was officially declared a failure.

After the ceremony all felt light-hearted; now nothing bound them any longer to the age from which they had come – or to the project, which, they all agreed, could have been a high point of human civilisation had it not been planned by ambitious military officials.

They left the main part of the equipment to the tribes, which were now united under the leadership of Senegal, Goodluck's son. He intended to go east to find new hunting grounds in the Tyrrhenian basin and on the Sicilian highlands.

Jerome was thinking of going to see Moses, and Goodluck and Snowball wanted to accompany him. Steve was still undecided.

They set out north with a few camels and their personal belongings, and waited for the barge south of what was later called Capo dell'Argentiera. It arrived on 2nd September and they embarked: Ricardo Ruiz and Nina Jamisson, Leonard Rosenthal and Elmer Trucy, Jerome Bannister and Paul Loorey, Goodluck and Rick Bailey, Snowball and Steve Stanley, a jeep with a trailer, fourteen camels – and Davy, of course.

Some colonists from the north who had heard that the

fortress had been dissolved, joined them because they no longer felt safe now. Also on board were a group of trader mercenaries who had come down from Africa and who paid for their passage with precious tiger skins and claws which would be worth a fortune in Atlantis, daggers of best Arabic craftsmanship, gold and silver jewellery of bizarre shapes and choice leather goods.

'From which age are these objects?' Steve asked one of the traders.

He shrugged his shoulders and answered in Arabic. Steve did not understand him.

'He says these objects are timeless,' someone else answered and squeezed his dark face into a smile. 'He doesn't understand your question.'

Steve nodded.

The barge was now heading north-west through the glittering light of noon, its mighty sail billowing in a strong south wind. The helmsmen in their dark burnouses and dark turbans were dozing in the noon heat, propped against the rudder. Most of the passengers had found shelter under the sun sail or had retreated below deck for a siesta.

Steve took Howard Harness's notes out and flicked through them. Davy kept him company and sniffed inquisitively at the tough, green-and-white striped computer paper.

A newspaper clipping fell out, marked *Newsweek*, 17th October, 1983. It was printed on rough paper, rather faded, and bore a photograph of a pompously dressed old man. The story underneath ran as follows:

### ASSASSINATION ATTEMPT ON MAXIMILIAN V

**Mexico City – AP:** Yesterday evening the aged Hapsburg Emperor miraculously escaped the bullets of an assassin, who had been waiting for the monarch when he left the cathedral at Empire Square after vespers on his way back to the National Palace. Nobody in the royal family was hurt, although one of the Emperor's bodyguards was killed in the gunfight. The assassin was arrested. According to reports issued by the Guardia Nacional, he denies belonging to one of the Leninist terrorist groups, although his evidence is confusing. Though he seems to be of Latin American origin, the accused seems to have lived abroad for a long time, as evidenced by his foreign accent as well as by some objects found in his possession when he was arrested.

'BAD WORK!' Harness had printed on the margin and underneath that: 'According to Murchinson he was decapitated.'

Steve pulled the loops of the computer paper through his fingers and examined the network of time-lines. A few points were clearly marked.

*March, 1867: Victory of the Mexican rebellion over the French invasion force, 19th June, 1867, Gueretaro: Ferdinand Maximilian, Archduke of Austria, from 1863 Emperor Maximilian I of Mexico, shot by firing squad under orders of Benito Juarez.*

On the margin: *Development most improbable. Successful correction of course?*

Higher up: *1519 – Hernando Cortes:*

Steve closed his eyes. On 16th August they had marched off from Zempoala – four hundred men, fifteen horses and six cannons; two hundred *tamenes* carried the muskets and other heavy weapons and the provisions, and only the riders and officers wore armour. For three days they had been fighting their way across the hot, humid plains and mosquito-ridden swamps of the *tierra caliente*. On the fourth day they started the ascent of the hazy slopes of the Colle de Perote. Now the path became steeper; exhausted, they reached Jicochimalco over steps hacked into the rock. In the evening light they made out to the south the massive mountain range of the Sierra Madre, overlooked by the immaculate pyramid of the Orizaba. Behind this mountain range lay the plateau, the promised land, the golden city of Tenochtitlán . . .

The night is bitterly cold. The soldiers in their sweat-drenched, cotton-quilted doublets shiver in the cold. Before the first light they strike camp, then climb up to the pass they call Puesto de Nombre de Dios. The porters move slowly, wearily now, and the horses have to be led by the reins; the air is thinner, icier. The breath of man and beast turns to clouds, while behind them the red sun rises from the haze on the coast. In front lies the snow-covered peak of the Orizaba, now lit up by the dawn. The valleys are covered in mist. The path zigzags upwards steeply, the valley narrows.

*Correction . . .*

Suddenly from the slope opposite comes a strange noise like the crackle of exploding fireworks densely packed for Carnival and strung up by the safety fuses on the cathedral steps. Light flashes at two points in the bushes, followed by the thud of explosions and the crack of musket fire.

A horse rises, frightened and neighing, toppling over backwards into the abyss and taking its rider with it. Bullets fly, flinging bodies into the air. Shell fragments tear up the cotton-quilted jackets, punching holes in armour as if it were cardboard, tearing open the bodies of horses, smashing rocks, screaming through the morning sky. Cortes is held in a sharpshooter's sights, doubles up and falls to the ground, hand on sword hilt, half-pulling the chiselled blade from its scabbard. Foaming blood bubbles from under his doublet. His wildly staring eye is pierced by a bullet and dissected in a split-second into its molecular ingredients. A helmet fills with blood, clotting albumen on splinters of bone. And above it all, an incessant hammering, the cruel rhythm of this dance of death.

Ten minutes later, it is all over. A time-line has changed its course. Death has come as if from nowhere; a merciless settling of accounts for the long and tragic history which is unfolding.

Steve's eye moved on to the next entry.

*Date: 29th August, 1519, nine o'clock local time.*

*Place: Cofre de Perote.*

*Mission: Four to five men, two heavy machine guns, mortars, sharpshooters.*

*Participants motivated by anti-colonialism, with romantic ideas about Aztec culture.*

*Realisation: Restructured B 747 with additional equipment (cage) disguised as radar unit. Drop combined with parachute jump.*

*Goal: To prevent fanatical Catholics from setting foot in Central America and wiping out ancient existing civilisation.*

Crusaders! Steve said to himself. As if the reformers who would follow them would be any better! As if it hadn't been high time to sweep away the bloody, priest-ridden regime of this Indian military dictatorship and dump it on the rubbish heap of history.

But perhaps America had not been discovered and colonised by white men. Perhaps Columbus sailed unsuspecting into the fire from Ahuizotl's coastal batteries which he had been persuaded to buy from some benevolent power, perhaps a small team of military advisers from Japan or China at the court of the Caciques. Suppose the seafarer went missing while searching a western sea route to the tempting shores of India and the Spice islands, and drowned in the Sargasso Sea? Suppose no news of the new continent ever reached Europe, no inexhaustible gold

treasure ever tempted the people there. Who would have paid
for the next expedition?

*Correction . . .*
   *Date: 12th October, 1492, two o'clock in the morning local time.*
   *Place: Guanghani.*
A shout from the masthead. Questioning voices in the
darkness, a torch is being lit. Men who have slept on deck rub
their eyes and climb halfway up the shrouds to get a better view
of the coast. Nothing in sight. In the sky the stars are still
glittering through gaps in the clouds. Creaking rigging, the
noise of water moving sluggishly along the ship's side.
   Another shout from the masthead.
   '*Land.*'
   Orders are given, a cannon is fired. There is an exchange of
signals between the ships, the helmsmen communicate.
   Yes. You can smell it now: land. It is a smell as of spice and of
rotten vegetation, wafted over by the wind. The noise of
breakers . . .
   The sails are hauled in, a plumbline is thrown out. The men
gather on deck, naked to the waist in the fresh air of early
morning. The stars fade away gradually in the lead-coloured
dawn. A coastline ahead. Everybody is staring at it, they touch
each other as if to make sure that they are not dreaming. They
have overcome infinity; they have not sailed over the edge of the
earth and fallen into the abyss. They have reached land, as
promised by the admiral.
   There is a light on the coast. Fire? A distant call. Human
beings?
   India. Will they be welcomed? Horny hands, weatherbeaten
by sun and salt water, make the sign of the cross. Here and there
a man stealthily touches an amulet, murmurs '*Salvador*' and
spits on the planks defiantly. Others can already smell the
exotic delicacies, the mild aroma of cinnamon and vanilla, the
pleasant, exciting scent of pressed tea leaves piled in packs on
the harbour wall, the cool smell of precious woods. The day
would reveal in fact what the widely travelled Venetian had
only described in words – the Empire of Cathay and the Island
of Zipangu, the towering cities made of marble, the golden
palaces over which flutter the silken dragon standards of the
great Khan, the ports teeming with big ships, the mile after mile

of winding coastline . . .

The Emperor's emissaries receive them respectfully and draw near. Then his dragon stirs, whipping the air as if with racing steel blades, the scaly armour on its squat body flashing brightly in the morning light. It's tail is raised high and decorated with a whirring silver disk, its roar can be heard for miles around. Majestically it approaches, its mouth open, spitting fire. It pours light on them. Not the flames of pentecostal illumination, but the fire of napalm . . .

In a flash the deck is turned into a living hell of melting faces and distorted mouths. Tortured screams ring out, cleaving the air. Rigging and masts plunge into the sea; people all ablaze leap overboard, but even the sea will not quench the flames. And the dragon goes on spitting until the water is covered with glowing driftwood moving in a shallow breeze. Then shots plough into the carpet of death until the last hands gripping planks or burnt bits of yard are gone . . .

'Are you asleep?' the voice of Paul Loorey asked him.

Steve opened his eyes.

'Daydreaming,' he said. 'Useless stuff. Look at it. Marginalia for a future history.'

'Howard's Summa?'

'He was writing away at it twenty years ago. Sometimes we talked about it.'

Paul sat down next to Steve in the shade. 'What's the point of it?'

'It's the most attractive historiography imaginable, Paul. Daydreams are important. They are the immense, never realised possibilities of history. The points where reality opens up in a moment of surprise give a momentary glimpse into another reality – they're points of departure for the human imagination. And if this world ever perishes, it'll be because of a lack of imagination on the part of its inhabitants.

'Of course, reality is important – far too important to be left to organising bureaucrats and arrogant military officials. But it was bound to come to that when *facts* became the main criterion. What do facts do to the human spirit? They turn reality into a ghetto for small minds – minds that can only believe in what they can touch. And that's such a small section from the broad spectrum of human existence.'

The wind had almost died away. The big, dark sail hung

limply, throwing a narrow strip of shade across the deck. The helmsman was asleep. Close by, dolphins were leaping up from the sea.

CHAPTER NINE

# REGARDS TO LEAKEY

The dolphins accompanied them on their journey, seeming to express in their movements a feeling of excitement at the conquest of new territories, a mood of gay abandon. They had not yet developed into the elegant smooth creatures which Steve remembered, and still had grey velvety fur and pointed heads from which sprouted bristly whiskers. Happy, playful animals with shrewd faces and claw-studded flippers, they leapt up from the waves, snorting disdainfully when they saw the boat and diving back into their element.

Meanwhile the barge crept on, a sleepy, hot south wind playing listlessly with the sail. The captain steered due west-north-west. On the seventh day of their journey the mountains of the Balearic Islands appeared on the horizon. The sky clouded over, the wind turned west. Rain beat down onto the wrinkled, slate-grey sea. The boat creaked.

Paul, Jerome, and Steve remained on deck, protected by a waterproof tarpaulin. Snowball and Goodluck sat on the ground between them, looking at the high sea with mixed feelings and examining the faces of their human companions for signs that might tell them whether or not their end had come.

It was impossible to fight the stormy west wind, and quite early in the afternoon the captain decided to steer close to the shore and look for a suitable landing place. Water swept on deck, and rain poured down on the planks, drumming on the tarpaulin under which they were sitting. The captain gave his orders, and the sailors in their dripping wet burnouses and turbans hurried up into the rigging to bring in the sail. A boat was let down into the water and fastened to the bow. The oars were dipped into the water. The captain ordered the barge to be towed against the wind.

'What's that?' Steve asked, pointing to a curious rock formation towards starboard, which rose up in the gloomy sky between two rain showers.

'The Shoulder of Hercules,' Paul said.

The rock indeed resembled a shoulder, pushing straight up from the water. The upper arm and the rounded top of the shoulder were clearly visible; then came the base of the neck, and above it the chin and ear, and the outline of a mouth in a cavernous, unformed face. The shoulder was pushing against the mountain as if it were propping up the land mass against the sea.

'Looks as if it was carved out of the rock,' Steve said, astonished.

'It was. It was created by a group of travellers who were sent much further back into the past. They wanted to leave some visible sign of their presence – some artefact that could be seen for miles around.'

'Has it been examined more thoroughly?' Steve asked.

'This is considered a dangerous spot by sailors. They refuse to go near it,' Paul said. 'Look. They're rowing as if their lives depended on it.'

Very slowly the barge moved past the rocky shoulder. The monument seemed to communicate a strange threat; it seemed powerful and defiant and yet like a reproach expressed in stone. How had these people felt when they found themselves thrown into this empty, uninhabited world, Steve wondered. Adam in an unfinished paradise. It was hard to imagine what they must have gone through. It made the achievement of the artist all the more admirable. In spite of all the misery of his daily life, he had found the strength to start this gigantic figure – and yet he had died before he finished it.

'There's a legend among the sailors,' Paul continued, 'that when this Hercules disappears under the waters, the last human beings will disappear with it.'

'That could happen today if it goes on raining like this,' Jerome said, wiping the water from his face and beard.

The barge reached the shore after dark, nosing its way through the driftwood. Shadowy figures jumped unsteadily ashore, throwing ropes. Wood grated against shingle.

The rain continued drumming on the tarpaulin all night. Next morning the animals were brought on land and put out to graze under guard, and Rick Bailey and Jerome set out hunting. Two trader mercenaries and a former colonist joined them. They killed a small tapir-like creature and an enormous stag standing about three metres high. Jerome shot a few wild ducks and tried to teach Davy to bring them back, but the dog was too headstrong and refused to obey his commands. The barge was moored. The captain had the water bags filled and made them fry meat to keep in reserve.

They sat under cover of temporary roofing made from leaves and gazed into the smouldering fire and at the pieces of meat frying slowly on the spit.

Two days later the wind changed and the sky cleared. Animals and provisions were taken on board, the ropes untied and thrown out.

Suddenly from among the bushes on the shore a creature appeared, light-skinned, with a bearded face and hair right down to the shoulders. He had short, very hairy legs and unusually long arms, was of a much stronger build than the average Chap and almost as tall as a fully grown human. He was dressed in tanned goatskin held together at the shoulder by a brooch made of bone, and he carried a water bag and a shoulder bag, also made of goatskin. A narrow, thin knife like a bayonet was stuck into his belt. In fact it was a bayonet, as Steve later discovered, but it was ancient and had not been sharpened for decades. In his right hand the strange man carried a coiled leather whip.

He ran up to the gangway which had not yet been fully hauled on board, held on to it and uttered an inarticulate shout.

'What do you want?' the captain asked brusquely, but the creature did not seem to speak a language and could only answer with throaty noises sounding like '*C'mon boy. Hey, c'mon boy.*'

Goodluck joined in and tried to communicate with throaty noises and gestures, but met with little success.

'He's not one of us,' Goodluck said finally. 'He's one of the last *foehst* and wants to be taken west to the mainland with his children. He says hunting is getting worse here every year.'

The captain shook his head. Two sailors tried to take the gangway away from the *foehst*, but he held on to it with his strong hairy arms and almost pulled the two men into the water. 'C'mon boy,' Hey, c'mon boy,' he kept on begging.

'Let him on board,' the captain said.

The *foehst* gave out a shrill whistle, and presently two young animals broke through the bushes and quickly approached.

Before the sailors could react, all three of them were on board. The *foehst* gave the captain a handful of long sabre-toothed tiger claws in payment for his passage.

'They'll be worth a fortune in Atlantis,' Paul murmured.

Steve watched the two young, a boy of about eight or nine and a girl two or three years younger. Both were naked, and considering their age, extraordinarily hairy. Soft, silky fur covered their bodies, not only around the private parts. They crept into a corner, clinging to each other and looking around shyly, and at once engaged in sexual play. The old *foehst*'s whip came down sharply, separating them. They let go of each other instantly.

'C'mon boy, hey, c'mon boy,' he growled. Ten minutes later they were together again.

'Hey, c'mon boy,' the *foehst* growled again, and cracked his whip.

Poor, wretched creatures, Steve thought as he watched them. He gave Elmer a pitying look. Is this how our descendants will look and behave? If so the galaxy will remain uncolonised for a long time to come. Perhaps it'll *never* be a place for human beings . . .

They pushed off from the shore and started to move again. The sea was blue and covered with white wave-crests, and a stiff breeze filled the sail.

On the twelfth day of their journey the plateau of the Iberian peninsula appeared in the west. They were sailing with a cool, dry north-easterly wind and were making good progress in spite of the slowly increasing counter-current produced by the waters gushing in at Gibraltar. They sailed close to the coast in a steady west-south-west course until they reached the mouth of the Almeria river after passing the Cape of Gata which stuck out far to the south. In the hazy distance to the south-west they made out the massive mountain range of Alboran, which rises up more than a thousand metres vertically from the sea.

The barge had made its last voyage. The captain and his crew were also planning to cross the Atlantic; they felt they would be more useful there, keeping up the link between the American mainland and the island.

'What will you do about the ship?' Steve asked the captain, a Navy man in his mid-sixties who had been sailing in the basin for more than thirty years. His pale grey eyes in the deeply tanned face looked at Steve disdainfully from under the faded blue turban.

'I shall leave it where it is,' he said. 'Perhaps somebody will find it useful.'

Steve nodded.

'Why do you ask?'

Steve shrugged his shoulders. 'It's just that I might need it.'

'Aren't you coming with us?'

'I'm not sure yet. I haven't decided.'

'You're in your prime. Over there you'll have a chance to make a future for yourself.'

Steve looked into the pale grey eyes with a smile. The captain lowered his eyes and pushed the turban from his forehead.

'Do as you like,' he said. 'Fasten the rudder when you sleep and never use more than a part of the sail. As long as you sail with the wind you'll manage by yourself. If it turns, it's best to bring down the yard, because you can't cruise against the wind. When it gets stormy you'll have to rely on prayer. That's all I can tell you. This thing isn't much more than a raft really. But it's a good raft. Ulysses wouldn't have had a better one. Good luck.' He turned away and gave orders to his men. The passengers disembarked, and the animals and goods were unloaded, Jerome driving the jeep ashore over swaying wooden planks. After a long silence the roar of the strong engine sounded barbarous, and the camels shied in terror, rolling their eyes. It was some time before the animals could be calmed down.

Two hours later the caravan started out in the direction of Cadiz, at first following the course of the Almeria upstream through winding gorges, then striking west, parallel to the densely wooded mountain range of the Sierra Nevada in the north. In the course of decades the mule track had been improved to a quite passable dirt road, on which heavier goods could be transported from the Atlantic coast to the basin.

'I gather you don't want to go with the others,' Jerome said to Steve during a rest. They had driven ahead a little in the jeep, and Goodluck, Snowball, and Ricardo were with them. They were preparing the camp for the caravan, collecting dry sticks and piling up stones to make fires.

'I feel the call of the wild,' Steve said, 'of the enormous

vastness of this unfinished world. One day man will come from Africa. The sixth day of creation started there. Perhaps I'll be allowed to experience a few seconds of this and be there as a spectator.'

'You'll get eaten up before you can take a look. And you'll be all alone.'

Steve shrugged his shoulders and raised his hands with a grin.

'And the Lord God said: it is not good for man to be alone . . . I shall give him a helpmate for company.'

Jerome snorted indignantly. 'Did you look at the hairy brats we had on board with us?'

'They're better of than we are. They're naked.'

'So you still believe you might be able to smuggle yourself into paradise without being noticed, eh?'

'It may not be as difficult as all that, Jerome. All you need to know is where it is.' After a short silence he asked: 'And how do you see your future?'

'I'm tempted by the vastness, like you,' Jerome said softly, putting his arm around Steve. 'I shall travel north and visit Moses. Perhaps I'll find him still alive. Goodluck and Snowball will come with me. Wouldn't you like to come with us?'

Steve shook his head. 'I have to find my own future,' he said firmly.

'I plan to go north with one of Moses' sons and look at those old ruins by the sea. I'll look for the shores of the legendary Lac Mer where the expanses of Asia open up, and watch the Himalayas being formed. Perhaps I'll find the land route to America and . . .'

'I can see that you have quite a big programme ahead of you.'

'I'd go mad if I had to live on an island.'

'You no longer believe in a return to the future?'

'It would be absurd,' Jerome said.


Twenty-one days later they reached Cadiz. The *New Atlantis* was already lying at anchor there, an ocean-going three-master made up from prefabricated parts which had been expedited into the past.

'Why did they never send us a ship like this for the basin?' Elmer asked indignantly.

'Because nobody ever thought it might be navigable,' Ricardo answered.

'They did damn little thinking, if you ask me,' Elmer growled.

Seagulls were circling over the miserable huts in the harbour, quarreling and screeching fiercely around the rubbish floating in the water of the bay. Far out in the glittering sea they saw some fishing boats.

During his time at college Steve had spent some time in Europe, including a few days in southern Spain. He remembered Cadiz as a bright, airy town; remembered the strong smell from the salt holes near the approach road, where the sun had dried up the sea and where men muffled up to their eyes were shovelling the grey-white salt into piles. He remembered an old restaurant he had visited there; recalled the clatter of cutlery, the echoing voices of the guests, and the coolness of its walls, even on hot July days. In Algeciras he had looked over with longing to the African coast, picturing the exotic towns full of costly objects made of gold and ivory, beautiful slave-girls and precious clothes made of brocade and silk . . . He had sworn to himself then that he would never enter these towns, in order to keep them intact in his imagination, with all their legendary splendour and magnificence.

Now he would never see them: even the possibility had been removed. But it was somehow comforting to think of them lying asleep and invisible in the lap of the future, instead of being rotten cadavers, pale shadows of their former greatness. Steve smiled to himself. At least the splendour of those towns lay ahead of them now, not behind them.

The *New Atlantis* had long since set sail and disappeared beneath the western horizon.

They stood on the rocky shoulder of the ridge of Gibraltar which once protected the basin from the waters of the Atlantic. Steve held five animals by the reins, while Jerome loaded his jeep and trailer for the journey with petrol cans and provisions, arms and ammunitions.

The waters were gushing down through a gap about eight kilometres wide; it had not yet reached its later dimensions. Every now and then Steve saw a flash of silvery fish bodies as they were swept over the edge by the strong current – life spilling from one bowl into another, the overflow from creation. In the east a misty haze of vapour swirled over the swift currents. The cool damp air was filled with a roar of rushing water that drowned all attempts at speech.

After taking his leave of Snowball and Goodluck and stroking Davy's hairy neck, Steve embraced Jerome, then climbed into the saddle. He lifted his hand.

'Give my regards to Leakey!' Jerome shouted and started the engine. 'I wish you a long life, Steve. But when the end comes, try and put yourself where he can find you.'

'Farewell,' Steve repeated, then urged his camel forward.

For some time he rode alongside the roaring waters and into the valley, following the river until he reached the bay of Almeria, where the barge was moored.

He did not hear the explosion.

Jerome had covered no more than three kilometres when it happened. During the fight for Gibraltar a brave soldier had had the idea of burying a mine on an uneven dirt track which formed the approach to the former mountain range.

Jerome died instantly. A mine fragment hit him under the chin, pierced the roof of his mouth, passed on to the right lobe of his brain and exited through the skull. Snowball, who was sitting next to the driver, was riddled with fragments, thrown from the jeep and also died a few minutes later. Goodluck, who had been sitting in the back was thrown out, lost consciousness and remained lying on the ground, gravely wounded.

The force of the explosion had torn the trailer from its coupling and turned it over on its side. The jeep, with Jerome dead at the steering wheel, swayed to the left on its torn tyres, slowly rolled off the track and down the slope and into a muddy pool, where it came to a stop. Then it began to sink slowly.

Davy barked furiously at the bubbles which rose to the surface. When they stopped, he turned round with an anxious whine and trotted up the hill. His nose was bleeding and he was shaking all over.

# CHAPTER TEN

# THE ENCOUNTER WITH THE ANGEL

Early that same afternoon Steve came to a stream and stopped to let his animals drink. While the camels were munching the juicy leaves of the bushes on the bank he sat down in the shade and helped himself to some cold fried fish.

Suddenly, among all the stamping and snorting of the animals, he thought he heard a dog bark. He looked up. A few seconds later Davy appeared, barking excitedly. He trotted down to the stream to quench his thirst, but seemed restless, barking at Steve as if begging him to follow him somewhere.

'Come here, Davy,' said Steve. 'What's the matter?'

The dog approached, whining and anxiously wagging his tail. Steve grabbed him by the scruff of the neck and examined him. He saw that he was wounded in the ear as if he had been grazed by a shot. He also discovered a further wound on his chest, below the right front leg, where it looked as if another bullet had winged him.

Davy wriggled free from his grip and trotted off the way he had come. He stopped a short way off and barked again.

'Do you want me to come with you, Davy? I understand now.'

Steve packed up his things, untethered the animals and got into the saddle. 'I hope you're not fooling me.' The dog followed his own scent and trotted on ahead. Steve felt suddenly anxious. In spite of the noon heat he drove his animals faster. Whenever they reached the top of a hill he stopped briefly and looked through his binoculars over to the west, but he could not see any signs of life.

Had they had second thoughts? Perhaps they had followed him in the jeep. It seemed unlikely. If they had, they would most likely have taken the dirt track into the Almeria valley; it was much easier to follow that than drive along the coast-line, even for a cross-country vehicle. Maybe Jerome had had an accident? Impatiently Steve dug his heels into the animal's flank.

Two hours later he found himself opposite the range of hills from where he had set out in the morning. To the left the waters of the Atlantic came pouring down. The air was full of water vapour. Salt was burning on his skin.

Suddenly Davy dashed off. A few minutes later Steve caught up with him. He was standing next to Goodluck, who was lying face down, panting and gazing westwards as if spellbound by the wonderful spectacle three kilometres away.

Steve jumped from the saddle, turned Goodluck over on his back and examined him thoroughly. He had two nasty wounds on his thighs, two more on his left hip and one in the shoulder. It looked as though he had been hit by shell fragments. He seemed to have lost a lot of blood and yet he had persisted in walking on until he collapsed. Was he trying to get help? Steve rested Goodluck's head on a rolled-up blanket, gave him some water to drink and washed his wounds as gently as he could. The pain brought the wounded man round again; he doubled up, whining, pushed his elbows into his stomach and pulled his knees up to his chin.

'Goodluck, it's me, Steve. What happened?'

The Chap looked at him, his eyes dark with fear. He licked his lips with his tongue and began to talk slowly.

'I shall go to them,' Steve said, when he had heard the full story.

Goodluck shook his head wearily. 'I have buried Snowball,' he said. 'Jerome drove into a mud hole. But he was probably dead already.'

Steve stared into the roaring waters for a few minutes.

'Listen, Goodluck,' he said. 'I can't get the fragments out of your body. Either they'll come out with the pus or they'll get embedded and stay in your body. You may have lost a lot of blood, but none of your vital organs is wounded. Otherwise you'd never have managed to get this far.'

Goodluck nodded.

Steve carried him over into the shade of an acacia tree and made a bed for him, then he lit a fire and cooked some food for him.

Next morning he felled a few young trees, built a makeshift stretcher on which he could carry Goodluck and fastened it onto the saddle of one of the pack animals. Steve knew that once on the barge he would have a better chance of nursing him; but he was reluctant to leave him behind alone while he went out hunting. There was a small chance he might pull through if he was fed on raw fish.

They started out eastwards again, moving forward very slowly. Steve travelled on during the night, and often during the day he would find himself falling asleep in the saddle, lulled by the leisurely, rolling movement of the camel as it picked its way confidently into the salt bowl of the Western Basin. The slopes, formerly sun-patched and covered in dusty thorn and ivy bushes, were now pale green as far as the eye could see. When a southern wind blew, the mists drifted northwards and came down over the slopes of the plateau forming the Iberian Peninsula. Most of the plants which once eked out a living in the dry air and salty soil of the former ocean died in the humid wind, but new ones arrived.

Soon the whole of Europe would be transformed. The palm groves north of the Alps would be covered with the enormous herds of antelopes and gnus would migrate south, and with them the lions, tigers, leopards and other predators which already existed from Darwin's master plan. Only the mastodons would remain, desperately roaming the snow forests in search of food, their passage home to the grazing grounds of Africa cut off by the waters of the Mediterranean. One long, hard winter and they would be extinct.

Man's ancestors would also remain, the Boisei as well as the Chaps, and they would learn to survive in the cold and ice, moving south in the footsteps of the migrating herds and learning how to overcome many obstacles. Slowly the human race would develop more and more skills, until at last it would find that there were no obstacles left to overcome: hostile environment, mountains, fast-flowing rivers, freezing weather, oceans, teeth and claws, space – and finally time. But wherever man went he would always meet one challenge and one immoveable obstacle: himself.

Steve looked up, tucking the kerchief that covered his mouth under his turban. For two weeks now they had been riding through what seemed like an endless summer, Goodluck sleeping fitfully on his stretcher and Davy trotting ahead, always keeping parallel to the shore of what would later be called the Mediterranean. Soon the waters would be rising by a metre a year; later, when the cataracts at Gibraltar had eaten further into the rock and the gap had widened into a channel, they would rise faster still. Even so it would take a thousand years before the enormous basin filled up, and even after two centuries there would still be land bridges to Africa south of Sardinia and Sicily, over which animals would be able to walk to safety into the warmer regions while Europe was swallowed up in the Ice Ages.

On the evening of the eighteenth day they reached the mouth of the Almeria and found the barge still moored among the drowning trees where they had left it. Steve put the camels out to graze and to let them eat their fill.

Using a provisional harness, he tied one of the camels to the mooring rope of the barge and pulled it up to the shore; then he made a comfortable bed out of mats and tarpaulin on deck and carried Goodluck on board. His condition was pitiful. One of the wounds on his thigh had become infected and the entire leg was now swollen. He was unable to walk and could barely crawl.

After he had filled all the available sacks with fresh water, Steve herded the animals on board and tethered them securely. He pulled the sail up on the winches, letting it billow in the gentle west wind, and steered out into the current. Then he fastened the rudder as the captain had told him, threw out some fishing lines in the stern and sat down next to Goodluck. He examined the festering wound, washed out the pus and bedded the leg high to make the swelling go down.

Goodluck was feverish now, hitting out at the air with his small fists, and growling. Steve wondered whether he should tie him up, but did not have the heart to do it. He knew now that he would never pull through, but he wanted to do everything in his power to make his last days easier.

Every few hours he checked the lines, pulled up twitching fish bodies, killing them for use as bait or preparing them for food by scraping the raw meat with the knife and picking off the bones.

It was difficult to feed Goodluck, but Steve never lost his patience. Davy watched him attentively and every time the Chap sicked up the food he registered this with a half-reproachful, half-greedy growl.

When Goodluck had been attended to, Steve rested under the sun-sail. Sometimes the wind died down altogether and all was silent except for the occasional creak of the rigging and the soft lapping of water against the hull of the barge. In these immeasurable intervals when time seemed to stand still, Steve remembered words which he thought he had forgotten hundreds of years ago, words about fallen suns and angels pouring their wrath upon the world. Sometimes anxiety gripped his heart so fiercely that he would stagger to the rail and vomit over it, hanging over the ship's side and panting until he found the strength at last to ladle cold water over his face and wet his forehead. Later, when the salt on his forehead had dried, he sometimes felt as if spiders were crawling in and out of the sockets of his eyes, spinning their webs in the darkness of his consciousness.

Again and again he had the same dream. From a high point – he never knew what was under his feet, but it felt like a tree rooted in a rocky island – he looked on to a shore which was washed by a dark, oily liquid, a lazy stinking brew into which all the waters of the earth had gone and in which all life on earth had died. From the shoreline to the horizon stretched dunes lit up by a chalk-white immensely bright light. There was a menacing black sky above it, as if an enormous wind had blown away the atmosphere and now the earth's face had become a helpless prey to cosmic storms. Suddenly the land began to move, heaving and lowering in the ripples of a mighty earthquake which came rolling in from the horizon, flattening the dunes and lifting the valleys up like waves. In spite of the lack of atmosphere there was a clear hissing noise as sand rose up from the waves like foam, as if the wind from the sun were beating photons from the flanks of crystals, transforming them into pure light. As always, Steve woke with the paralysing feeling that he had seen that earth without a future, of which Paul had spoken.

It was evening when he woke up. The sun had set. He was sweating and exhausted. On all fours he crept over to Goodluck, certain that the Chap had died. But Goodluck was alive. His breath was shallow but regular. He was fast asleep.

Now a dark bank of clouds hung over the African coast, lying transversely, leaning against the flanks of the mountains, their edges a pale yellow.

Steve took a deep breath and wiped his forehead. The heat

made him feel dizzy. He stared out into the descending gloom. Was this patchwork really my life? he asked himself anxiously. Somehow he had always thought that everything so far had been a dress rehearsal, at the end of which the curtain for the *real* performance would go up, with all the parts properly shared out and everybody acting his role to perfection. Surely nobody could be forced to stumble onto the stage completely unprepared and take part in a play he had not read before and whose plot made no sense.

Now he knew with frightening certainty that this *was* his life; and that far from being about to rise, the curtain was about to fall, bringing it to an end once and for all. It was happening *now*. Not one second in it could be lived again; all the choices he had taken so casually in the fond belief that the decisions they involved could be corrected later, were irreversible. And this certainty weighed on him as heavily as a rock, the rock of time itself. And all because he had not returned his plastic card that morning; because he was still drunk from the whisky of the night before, and because he was thoughtless, like all the others who had set out on this crazy adventure.

He felt as if he were sitting at the controls of a space-shuttle, in a space-suit which was far too tight for him, and with ill-functioning life-support systems. Below him he could see a dead earth, a burnt-out cinder like himself, drifting into the future, lifeless. The radio was silent; nothing could be heard apart from the electromagnetic song of the stars, the echo of creation returned from the edge of the universe like the sound of breakers on a distant shore, and his own rattling breath in the mouthpiece of his oxygen mask. He was drifting, drifting noiselessly over the abyss, with the earth's atmosphere wafting beneath him like a diffuse whirl of photons.

Then the first rays of the rising sun quivered on the horizon – and sank back again. He examined his controls hastily. They were all dead. The indicators had gone back to zero.

A smell of decay hung in the air. Stale air filled his lungs. He felt as if earth could not hold him any longer, as if he were floating up towards midnight, without stopping, in a race for the stars . . .

'What's the matter with you, Goodluck?' he panted, staring aghast at the dark, straight figure that stood before him, blotting out the stars. He smelt the rotting wounds, the wet fur drenched by the sweat of death.

The animals which were tethered in the stern had become restless and had got up. Davy came towards him, his claws clicking on the planks, sniffing and snorting and nuzzling against him to wake him up. The moon broke through the clouds.

Steve stared at the mast and saw now that in his dream he had mistaken it for the raised-up figure of Goodluck. Far over in the east he could see blood-red flashes of lightning, but no storm arose. Next morning only a few narrow, smoky banks of cloud bore witness to the battle of the air-currents which were quickly melted down by the rising day.

Goodluck was alive. Steve washed him and gave him drink, stilled his hunger and quenched his thirst.

They were drifting east. The sky was dazzlingly bright and full of gaiety, the rippling water stippled by quivering silver lances of sunlight. And so they sailed on, day after day, drifting through an endless twilight of hazy brightness which was almost imperceptibly overlaid by the starry night as if by a blanket of light clouds.

Swarms of birds crossed their course, flying very high, but Steve could not identify them.

'We'll follow them south, Goodluck,' he called out.

In the night they could hear them scream between the stars.

The shore glided past as they continued their journey: forests dappled in autumn colours; evergreen gingkos, golden glowing cork trees, flaming maples, pale green cinnamon trees, the black flame of cypresses, pale yellow bushes dominated by dark cedar trees and protected by pines . . .

Steve went ashore at the mouth of the Soumman. In the haze over to the east he knew there lay the former landing zone and beyond it faraway La Galite. There it had all started; there the heart of the whale had exploded, showering them with its blood; there the galaxies of reality had first begun to move apart.

He carried Goodluck on land, then he disembarked the camels and the rest of his provisions and belongings, and set about making a camp.

After putting the famished animals out to graze and attending to Goodluck, Steve lay down to get some rest. After sleeping like a log, he was awoken by a strange whirring sound. Davy was growling and Goodluck was throwing his head restlessly from side to side, as'if in terror.

Steve raised his hand to shield his eyes. Before him was a brightly shimmering apparition, about ten metres high and five or six metres long. It was almost transparent and in it a figure appeared to be floating. He was dressed in a scarlet space-suit with a white tool pack on his back, and his hands rested on a set of instruments like silver encrustations, built into the transparent material at the head of the pressure seat.

With a soft *ping* three thin telescopic legs snapped out of their brackets on the underside of the glowing craft and spread out. The moment it touched ground it became opaque and yellow on its upper side, while the area below the arrow-shaped stump wings, which stabilised the vehicle during flight, was coloured white. On the nose Steve could clearly see the insignia Harald had described. On the roof a laser gun moved out and swivelled gently round to aim at Steve.

He lifted his hands protectively. 'Don't shoot,' he shouted.

The lower part of the craft burst open and from the gap a short ladder descended on which appeared a pair of scarlet boots.

Davy bared his teeth and growled. Immediately the laser gun pointed at him.

'Don't shoot!' Steve called out again, the figure emerged from underneath the vehicle's belly and walked up to him.

'Have no fear,' the pilot said in his strange hard Italian. He lifted his gloved right hand, whereupon the weapon swivelled upwards, pointing harmlessly into the sky. It remained there when he lowered his hand again.

The pilot was an unusually tall and broad-shouldered man. He must be at least two metres high, Steve thought, and tried in vain to recognise a face behind the golden steam on the visor of the helmet. For a second he believed he had seen a beautiful dark-skinned face, perhaps the proud face of a Nubian. But he might have deceived himself.

Steve looked at the insignia on the sleeves of the space-suit. On the right was the lamb, on the left a key crossed with a laser gun; written above it were the words: CHRISTO SALVATORI.

'Who are you?' Steve asked in his bad Italian.

The pilot pressed a switch on his helmet and answered into his microphone: 'Do you speak our language?'

'Only a little.'

'You are from a future which is not in God's hands.'

His hand was heavy on my world, Steve thought. 'Who are you?' he asked once again.

'I am the Lord's pathfinder,' the pilot said. 'I am looking for one of our soldiers who operated in this era and did not come back.'

'Does that mean that you are able to return into the future?' Steve asked breathlessly.

The pilot hesitated.

'Certainly,' he said. 'Into *my* future. Into the future of the Lord.'

'Could you take me with you?'

'I could take you, but it is not for me to decide.' He pointed at Goodluck. 'The hominid has to stay here.'

'He's in desperate need of medical help.'

Goodluck had woken up. He propped himself up and stared at the pilot as if at a ghost.

The pilot came and knelt down beside him. He adjusted something on his glove and touched Goodluck's upper arm with his fingertips. Sand-coloured hair flew off and a hand-sized area of dark skin emerged. The pilot undid his tool pack, took out a semi-spherical tortoise-like object and clamped it against the spot. It stuck and started to hum. Goodluck stared at the apparatus in a mixture of curiosity and horror, baring his teeth. His dark lips trembled, but he suppressed his usual growl and did not bat an eyelid when it was taken off a few minutes later. In three places there were drops of blood oozing from his skin.

The pilot straightened himself up and turned to Steve, touching his naked upper arm with the fingertips of his glove. They felt rough and pleasantly cool on the skin; then the 'tortoise' gripped, but the pain was barely perceptible.

'It's almost forty years now,' Steve said. 'Your comrade got caught in a battle between our troops and the other side. He must have been killed. I was told by an eye-witness.'

It was hard to gauge the pilot's reaction, since the visor of the helmet remained dark and impenetrable. Steve could see only the mirror image of his own face, distorted by the convex surface of the glass.

He rubbed his upper arm when the apparatus had been taken off. The skin was itching, and three tiny wounds were visible where the probes had pierced the flesh.

'I'll see what I can do for you,' the pilot said. 'Shall I find you here?'

Steve nodded.

'Wait for me, then. I shall return.'

He got back into his vehicle. The invisible engines whirled up the dust, the body became transparent and ascended quickly in a diagonal line up into the midday sky, with a dangerous growl, as if the gates of hell in the baptismal chapel of the Lateran Palace were clanging open.

Steve raised his hand involuntarily, as if to recall the glittering vehicle, then he dropped it and turned to Goodluck. He saw that the Chap had fallen asleep. He decided to lie down in the shade, too, and fell asleep immediately.

Steve was woken up by Davy nuzzling him with his nose. He stretched himself and felt rested and strong, relaxed and full of initiative. How long had he been asleep? He remembered the encounter with the angel, like Harald's before him, remembered a roaring in the sky, as if . . .

He sat up abruptly and stared at his upper arm. Hastily he scraped off the scab. The tiny cuts underneath had healed now and were barely noticeable.

Goodluck had lit a fire and was frying a piece of meat on a pointed stick which he held over the flames.

Steve got up, went over to him and looked at him across the fire, amazed. Goodluck looked terrible. His body was emaciated, the skin stretched taut over the rib-cage, the shoulderblades protruding; his hair had fallen out in bushels, and on his left upper arm he had a bare patch the size of a man's hand . . .

As if he felt Steve's gaze, Goodluck started to scratch there.

'Davy killed a snake,' he said.

The twigs were crackling in the fire. Steve shook his head slightly and tried to catch Goodluck's gaze. He looked deeply into the hazel-coloured eyes and saw a new vitality there.

The Chap pulled his lips into a smile. Steve smiled back.

What is 'reality' for the mind? A ghetto, according to Paul. Goodluck as if he had understood Steve's thoughts, briefly wiped his forehead and eyes as if to remove the cobwebs of an Indian Summer.

Steve got up and started to saddle the animals. Goodluck watched him with astonishment.

'Are we going to start out on the ride?' he asked.

'Do you feel strong enough?'

'I'm strong.'

'OK. Let's go then.' With a decisive jerk he tightened the saddle straps. 'I can't leave you here where I need you most.'

Goodluck looked west, where the sun was already low on the horizon. 'We shan't get far today.'

'Then we'll ride through the night. I can't stay in this place, it frightens me.'

Goodluck looked around hesitantly and nodded. He cut the fried snake into three pieces and offered two of them to Steve and Davy. Then he put out the fire.

The sun was setting as they rode upstream along the valley of the Soumman. By midnight they had reached the edge of the plateau and they decided to give the animals a short rest. The crescent moon was drifting towards the distant hills in the west, pouring its light over the rippling grasslands of the Sahara, which stretched right as far as the eye could see, beneath a limitless sky.

'I'd like to open my wings and fly,' Steve said.

Goodluck gave him a searching look, bared his teeth and produced a laughing sound. In his night-black eyes could be seen the reflection of the stars.

Steve joined in his laughter, pushed his heels gaily into the flanks of his camel and urged it on. He felt as if somewhere beyond the horizon, beyond the darkness, beyond the twinkling of the stars something or somebody was waiting for him. And he was full of joy.

By the time the sun rose they had been received into the wide, bright heart of Africa.

## by BRIAN W. ALDISS

The tale of adventure is the oldest kind of tale. It made life bearable in a leaky Ice Age cave – I know because I was there in spirit – just as it makes life in a sixth-floor three-room apartment bearable today. Tales of adventure remind us that inside every commuter there is a man of action screaming to get out.

'The Last Day of Creation' is a splendid tale of adventure. Here are men in trouble, overcoming hardship, confronting the unknown, remaining undaunted despite all difficulties. So the tale is traditional, and eternally welcome for that.

At the same time it is also science fiction. And that gives it an extra dimension. Wolfgang Jeschke has been very clever. He has discovered an unvisited part of the world in which to stage his tale of adventure – the bottom of the Mediterranean Sea, five million years ago. What a setting! This is the liberty that science fiction allows: it can present us with new locations when old locations are used up. For instance, it would have been possible a couple of decades ago to set the story in the basin of the River Amazon. No longer. Now the Amazon is tamed. Roads are being hacked across the South American continent, the virgin forest is being destroyed at the rate of so many hectares a day (which, incidentally, could kill us all, in case you hadn't heard), and in the evening men sit down in bars and drink beer or Coke or read comic strips just like men anywhere. The Amazon is becoming as prosaic as the nearest car park. Not so the bed of the Mediterranean, five million steaming years ago.

Having picked his exotic setting, a writer has to do two things. He has to get his characters there, and he has to give them a good reason for going. This is where 'The Last Day of Creation' wins prizes! Jeschke's time-device is perfectly plausible within the limits of the novel. I like it; I admire the way men find the device cumbersome and difficult to operate and then, when it does work it doesn't do so very efficiently – as is the way with all prototypes.

This device also gives the author a chance to put across a message that most of us (particularly if we have been soldiers) find sympathetic. The time-device would have worked better if its operators had been more concerned. In other words, forward troops are once more let down by the generals back at base. This ironic realism permeates the book and lends the whole fantasy the colour of truth.

Then the question of giving the characters a good reason for embarking on their adventure. They're after oil for the West. Just that simple. Brilliant ideas are always simple.

I've been reading science fiction for a long while. I recall many stories where, as a result of surplus energy, there is complete automation of the planet and work is a scarce commodity. Curiously enough, considering how SF is in effect energy-based, I recall few novels where oil is scarce and has to be searched for. In fact, I recall one: an early Frank Herbert novel called 'Under Pressure' (also 'Dragon in the Sea'). There the Americans syphon oil from under the Polar ice cap.

'The Last Day' has a delightfully simple solution to the current oil shortage – which shall not be itemised here, in case any reader is rash enough to turn to the unimportant afterword before the all-important story. All I will say is that it is a splendid idea, and I wish Jeschke could get a patent on it and put it into practice.

This serious case of oil-smuggling lends the novel great topicality. Such a remarkable mix of a story set five million years ago and a message as up to date as tomorrow's breakfast cereal leaves us with an engaging sense of paradox. The exciting tale of adventure carries an intellectual punch. This butterfly has a kick like a mule.

Perhaps I've carried on too long about the infrastructure of the novel. It's something that the average reader, getting on with the story, will scarcely bother about. Let me redeem myself by saying that infrastructure is nothing unless the story works as a story – and work this one certainly does. It thunders on at an heroic pace, like a John Wayne movie, like one of the great SF adventures of Harry Harrison (which is curious, because I can tell you, reader, that Mr Wolfgang Jeschke in person resembles Harry Harrison in person – so much so that I once bought him a drink by mistake).

One of its great assets is the mixed pack of early men who come and go throughout the thickets of the story. Who *they* remind me of I will not say. Their presence adds mystery to the proceedings. It also reminds those of us who are historically inclined that all stories have predecessors, and predecessors here include Stanley Waterloo's 'The Story of Ab' (1897) and Jack London's 'Before Adam' (1906).

The early men reinforce my belief that 'The Last Day of Creation' celebrates mankind. Mankind's guts and ingenuity are really the theme of the book, as of all true adventures.

It's a good theme, and a good book to go with it. Read it fast, before the oil runs out.

Brian Aldiss

Oxford
August, 1979